Makers of Puritan History

Makers of Puritan History

MARCUS L. LOANE

FOREWORD BY
PHILIP E. HUGHES

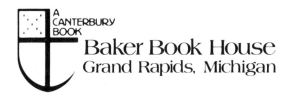

A CANTERBURY BOOK

Baker Book House
Grand Rapids, Michigan

PHOTOLITHOPRINTED BY CUSHING - MALLOY, INC.
ANN ARBOR, MICHIGAN, UNITED STATES OF AMERICA

To

HELEN McGREGOR RAMSAY

DOCTOR AND MISSIONARY
AT LAKHNADON AND CHHAPARA
IN INDIA

*in token of friendship
this book is inscribed.*

*"For Himself hath said,
I will in no wise fail thee,
neither will I in any wise forsake thee."*
HEBREWS 13:5 R.V.

Canterbury Books (series editor, Philip E. Hughes) are written by Anglican (Episcopalian) authors and offered as contributions of authentic Anglican thought and theology. The series will include important reprints as well as works by contemporary scholars. The significance of the subject matter, together with the quality of the writing and the reputation of the writers, is expected to ensure a wide readership for **Canterbury Books** not only among Episcopalians, but also among Christians of all denominations.

Philip Edgcumbe Hughes, Anglican scholar and author, is currently Associate Rector of St. John's Episcopal Church, Huntingdon Valley, Pennsylvania, and Visiting Professor at Westminster Theological Seminary, Philadelphia. Previously, he served in England as Vice-Principal of Tyndale Hall, Bristol; Executive Secretary of the Church Society; and Editor of The Churchman.

FOREWORD

THE CHURCH OF OUR DAY HAS BEEN AND
continues to be enriched by the finely conceived and deeply Christian
writings of the Archbishop of Sydney, and the appearance of this new
edition of his book *Makers of Puritan History* should be an occasion
of rejoicing for all who value the treasures of our evangelical heritage. The volume is, in effect, the third in a trilogy of biographical
studies, the two other volumes being *Pioneers of the Reformation in
England* and *Masters of the English Reformation,* in which the story
is told of some of the great men of the sixteenth century, who lived
and died for the cause of reforming the Church of England in accord-
ance with the evangelical principles of the New Testament. Here in
this present volume Archbishop Loane takes us into the seventeenth
century as he absorbingly mirrors the religious issues of that turbulent
era in the lives and labors of four spiritual giants — two of them
Scotsmen and two of them Englishmen.

To read of God's dealings with his servants in a past age, men as
frail and fallible as we still are, and to be reminded of the manner in
which, through trials and conflicts, they were fashioned into polished
shafts for the use of the Master, is always a salutary and searching exercise. It convicts us of our own lukewarmness and little faith; it con-
firms the tremendous potential for lasting good of a life that is self-
lessly and holily dedicated to the service of Christ and his truth; it
challenges us to play our part more boldly and trustingly in the spiritual drama of our own age, realizing that, however much outward
circumstances may change, the human heart and its deepest needs
remain the same; and, finally, it convinces us that in the front line of
the army of Christ there are always places to be filled.

In every generation the Church of Christ stands in need of men
who possess the statesmanship of an Alexander Henderson, the devotion of a Samuel Rutherford, the vision of a John Bunyan, and the
learning of a Richard Baxter — statesmanship, devotion, vision, and

learning, coupled with genuine humility, unselfconscious sanctity of life, and an evangelical and pastoral concern for others. This book will be a blessing and a challenge to every reader who hears the call of God to step forward into the battleline of Christ's army and play a part in the making of the history of our day.

PHILIP EDGCUMBE HUGHES
Rydal, Pennsylvania

Makers of Puritan History

PREFACE

THE FOUR STUDIES IN THIS BOOK ARE
concerned with men whose lives belong to the seventeenth century and who reflect the long struggle on the part of Scottish
Presbyterians and English Puritans with the Stuart regime. Henderson and Rutherford, who represent the struggle north of the
Tweed, cover the reigns of James I and Charles I. Bunyan and
Baxter, who represent the struggle south of the Tweed, cover
the reigns of Charles II and James II. The two Scottish leaders
were in London as members of the Westminster Assembly of
Divines and were known to all the leading Puritan ministers in
the England of that decade; and they never varied from a rigid
adherence to the primary convictions which were embodied in
the Solemn League and Covenant. The two English preachers
knew little of Scotland and were wholly absorbed in the spiritual
conflict which was taking place in their own country. Henderson
and Rutherford were prominent in Church and State alike, Presbyterian to the backbone, virtually incapable of all ecumenicity in
Church affairs; men of profound reverence and intense piety who
were to contribute much to the spiritual inheritance of their Kirk
and country. Bunyan and Baxter were never implicated in the religious policies of State and Crown as their northern neighbours
had been: Bunyan indeed had no political pull or contact at all;
Baxter only for a short time and on the fringe of things. They
were destined to spend many years in forced silence, under a
severe penal code, subject to fines and confiscation, and in prison.
Nevertheless they were both to become figures of national importance in view of their spiritual stature. They were Puritans
and patriots of the finest order, with a large-hearted tolerance which
went greatly beyond that of most men in their own age; and their
personal devotion as well as their astonishing intellectual fertility
has left the whole Church in their debt. Thus all four men reflect in some degree the great struggle which still dominates the
whole century; and that was a struggle which the Stuarts them-

11

selves provoked by their ecclesiastical policy. There was temporary respite under the iron rule of Cromwell, but there was no lasting relief until the last Stuart had been forced to leave the throne by the Revolution of 1688. These four men were all in the van of the freedom-fighters in their own age, and they fought for freedom of truth and conscience, freedom for life and worship, freedom both as citizens and as Christians. It would not be hard to point out their limitations and imperfections, their mistakes and failures; but they were fired by an inner nobility of motive and ideal which lifts them far above petty criticism and gives them a lasting title to be known as men who were like Bunyan's pilgrim, Valiant-for-Truth.

M. L. L.

CONTENTS

(*From the portrait belonging to the Hendersons of Fordel*)

ALEXANDER HENDERSON

ALEXANDER HENDERSON
The Chief of the Covenant

1583—1646

I bless Thee for the quiet rest Thy servant taketh now;
I bless Thee for his blessedness, and for his crowned brow;
For every weary step he trod in faithful following Thee,
And for the good fight foughten well, and closed right valiantly.

—Mrs. A. Stuart-Menteith: *Lays of the Kirk and Covenant*

ALEXANDER HENDERSON WAS BORN IN THE parish of Creich in Fife some time during the year 1583, and we learn from his will that he had at least two brothers and three sisters.[1] But no details of his home life or his parents have come down to posterity, and we know but little even of his adult activities before the last crowded years of his life. He left no heir to preserve his memory, and wrote no book to disclose his character; few of his letters have survived, and there is no private journal to open a window into his soul. How great is our loss we may learn from the grateful words of Samuel Rutherford: "I received your letters; they are as apples of gold to me."[2] It was almost two hundred years before John Aiton was induced to write his life, and the details had by then more or less vanished. Robert Baillie, who could have done it, did not for want of time; Robert Wodrow, who would have done it, did not for lack of material. Thus we now have to trace the man through the maze of events in which he was the firm but unostentatious leader. It is a great story, but it lacks a sense of nearness; it lacks the light and warmth which would have been supplied by his private letters or a personal narrative. He was honoured as a scholar and a preacher in his own age, but he is now better known as a great statesman and a man of affairs. He had a strong love for Fife and for St. Andrews, and would gladly have spent his life in that part of Scotland; but he was called upon to take a large share in the great struggle of the Church for faith and freedom, and he was the moving spirit in some of the greatest events which have ever transpired north of the Tweed. His name indeed belongs to the whole of Scotland, for he poured out his life in the cause of spiritual freedom and national independence.

1. See John Aiton, *The Life and Times of Alexander Henderson*, pp. 662, 663.
2. A. A. Bonar, ed., *The Letters of Samuel Rutherford* (Letter 115), p. 233.

We learn from the records in the University of St. Andrews that he matriculated at St. Salvator's College in December, 1599, and that he took his degree as a Master of Arts at the age of twenty in 1603. He then became a Regent or Quaestor in the Faculty of Arts and taught philosophy for some eight years "with no little applause."[3] There are occasional references to him in the records, and he held his office as a Regent until 1611 when he became licensed as a preacher of the Gospel. It was then forty years since James Melville had been so stirred as a student at St. Andrews by the visit of John Knox in 1571. "I saw him every day of his doctrine go hulie and fear, with a furring of matriks about his neck, a staff in the one hand, and good godly Richard Ballantyne, his servant, holding up the other oxtar, from the Abbey to the Parish Kirk; and by the said Richard and another servant, lifted up to the pulpit, where he behoved to lean at his first entry; but or he had done with his sermon, he was so active and vigorous that he was like to ding that pulpit in blads, and fly out of it!"[4] James Melville could never forget the power of those sermons: "In the opening up of his text, he was moderate the space of an half-hour; but when he entered to application, he made me so to grew and tremble that I could not hold a pen to write."[5] And there were memories more sacred still: "Mr. Knox would sometimes come in and repose him in our College yard, and call us scholars unto him, and bless us, and exhort us to know God and His work in our country."[6] There were no such episodes to cheer or to inspire Henderson either as scholar or Quaestor; but he must have shared to the full in the inspiration which James Melville's uncle, the great Andrew Melville, had brought to St. Andrews.

Andrew Melville had been a frail child and orphan whose chief delight was in his books, and he left St. Andrews with a brilliant reputation as a student in philosophy and literature. He then travelled on foot, first to Paris for the study of Greek and Hebrew, and later to Poitiers and to Geneva for the study of law and

3. See G. Webster Thomson, *Alexander Henderson*, p. 89.
4. James Melville, *Autobiography and Diary*, p. 33.
5. *Ibid.*, p. 26.
6. *Ibid.*

theology. Letters from home at length induced him to return in the summer months of 1574, and he addressed himself to the need to revitalize the life and work of the University of Glasgow. Then in 1580 he was appointed Principal of the University of St. Andrews and he devoted all his energies to this field of education. "As to that he brought home with him," so his nephew wrote with regard to his years of study abroad, "it was that plentiful and inexhaustible treasury of all good letters and learning, both of human and divine things; and that which super-excels, a profound knowledge, upright sincerity, and fervent zeal in true religion, and to put the same in use for his kirk and country; an unwearied painfulness and insatiable pleasure to give out and bestow the same without any recompense or gain."[7] But James Melville grew more ardent still when he went on to speak of his books: "The next summer came home his library, rich and rare, of the best authors, in all languages, arts and sciences; clearly declaring by his instruments what a craftsman he was."[8] Andrew Melville was an enthusiast who led the way in an academic revolution; mediaeval methods were thrown to the winds and a new type of education was put into effect. But in 1606 the two Melvilles were summoned to London by James I, and in 1607 Andrew was removed from office at St. Andrews; they found themselves driven by the King from pillar to post, first into prison, then into exile.

Alexander Henderson must have felt the impact of Melville's great reputation in St. Andrews and may have heard his lectures in theology. But he did not yield to his spell as a teacher, for the time had yet to come when he would revere his name and his massive authority. Meanwhile he was known to be in favour with the very men who had been at work to oust Melville, for he was a member of that party which stood for the Episcopal way of things in Scotland. His first extant letter is a witness to his friendship with George Gladstanes, the Archbishop of St. Andrews, and he was looked upon as a rising man in the ranks of the Episcopal party. Thus in 1612 he was chosen as one of the Procurators of the Nation of Fife, and in 1613 he was named as one of the three Assessors to the Rector of the Nation. It was

7. *Ibid.*, p. 44.
8. *Ibid.*, p. 45.

apparently in December, 1613 or in January, 1614 that he was presented to the parish of Leuchars, a small country village which lies about six miles to the northeast of St. Andrews. Leuchars was a living in the patronage of the Archbishop, but an Archbishop's presentee could not hope for a kind welcome. No part of the Kingdom was more hostile to the Bishops than the County of Fife, and the parishioners would look on him as a hireling and a stranger. Thus they made the only protest at his induction which the stringencies of the time would allow, and the doors of the church were nailed up on the day of his ordination. The whole party had to climb in through a window and the ordination took place in an empty building. We do not know his thoughts at the time, but there can be no doubt as to the personal reference in his address as the Moderator of the famous Glasgow Assembly in 1638: "There are divers among us that have had no such warrant for our entry to the ministry as were to be wished. Alas, how many of us have rather sought the kirk than the kirk sought us!"[9]

It was a bleak welcome for the new minister, and two or three wretched years must have ensued. But out of the darkness, one bright event was soon to shine like a star in the night. The death of George Gladstanes in June, 1615 and the studied indifference of his successor Spottiswoode may have helped to dispose his heart for this event. It came to his ears that Robert Bruce, one of the greatest figures of the age, was to preach in the nearby Church of Forgan. He knew that Bruce had been with James Melville at St. Andrews at the time when John Knox paid his final visit there in 1571. He knew too that Bruce was the most distinguished disciple of Andrew Melville in the struggle between the Church and Crown. Had not King James expelled him from his own pulpit in Great St. Giles? Was not that the reason why he was now preaching in a place like Forgan? Thus one memorable Sunday morning sometime between June, 1615 and July, 1616, Henderson made his way from Leuchars to hear the man whose praise was in all the churches. He sat in the darkest corner of the church beneath the gallery and watched Bruce as he took his place in the pulpit. Bruce was a man with a calm and im-

9. See John Aiton, *op. cit.*, p. 94, footnote.

posing appearance, and he stood a while in silence. Henderson was a little astonished at this, but there was a greater surprise in store. With an air of impressive dignity, he gave out as his text the words of the Saviour: "Verily, verily, I say unto you, he that entereth not by the door into the sheepfold, but climbeth up some other way, the same is a thief and a robber" (John 10:1). We do not know whether Bruce chose those words with the story of the Church at Leuchars in mind, but they went home like the thrust of "drawn swords" to the heart of the man who was trying to hide in the darkness of a corner. That text, and the sermon which Bruce went on to preach, had its issue in a true and abiding conversion. "He worshipped God," as Thomas Mc-Crie wrote, "and going away, reported that God was of a truth in those whose ways were so opposite to his own."[10]

This great crisis of faith also led to Henderson's conversion to the Presbyterian cause, for he became aware of the spiritual issues which lay behind the King's plans for Scotland. James VI, born in 1566, crowned in 1567, grew up under a series of regents until he was able to grasp the reins of power in his own hands. His marriage in Denmark took place in the early winter months of 1589, and James Melville quaintly tells how they "made good cheer, and drank stoutly till the Spring time."[11] When the union of the Crowns took place in 1603, it was welcomed as a triumph, but it did not improve matters for his northern subjects. Thus when the two Melvilles were at the Royal Chapel in London in 1606, they were dismayed to see "the King and Queen offer at the altar which was decorated with two books, two basins, and two candlesticks."[12] These were traits of personal character; but they had foils in his national policy. James had convinced himself that he ruled by Divine Right, and that no true subject ought to question this absolute authority. He held that the King was above the law and could do no wrong, and he could not forgive the Church in its stand for freedom. The case between the King and Kirk had been summed up in the famous words of Andrew Melville at Falkland in 1596. Calling him "God's silly

10. Thomas McCrie, *The Life of Alexander Henderson*, p. 7.
11. Melville, *op. cit.*, p. 277.
12. *Ibid.*, p. 664.

vassal," he took him by the sleeve and said, "Sir, as divers times before, so now again I maun tell you there is twa Kings and twa Kingdoms in Scotland; there is King James, the head of this commonwealth; and there is Christ Jesus the King and His Kingdom the Kirk, whose subject King James the Sixt is, and of whase Kingdom nocht a King, nor a lord, nor a head, but a member."[13] James found that his style of kingcraft was in opposition to the very essence of the Scottish Reformation, and that he could never rule as he wished to rule while the Kirk retained such an independent spirit. It was James who said that "Presbytery agreeth as well with Monarchy as God with the devil"; it was James who laid down the dictum, "No Bishop, no King."[14] Therefore he set out to subdue the Kirk and to restore Erastian and Episcopal forms of government in the land of John Knox.

This was not an easy matter, but the King meant to have his way. He refused to summon a free General Assembly; he procured his legislation through a servile Parliament. He gagged or banished the best men in the Church; he bribed or muzzled the chief men in the State. The two Melvilles, and John Welsh, and Robert Bruce of Kinnaird were all forced out of the struggle. Thus in 1607 James increased the Scottish Episcopate to the exact number of pre-Reformation Bishops, and in 1610 a carefully packed Assembly met at Glasgow to vote in an Episcopal constitution for the Church of Scotland. This was formally ratified by the Parliament of 1612 and no further meeting of the General Assembly was held until 1616. Thus Henderson threw in his lot with the Presbyterian Kirkmen just at the time when their fortunes were at the ebb, and we cannot doubt that God had brought him into the full tide of intelligent belief for such a time as this. He was soon on terms of warm and earnest friendship with men like the veteran William Scott of Cupar, and he became known and trusted in Fife. He was only a new recruit and he belonged to the younger generation; but the change was felt in Leuchars at once, and he was soon called out to stand

13. *Ibid*. Cf. Thomas McCrie, *The Life of Andrew Melville*, p. 181.
14. See R. L. Orr, *Alexander Henderson: Churchman and Statesman*, p. 20.

before the world. The King issued a new summons for a General Assembly to be held at Aberdeen in August, 1616, and Henderson was a member for the Presbytery of St. Andrews. It was the King's avowed desire to work through this Assembly for the furtherance of the episcopate, and the Bishops hoped to manage affairs on their own terms. It was resolved to take certain measures for the preparation of a new confession, catechism and liturgy, but the Assembly failed to accomplish most of what James had planned. It was significant mainly because it gave Henderson his great chance to declare himself for the cause which he had once so strongly opposed. The part which he took in private meetings of the brethren as well as on the floor of the Assembly was a happy omen for the future.

A more important Assembly was held at Perth during August, 1618, and Henderson was once more a member for the Presbytery of St. Andrews. This Assembly only sat for three days, but it set in motion a long train of controversy which did not end until the whole episcopal order was in fragments some twenty years later. Its work was to endorse a series of regulations known as the Five Articles of Perth: they dealt with such matters as kneeling at the Lord's Table, private celebration of the Sacraments, Confirmation by the Bishops, and the observance of Saints' Days. Threats were freely employed to force the Five Articles through the Assembly, but there was a solid minority of forty-five members who refused their assent. Henderson, Scott and Carmichael were the key men in the opposition, and their firmness was a demonstration of the strength of moral fibre. They were summoned before the Court of High Commission at St. Andrews in August, 1619 and were charged with having written and published a hostile criticism of the Perth Assembly. But the author was David Calderwood, and the charge could not be sustained. Three months later, a three-day Conference was held at St. Andrews between the two Archbishops and nine Bishops on the one hand and the clergy who refused to conform to the Perth Articles on the other. Henderson was the spokesman for the latter and made it clear that they would not yield to the King's demands. The Articles were ratified by Parliament in 1621 and the King at once wrote to the Bishops to say that since the sword had been unsheathed, they must not let it rust. But there was no further interference during his reign, and he died in 1625. Henderson, however, had now become a man of mark, and his name was known far beyond his own County of Fife. Various proposals were made to move him to some more influential parish; the Town Councils of Edinburgh in 1618 and of Aberdeen in 1623 held out their hands. But his heart was still in Leuchars; he that came in like a hireling felt a special obligation to serve his flock as a shepherd.

Charles I came to the throne in 1625, but there was no change in religious policy. His aim was to enforce all his father's laws with regard to Church affairs, and this aim was strengthened by an Act of Revocation which revoked and annulled all grants of Church and Crown lands in Scotland made since the year 1542. This Act was passed within the first year of his reign and was to prove the root cause of all his later troubles. Time was to show that Charles was in many ways much superior to his father, but he lacked his strength and self-reliance. He would always need the support of a stronger man to carry out his projects, and it was the misfortune of his reign that he had already begun to lean on Laud, who had become Bishop of St. Davids in 1621. James had felt grave mistrust for Laud and had only agreed to make him a Bishop after he had voiced a remarkable protest: "The plain truth is," he said, "I keep Laud back from all places of rule and authority, because I find he hath a restless spirit and cannot see when matters are well, but loves to toss and change and to bring things to a pitch of reformation floating in his own brain which may endanger the steadfastness of that which is in good pass."[15] But Charles took Laud into his heart and gave him a free hand in Church affairs. He was transferred from St. Davids to Bath and Wells in 1626, and from there to London in 1628; and he had more authority in this office than Abbot himself at Canterbury. It was Laud more than all others who nursed Charles in that concept of the kingly office which was to spell his ruin in England, as well as in that twin concept of the priestly office which was to spell his ruin in Scotland. Charles knew little enough of

15. C. V. Wedgwood, *Strafford*, p. 83.

his northern kingdom; Laud knew less still. But there can be no doubt that Laud had a definite animus against Scotsmen; his pen-portraits of the Scottish leaders are all etched with the same virulent prejudice. This may have been linked with one of his first visits to Court when the Scottish jester, Archie Armstrong, said grace at the royal table in the words: "All praise to God, and little Laud to the devil."[16] At all events, the old struggle between John Knox and Queen Mary, between Andrew Melville and James, was to break out again with Charles and Laud. And the Church with Henderson's leadership was to do for Scotland what the army under Cromwell was to do for England.

Very little is known of Henderson during the first twelve years of the new reign. Those years were like the lull before a storm, and he spent them in the labours of his country parish. They were years in which he poured out his strength in the cure of souls and the world of books. He was patient, thorough, a man of prayer, building up his people in the knowledge of truth, nursing his own soul in the grace of God. Meanwhile he stood alert on his watchtower and tried to judge how the situation would move to a climax. In August, 1625, Charles had issued a Royal Proclamation which was nailed to every Church door throughout Scotland and which required a strict conformity to the Perth Articles. In July, 1627, Henderson came up from the Presbytery of St. Andrews to attend the Edinburgh Conference, and he again showed great moral courage in his stand for the Kirk's independence. He won fresh praise in the lower courts of his own Presbytery, but no further public event in that decade summoned forth his strength in wider spheres of activity. In 1631 he received a call from the Kirk Session of Stirling, and in 1632 from the Kirk Session of Dumbarton; but he loved his parish and was without personal ambition, and he remained on at Leuchars although its low-lying marshes were a potent source of danger to health and strength. Archbishop Spottiswoode had shown himself anxious not to stir up needless difficulties, and the non-conforming clergy were still on the increase. Nevertheless severe measures were in operation, and it was a mark of Henderson's fortitude that he

16. Hugh Watt, *Recalling The Scottish Covenants*, p. 44.

refused to be subdued by the fate of others. The two Melvilles and John Welsh had died in exile during the reign of James I. Robert Bruce had died in 1631 after years of enforced silence. Carmichael's death and Scott's age now left Henderson almost alone as a captain in the Church's fight for freedom, and he must have braced his mind for the great struggle which he knew was at hand.

In June, 1633, Charles went north for his long delayed coronation in Scotland and Laud travelled with him to deal with the problems of Church worship. It had been hoped that this visit would do much to heal old quarrels, but its only result was to provoke the chief quarrel of all. Laud set up an altar in the Abbey Church at Holyrood for the coronation ceremonies, and thus disclosed his real purpose: for "at the back of this altar, there was a rich tapestry wherein the crucifix was curiously wrought, and as those bishops who were in service passed by this crucifix, they were seen to bow their knee and beck."[17] Laud then preached a sermon on the need for conformity and plans were launched to draw up a Book of Canons and a Liturgy for the Church in Scotland. A draft was first to be compiled by the Scottish Bishops, and then approved by Laud, and then imposed on the Church by the King's authority. On his return to London in August, Charles was able to greet Laud with the words: "My Lord's Grace of Canterbury, you are very welcome."[18] As the Primate of All England, he was thenceforth supreme, and his supremacy was soon felt in Scotland. "This little man, with his horse-shoe brows, and prim mouth, and sharp restless eyes,"[19] put an end to all wise moderation and pressed on with his plans for Church reform. At length, in May, 1635, a new Book of Canons for the Church of Scotland was confirmed and enjoined under the Great Seal by letters patent, and a complete code of regulations was thus promulgated on the sole authority of the King. This meant that by one stroke Laud had displaced the two Books of Discipline which had embodied the constitution of Presbyterian Church Government. Perhaps the most dangerous element

17. See R. L. Orr, *op. cit.,* p. 52.
18. *Dictionary of National Biography,* "William Laud."
19. John Buchan, *Oliver Cromwell,* p. 87.

in this innovation was the fact that the Church had not been asked for her consent. It was with some reason that a punning critic presumed to say that Laud's Canons would soon make more noise than all the cannons of Edinburgh Castle.

But it was not until Charles and Laud took steps to impose a new form of worship on clergy and people that the real storm burst in Scotland. The Book of Canons was a bad omen, but the Romanised Liturgy was a deliberate threat to the whole Scottish Reformation. In April, 1635 the draft of this Service Book was endorsed by the Scottish Bishops, but it was not until December, 1636 that it was finally authorized by the King's letter and a proclamation of the Privy Council. There were immediate signs of trouble when this became known in Scotland. It was not as though there were a rigid hostility against all forms of prayer in Church worship. People were quite ready to hear the prayers compiled by John Knox read in their churches. But they opposed Laud's Book because it was meant to exclude all prayers of an extempore kind and because it would promote what they believed to be unsound in doctrine and teaching. They felt that the only way in which it differed from the English Prayer Book was by closer spiritual proximity to the Roman Mass Book. There was also the fact that it would be forced on Scottish congregations by royal mandate and this would raise the whole question of the authority of the King with regard to Church affairs. Nothing could prevent a national explosion when it was known that a day had been fixed for the introduction of the Book to public worship. On that fateful Sunday, July 23, 1637, the two Archbishops and the Chancellor, other Bishops and the Lords of Session, members of the Privy Council and the City Magistrates, made their way in robes of office to the Cathedral Church of St. Giles in Edinburgh. But the people also had poured into the Church, and they meant to welcome the use of the new Book with an uproar. The Dean's courage failed him, but the Bishop ordered him to proceed with the Collects. It was then, according to tradition, that Jenny Geddes, a poor woman who kept a herb stall near the Tron, flung her stool with a curse at the head of the Dean. The whole Service broke up in a tumult; the Scots had been stirred to the white heat of spiritual indignation.

It was this great crisis which at last brought the most able man in the Kirk out of his quiet manse at Leuchars. He was fifty-four years old when he found himself at the head of a great movement which was to shake the whole nation, and the nine years of life which still remained were to be spent without reserve in the public service of the Church and State in Scotland. He had ceased to be a merely private figure long before that July day at St. Giles, and had plainly been marked out for wider activities. He had been the object of close and jealous observation by those in authority, and they had been eager to seize on the slightest mistake which might have vexed the cause for which he stood. Not many weeks before, on March 9, Samuel Rutherford had sent him a friendly warning from his place of exile: "As for your cause, my reverend and dearest brother, ye are the talk of the north and south; and looked to, so as if ye were all crystal glass. Your motes and dust would soon be proclaimed, and trumpets blown at your slips; but I know that ye have laid help upon One that is mighty.... God hath called you to Christ's side, and the wind is now in Christ's face in this land; and seeing ye are with Him, ye can not expect the lee-side or the sunny side of the brae.... Let us pray for one another. He Who hath made you a chosen arrow in His quiver, hide you in the hollow of His hand."[20] Rutherford knew, as others knew, that Henderson combined a clear mind with a firm grasp of affairs. He was known as a man with a high-minded sense of courtesy in debate and a clear-sighted gift for promptitude in action. He was quiet and grave in manner, but he spoke with fluent ease and authority. He had always excelled as a spontaneous speaker, yet his utterances were so clear and rounded that they always seemed to suggest full and careful preparation. He was indeed the talk of the north and the south when the fracas at St. Giles burst upon Scotland.

Protests against the Book poured in from all quarters; the nobles and gentry as well as the common people flocked into the city. A deep sense of anxiety was felt as a Supplication was drawn up and sent to the King. It asked for the suppression of the

20. A. A. Bonar, *op. cit.*, (Letter 115), pp. 233, 234.

Liturgy, and it was signed by the leading men in Scotland. But Charles and Laud had learnt nothing, and the struggle went on. On August 10 clergy in Fife received orders to buy copies of the new Book for use in their Churches within fifteen days on pain of imprisonment. Henderson, with two others in the Presbytery of St. Andrews, at once stood out and refused to comply. He was willing to buy the Book and read it for his own information, but he would not promise to make any further use of its forms of prayer. Thus he entered the lists and threw down the gauntlet in a challenge which the Bishops could not evade. He was the first man of mark to resist episcopal authority on this issue, and the result was that his case became a test for the Church as a whole. A messenger-at-arms served him with an order to buy and use the Book within fifteen days on pain of imprisonment; but the threat fell on a man with a heart of steel, and its force was broken and turned aside. Henderson determined to test the whole matter by the Laws of Scotland, and on August 23, he lodged a petition with the Privy Council to suspend the order on the ground that the Book had not yet been approved by a General Assembly nor by Parliament. When the Privy Council met on August 25, his appeal was upheld: it was affirmed that the order extended only to the purchase of the Book "and no farder,"[21] and an address to the King was prepared, asking him to summon a deputation to London. This not only delivered Henderson from the threat of imprisonment; it changed the whole situation, for it meant that within the space of a few days, the cause of one man had become the cause of the whole Church.

It was by this courageous step that Henderson took his place in the field of Church affairs where he was to prove the foremost figure in the fight for freedom. He had in fact compelled the Church to give up its merely passive opposition and to commit itself to an implacable conflict. The next ten years were to form one of the decisive periods in the historical development of England and Scotland alike, and he was an avowed leader in Church and State throughout the whole of that crowded decade. The swift

21. *Dictionary of National Biography*, "Alexander Henderson."

rush of events north of the Tweed was to produce wide and instant repercussions in the Southern Kingdom, and we tend to lose sight of the minor details of that epoch while our eyes are focused on deeds of more renown. But we see Henderson behind the scene or on the stage at each new turn of this living drama, for both in private and in public, he was guide and captain of his party and the movement for which it stood. He was always ready for counsel or action; his was the chief mind in the one, and the strong hand in the other. The full stature of the man is never seen so clearly as when we take stock of those who were his fellows. Some of them brought to their party the strength of rank and name as well as their private worth and talents; he had nothing but his moral integrity and his native ability. These were assets which must have been of the highest order, for they transformed him from a quiet rural minister into the most prominent man in Scotland. Nobles like Rothes and Loudon would have graced any country; preachers like Blair and Dickson would have cheered any party. But they would have been the first to acknowledge Henderson's superior ability in the affairs of Church and State. "They had all to consult him," so David Masson affirmed, "in every strait and conflict he had to be appealed to, and came in at the last as a man of supereminent composure, comprehensiveness, and breadth of brow."[22]

Henderson and Lord Balmerino arranged to keep in touch with the course of events through the Lord Advocate, Sir Thomas Hope, and thus were ready to act when the King sent down his reply in mid-September. Charles had refused to make the least concession, but had issued orders to have the use of the Liturgy enforced at once. Henderson and Balmerino conferred with Sir Thomas Hope, and a Supplication was drawn up and handed in as from no less than two hundred parishes. But Charles and the Bishops who were members of the Privy Council would not relent, and on October 17, an order was proclaimed at the Cross by sound of trumpet to compel the Petitioners to leave the City within twenty-four hours on pain of treason. But this only served to stimulate Henderson and his friends in opposition, and they

22. David Masson, *The Life of John Milton*, Vol. III, p. 16.

fastened on the Council order as the ground for a more decisive remonstrance. Whereas so far they had only sought to suspend the order with regard to use of the Liturgy, they now resolved to proceed against the Bishops themselves as the real authors of all the troubles which the Liturgy had entailed.

David Dickson and the Earl of Loudon drafted the terms for a formal complaint which was ready for a meeting of the Petitioners the day after the Council had ordered them to disperse. Thus on October 18 this document was accepted by the Petitioners, and it was soon subscribed by thirty-eight nobles, several hundred ministers, gentlemen without number, and all the Burghs in Scotland except Aberdeen. This was a far-seeing course of action, for it combined all classes into a solid and impressive unity. It would encourage a strong sense of cohesion at a time of common danger and it carried the whole struggle into the camp of their veteran opponents. Bishops would no longer sit in judgment on the Petitioners, but would stand their own trial as the major trouble makers in the life of Scotland. Thus by the end of October the whole of the Lowlands was aflame with indignation, and the quarrel had spread far beyond the Service Book and its first issues.

The whole situation was full of grave alternatives, and the King's cause required a firm hand in control; but there was none. Members of the Privy Council waited on Charles, and the only course of action of which Charles could think was to issue a series of foolish and irritating proclamations. Large crowds still thronged the streets and kept the whole city in a state of ferment, and the Petitioners did not disperse until November 17, when the tension was eased by a compromise arrangement. A large majority of the Petitioners then left Edinburgh, knowing that it had been agreed by the Privy Council that a certain group should remain. This group was to consist of a representative body of sixteen Presbyterians who were to meet at four tables in the parliament house: the nobles, the gentry, the ministers, the burgesses, were each to have their own table. These four Tables, with four members for each Table, formed the central group of sixteen, and one member from each Table formed a supreme council of four members only. These four Tables had no legal standing, and had only been called into being by the Privy Council in the hope that they would divide and break up the Petitioners: but they gave the Petitioners direct access to all kinds of information, and they were soon in full control of all Scottish affairs. It was not long before the main Table was in effect manned by Loudon and Dickson, Warriston and Henderson. Robert Baillie liked to say that Henderson and Dickson were "the two Archbishops" in this cabinet of the Presbyterian party.[23] It was undoubtedly under Henderson's management that they discovered and developed their authority. If the Privy Council were the recognized Government, the four Tables were the unofficial Opposition; the party in office was the Privy Council, but the real power lay with those in opposition. The great mass of Scottish feeling was ranged behind the four Tables, and the virtual government of the country soon passed into their hands.

In due time it became clear that they would have to contend with Charles himself rather than the Privy Council or the Bishops. On February 19, 1638, the Earls of Traquair and Roxburgh made a proclamation for the Privy Council with flourish of trumpets at the Cross of Stirling. It was announced that the King had confirmed the use of the Service Book and that all meetings of the Petitioners would now be held treasonable. Three days later, on February 22, the same proclamation was issued in Edinburgh, and it became impossible to avoid an open rupture. Men of high rank had been involved in an overt act of wilful opposition to the King and Privy Council as a result of their part in the General Supplication. It was now to become treason to keep up the agitation; therefore they were compelled to face the odds. Either they would have to submit to the King's terms, or they must needs prepare for war. And such preparation would have to be on the widest scale if they were to cope with the forces which the Crown could marshal for their destruction. Such an alternative would be a most perilous enterprise, but the great qualities of men like Henderson were to match its demands. His task was to defend the Church in its doctrine and government from the assaults of Charles and Laud; this would need skill,

23. *Dictionary of National Biography,* "Alexander Henderson."

tact, shrewdness and courage. He saw that the least sign of a modified attitude on the part of Laud might yet save the day for the Bishops and he saw that it was imperative to stave off all attempts to drive a wedge between the ranks of the Presbyterians. Thus the idea of a National Covenant took shape in his own mind, and this was to prove the master-stroke of his policy — decisive, effective, and great beyond his dreams. It was a grand design to link all ranks in a bond of union which would commit them in absolute loyalty to Christ's Crown and Kingdom.

Henderson knew the risks of exile or of imprisonment in the lonely cells of Blackness Castle, but he counted not his life dear unto himself in the service of his Master. Thus on February 23, in spite of the proclamation, Henderson made his proposal in the midst of a fresh and vast concourse of the Presbyterian party in Edinburgh. He asked for a national subscription to a common bond of faith and action, and the response was a tremendous resurgence of the people's good-will. There was nothing new in the main idea; James VI himself had subscribed the Covenant of 1581 in favour of the Reformation doctrines. Good men throughout Scotland were grieved at the decline from this older Covenant and proved eager to take up the latest proposal. Thus Henderson and Warriston were asked to draft the terms of this historic document, and they made the first part consist of a verbatim copy of the older Covenant: this was followed by a section in which Warriston summarized all the legislation which had been passed in its favour and a special section in which Henderson endeavoured to link the whole bond with current circumstances.

On Sunday, February 25, congregations were called upon to mourn for the breaches of the earlier Covenant which had brought God's wrath on the land. On Tuesday, the 27th, the new document was amended and accepted after it had been read in the people's hearing. The great burden of this famous statement was that of full personal and national dedication to God. This alone can explain all the later scenes of enthusiasm among people whose tradition for reticence is so strongly rooted in character and history. "From the knowledge and conscience of our duty to God, to our King, and country, so far as human infirmity will suffer, wishing a further measure of the Grace of God for this effect," so the Covenant asserted, "We promise and swear by the Great Name of the Lord our God to continue in the profession and obedience of the foresaid religion."[24]

The next day, February 28, was the day fixed for signature and subscription, and there have been few more memorable days in Scotland than that Wednesday. There is no more famous scene in Scottish annals than the scene on that chill afternoon in the old Church of the Greyfriars. A fast had been proclaimed and the Church was filled with nobles and barons from all over the country. At two o'clock, Rothes, Loudon, Dickson, Henderson and Warriston arrived with a copy of the Covenant for signature. Proceedings were opened by Henderson when he engaged in a prayer of sublime thought and feeling: he stood with face upturned amid the bowed heads of hundreds and poured out his prayer "verrie powerfullie and pertinentlie."[25] Then the Earl of Loudon gave a solemn address, and Warriston read out the terms of the Covenant. This was followed by a long pause and a profound stillness, until the Earl of Rothes asked if there were anyone who wished to object. At four o'clock, the first name was subscribed and the signing went on until near eight o'clock that night. The old legend of the immense numbers who signed their names on an up-turned tombstone in the church-yard has been discredited; it was only the nobles and barons who signed that day and they did so inside the Church. But long pent-up feelings swept through their minds, and they confirmed their signature and subscription with an oath of tender solemnity. Tears coursed down the cheeks of many when they lifted up their right hand as the sign of a vow before the great Searcher of all hearts that they would defend His Crown and His Kingdom. It was a bold affirmation that the spiritual duties of the Church ought to be free from interference, and Henderson was elated when he declared: "This was the day of the Lord's power wherein we saw His people most willingly offer themselves in multitudes like the dew-drops of the morning,... the day of the Redeemer's strength, on which the princes of the

24. See R. L. Orr, *op. cit.*, p. 127.
25. See John Aiton, *op. cit.*, p. 254.

people assembled to swear their allegiance to the King of kings."[26]

The people of Edinburgh signed the next day, and on Friday, March 1, copies were despatched to every shire and parish in the Kingdom. It was received in all but one or two places with the same enthusiasm and was subscribed by so many that the whole realm was as one man in the good cause. John Livingston tells us what he saw with his own eyes at Lanark: "I may truly say that in all my life-time, excepting at the Kirk of Shotts, I never saw such motions from the Spirit of God.... I have seen more than a thousand persons all at once lifting up their hands, and the tears falling down from their eyes."[27] The Universities of St. Andrews and Aberdeen stood out at first with a formal condemnation of the National Covenant, but mid-summer found the city and shire of Aberdeen almost alone in opposition. Henderson was a leading member of a deputation which was sent to visit Aberdeen in the month of July and he secured five hundred signatures for the Covenant in the city as well as those of some fifty ministers in the district. Henderson had now become the first man in his country, and his country had made its stand. His quiet days at Leuchars, his love of retirement, his lack of ambition, had to be laid aside. He was busied henceforth with all kinds of public duties, for no step was taken without consultation with him. His voice was heard in all the private assemblies which were arranged; his hand was seen in all the public documents which were compiled. He dealt with the agents who came from the court: he drew up the statements which went to the press. But his greatest contribution was to seek the immediate restoration of the General Assembly and to urge the calling of a National Parliament so that measures taken for the Church's freedom could be sanctioned by law. Thus he drew up a new Supplication and sent it to London. He was led by a sure instinct in the formation of this policy, although the King only spat out his wrath at the "damnable Covenant" and sent it back unread.[28]

Charles knew that he would have to come to terms or go to war. And his mind was resolved for war. But he was in need of

26. *Ibid.*, p. 257.
27. *Ibid.*, p. 259.
28. See R. L. Orr, *op. cit.*, p. 132.

men and money, and he hoped to spring a trap by keeping them in suspense until he was ready. Thus he appointed the Marquis of Hamilton as Commissioner for Scotland and sent him north to waste time and deceive the Scots with fair speeches. On June 9 the Marquis made an almost regal progress through the streets of Edinburgh and set to work on his thankless mission. His task was to wean the nobles away from the commons and then persuade them to renounce the Covenant. His plan was to shuffle as long as he could on each point in debate and then move on to some new shift. The next three or four months were spent in a diplomatic struggle between Hamilton on one side and Henderson on the other, and the Marquis found himself out-witted by the Covenanter at each new point in the conflict. He was hustled from post to post until he had lost all his original ground, and he did not even gain time, much less command respect for the King's cause.

Henderson's consummate ability was proved by the skill and firmness with which he matched and foiled all the Commissioner's tactics. He told Hamilton from the beginning that the King would have to summon a General Assembly and National Parliament, and that the next step would be to sanction the trial of the Bishops as the cause of all the trouble. Hamilton finally agreed, but he wished to impose restrictive conditions which would have placed them in a most awkward situation. Henderson's reaction was to take steps for a General Assembly — with or without the King's sanction — and the Tables at once required all Kirk Sessions and the Presbyteries to proceed in conformity with the Act of Dundee of May, 1547. Thus the King's hand was forced, and he gave in. The Privy Council issued a summons for a General Assembly to meet at Glasgow on November 21, 1638 and for Parliament to meet in Edinburgh on May 15, 1639. A Royal Declaration absolved Scotland from the five Perth Articles and the Court of High Commission, from the Book of Canons and the Liturgy, and made the Bishops subject to the censure of the Assembly.

The air was tense with excitement and emotion when the General Assembly met at last on that November Wednesday in the Cathedral Church of Glasgow. All men knew that it would provide the field for an intense struggle: a struggle not merely to resolve the merits of episcopal and presbyterian forms of government, but to decide whether it would result in peace or war. Both sides prepared for the contest with the utmost activity; the King's Commissioner did all that he could to guard the future. But the Assembly was largely composed of men who were committed to the Covenant and all the most influential of the Presbyterian leaders were among its members. The handful of Petitioners led by Henderson twelve months before had now increased in numbers and prestige in such a way that they could speak with their foes in the gate. The King had found no one in Church or State who could handle his cause with the tact it required or who could serve the Crown with skill equal to the emergency. But we can judge what the private anxieties of the Petitioners were like before they met from the words of Robert Baillie: "We were somewhat in suspense about Mr. Alexander Henderson; he was incomparably the ablest man of us for all things. We doubted if the Moderator might be a disputer; we expected then much dispute with the Bishops and Aberdeen Doctors. We thought our loss great and hazardous to tyne our chief champion by making him a judge of the party."[29]

Henderson was elected as Moderator on Friday, November 23, with no vote in opposition except his own, and there could have been no better combination when Warriston was elected as Clerk of the Assembly. A clear mental picture of that famous body, in those days of early winter, would show us a little table placed just in front of the Commissioner. Behind that table sat Henderson, a man in the middle fifties, his face "yellow from the fevers of the Leuchars marshes, lined with thought, and burning with a steady fire."[30] Beside him sat Warriston, at the age of twenty-seven, canny and lynx-eyed, lawyer and mystic, apt to forget time on his knees, a man of power with his brethren.[31]

The main struggle began when the Moderator proposed to bring forward the trial of the Bishops. Hamilton at once inter-

---

29. See G. Webster Thomson, *Alexander Henderson* (in *The Evangelical Succession,* Second Series), pp. 111, 112.
30. John Buchan, *Montrose,* p. 89.
31. *Ibid.,* p. 75.

vened and made a strong statement: "I stand to the King's prerogative as supreme judge over all causes, civil and ecclesiastical.
To him the Lords of the Clergy have appealed, and therefore I
will not suffer their cause to be farther reasoned here."[32] He urged
Henderson to end proceedings with prayer, but the Moderator was
not to be deterred. This was now the supreme test of his power
as a leader and he refused to shrink from its challenge. The eyes
of all were fixed upon him as he faced the King's Commissioner;
no one was in any doubt as to what a firm line of conduct
might cost. Neither could they have guessed from the modest
exterior of the man what courage and what wisdom were locked
within. He stood his ground with firm intent, dignified, courteous, resolute; it was a stand both for freedom and for duty.
The King's Commissioner renewed all his former protests in
the King's name, and laid it down that no Act passed in that
Assembly could be held valid in law. Then, on Wednesday,
November 28, in the name of the King, he dissolved the Assembly and retired. Henderson's leadership did not fail him
when the Marquis withdrew, and he ignored the dangers of
treason as he addressed himself to the Assembly. "All who are
present," he said, "know how this Assembly was indicted, and
what power WE ALLOW to our Sovereign in matters ecclesiastical."[33] All the members of the Assembly with the exception of the three or four from Angus then raised their hands in
a formal vote to remain until they had finished the work in
hand. Then they proceeded with the conduct of their business on the ground that the Church had the right to govern
its own affairs. But this was a course of action in circumstances
which implied little less than revolution. The King's authority
had been disregarded on the ground that the Church was bound
to yield to the higher authority of Him Who is invisible.

Thus this General Assembly sat at Glasgow for a full month,
and its work was thorough. It annulled the six corrupt Assemblies which had been held since the accession of James to the
English Throne in 1603 and it declared that the episcopal

32. John Aiton, *op. cit.*, p. 356.
33. *Ibid.*, p. 357.

system of Church Government was not consistent with the Confessions of the Church of Scotland in 1580, 1581, and 1590. It renounced the Perth Articles, the Book of Canons, and the Liturgy; it restored the old forms of worship in their original simplicity. Perhaps the main object which occupied the Assembly was the trial and censure of the Bishops. Fruitless efforts had been made to induce the King's Commissioner to summon the Bishops before the bar of the Assembly and it is not surprising that, with the King's express authority, they had refused to accept its jurisdiction. They were arraigned by name in their absence, and the words of Robert Baillie make it clear that something rather less than justice was done.[34] But they were found guilty and were sentenced in terms of marked severity: six were to be deposed, and the other eight were to be excommunicated as well. It fell to the Moderator to pronounce the sentence, and this was done with great solemnity. On Tuesday, December 13, Henderson preached before the Assembly on the words of David: "The Lord said unto my Lord, Sit Thou at my right hand until I make Thine enemies Thy footstool" (Ps. 110:1). This grave sermon was known as "The Bishop's Doom,"[35] and it was followed by the words of deposition and of excommunication "in a very dreadful and grave manner."[36] The whole programme which had been envisaged by the National Covenant was thus carried into effect and the Second Reformation (as it has often been called) was complete. No two men could have done more to guide it to a successful conclusion than Henderson and Warriston. Their work was, in fact, to form the basis on which the whole structure of the Church of Scotland has since been built. We ought not to forget Henderson's words of dismissal when he dissolved the Assembly on December 20th: "We have now cast down the walls of Jericho; let him that rebuildeth them beware of the curse of Hiel the Bethelite."[37]

Henderson's leadership had been confirmed by his wise and able guidance of that historic Assembly; he had won the admiration of all

34. See R. L. Orr, *op. cit.,* p. 184.
35. *Ibid.,* p. 184.
36. See John Aiton, *op. cit.,* p. 361.
37. *Ibid.,* p. 368.

in the discharge of his duties. He had never lost the vision of things unseen and he had kept the tone of the Assembly on a level of high dignity. He had met in private with his closer friends each evening and had often consumed a large part of the night with them in prayer. Many evenings were spent with the young Lord Lorne of Argyll and the future Marquis traced his conversion, or the assurance of it, to Henderson's quiet ministry.[38] This man, with his slender frame and pensive features, had now become the most trusted leader of the Scottish people, and it was felt that he must move from his country Church at Leuchars to a central and more commanding position. Edinburgh and St. Andrews both applied to the Assembly for his appointment as one of their ministers, but he was loath to go either to the one or to the other. But it was quite in vain for him to plead that he was too old a plant to take root in such fresh soil or that he might bear more fruit where he was than in the heart of a city.[39] It was of no avail even to say that if he must take his leave of Leuchars, he would prefer to go to St. Andrews rather than to Edinburgh. It was resolved by the Assembly on December 18, 1638 that he should be moved to Edinburgh, and a few weeks later, on January 10, 1639, he was installed as the minister of the Cathedral Church of St. Giles. His own subsequent reflections on the guidance of God in this matter are an authentic example of true Christian piety. "When from my sense of myself and my own thoughts and ways," he wrote, "I begin to remember how men who love to live obscurely and in the shadow are brought forth to light, to the view and talking of the world; how men that love quietness are made to stir and to have a hand in public business; how men that love soliloquies and contemplations are brought upon debates and controversies; and generally, how men are brought to act the things which they never determined nor so much as dreamed of before: the words of the Prophet Jeremiah come to my remembrance, 'O Lord, I know that the way of man is not in himself; it is not in man that walketh to direct his steps.' "[40]

38. See Alexander Smellie, *Men of the Covenant*, p. 63.
39. John Aiton, *op. cit.*, p. 364.
40. *Ibid.*, p. 365, footnote.

War was now imminent, and the Covenanters set their house in order; the call to arms sounded in village and hamlet while the Scottish leaders still did what they could to conciliate the King. The whole idea of war was so distasteful to a man like Henderson, and some of his statements were so conciliatory that they caused real offence within his own party. But Charles sent a fleet to blockade the Firth of Forth and marched at the head of his troops to the Lowland borders. The Commons had refused to grant supplies for this expedition, but the Bishops had come forward under Laud with large-scale contributions. Thus in England this was called the Bishops' War and Charles was ridiculed as Canterbury's Knight. Charles reached Berwick on May 28 and the Scots pitched their camp at Dunse Law some six miles away. The hill-top was garrisoned with forty mounted cannons and the slopes were covered with regiments. A new pennon fluttered at the captains' tent doors, embossed with the arms of Scotland and a motto wrought in letters of gold: "For Christ's Crown and Covenant."[41] The whole force was under the command of Alexander Leslie, "that old, little, crooked soldier," who had been trained in the school of Gustavus Adolphus.[42] A Council of War took place each day in the Castle of Dunse, and a daily meeting of the regimental chaplains was held in the tent of the Earl of Rothes. Each morning and evening, 20,000 men were summoned by sound of trump or beat of drum to prayer and the exhortation to put their trust in the sword of the Lord. But the two main armies never met in battle, for their leaders resolved to treat for peace. On June 18, the Pacification of Berwick was signed, and its terms make it clear that the affairs of Church and State were now treated as one. It confirmed the abrogation of the Perth Articles and the Court of High Commission; it approved the abolition of the Book of Canons and the Liturgy; it affirmed that the Bishops were answerable to the General As-

41. See Alexander Smellie, *op. cit.*, p. 110.
42. *Ibid.* Gustavus Adolphus (1594-1632), King of Sweden, a great soldier and trainer of generals, who won wars against Denmark, Russia and Poland and supported, through his religious interest, the Protestant cause in the Thirty Years' War.

sembly; and it agreed that a General Assembly and a National Parliament should meet at least each year.

Henderson was one of the six Scottish Commissioners who drew up and signed the terms of this peace treaty, and it brought him for the first time into direct contact with the King, with whom he had much personal discussion. Charles seems to have felt a genuine attraction to the Earl of Loudon and Henderson, and on their knees they begged him to agree to the final abolition of the episcopal system. Charles was convinced of their personal loyalty, and spoke highly of their prudence and skill. Henderson was so favourably received that Mr. Secretary Coke's clerk, Edward Norgate, wrote of him as follows: "Indeed, for Henderson, he is so highly commended for a grave, pious, and learned man, he has made one at every conference; and Mr. Secretary (Coke) tells me that in all his speeches, you may find as much devotion, wisdom, humility and obedience as can be wished for in an honest man and a good subject."[43] Henderson had in fact proved himself as the greatest statesman north of the Tweed, and his prestige had reached new heights when the Assembly met in Edinburgh during August. The Earl of Traquair was the King's Commissioner, and David Dickson was chosen as the Moderator. Henderson's name had been proposed, but he declined on the ground that he had held the office on the last occasion; but he was the ruling member, always at hand with his wise and prescient suggestions for the welfare of the whole Church.[44] This Assembly had none of the splendour of the Glasgow Assembly the year before, although it renewed the Covenant with the express sanction of Charles himself. But the Earl of Traquair was more skilful in his management of the Parliament which met as soon as the Assembly had been dissolved. Henderson preached before the Parliament on August 31, and it was then prorogued before it could ratify what the Assembly had done. This meant that the Pacification of Berwick had failed in its purpose; it had settled

43. See R. L. Orr, *op. cit.*, pp. 207, 208.
44. J. Pringle Thomson, *Alexander Henderson: The Covenanter*, p. 75.

nothing on a lasting basis, and the threat of war had now been revived.

In January, 1640, the Earl of Loudon journeyed south to wait on Charles at Whitehall, but he was sent to the Tower of London because Charles was in the midst of preparation for war. Henderson was well aware of the danger ahead, and issued a warning to his colleagues. He would not leave Edinburgh even for the General Assembly when it met at Aberdeen in July, for the English army was once more close to the border. But he joined "the little crooked soldier" Leslie at the end of the month when he reoccupied his old camp at Dunse Law. Then, on August 21, the Blue Bonnets crossed the Tweed and mastered Newcastle and Durham within the next few days. The Scots were now on the soil of England, and Charles was forced once more to treat for peace. Henderson was one of eight Scottish Commissioners who were sent to Ripon to meet the King's Commissioners on October 1, but the business was then transferred from Ripon to London. Henderson was delayed by illness and only arrived in London on November 14. But things were to drag on until July, 1641.

Meanwhile the Town Council of Edinburgh had taken steps in January to revive the office of Rector of the University, and he was to hold this office by his re-election each year until his death. It was while in London that he proposed to Charles his plan for a financial subsidy for the Scottish Universities from the revenues of the Scottish Bishoprics. This plan did not succeed, but he gave of his best to the cause of education in his country. Sir Alexander Grant affirmed that he was "the ablest educationist and the man of clearest insight" of all those who had been concerned with the development of the University of Edinburgh.[45] He had the eye to see what was wanted, and the tact and drive to carry it out. He introduced to Edinburgh the teaching of Hebrew and the honour classes known as "circles." He encouraged the colleges in the teaching of Greek and of Logic, and he left two thousand marks Scots as a bequest for a school at Luthrie in the parish of Creich.[46] He was indeed a right true son of John

45. See R. L. Orr, *op. cit.*, p. 386.
46. *Dictionary of National Biography*, "Alexander Henderson."

Knox and Andrew Melville in his desire to promote the learning and literature of Scotland.

These nine months in London brought the Scottish Commissioners into contact with the leading men in England, and their stay was coincident with the first months of the Long Parliament. On November 11 the Earl of Strafford was accused by the House of Commons, sequestered from the Upper House, and confined by the Usher of the Black Rod. On December 18 Archbishop Laud was disgraced in the same way, and not a voice was raised in his defence in the Commons. Robert Baillie could not refrain from an exclamation full of triumph: "God," he wrote, "is making here a new world."[47] Baillie and the Earl of Loudon framed the Scottish charges against Laud and Strafford; Henderson and Warriston were employed to revise and abridge their draft. The Scots were at Strafford's trial each morning at five o'clock once it began on March 22, 1641; they were seated with the Commons just behind the platform on which he stood in the midst of Westminster Hall. When his execution took place on May 12, they made their way through the crowded city to the King at Whitehall and were surprised to find him, once the long strain was over, calm and cheerful. Meanwhile long and anxious conversations had been in full progress and it had been Henderson's task to draft the papers which came up for discussion. The King and the Scottish Commissioners all hoped for a uniform settlement for the Church in the three Kingdoms, and the only point in debate was the question whether it should be an Episcopal or Presbyterian uniformity. Charles had stood out against all compromise when compromise would have brought peace, and there was now no concession which he would not make when concession had ceased to be enough. Thus Henderson was invited to see him in private; several interviews took place and on August 7 a new treaty was signed. Henderson understood it as a pledge of full Presbyterian uniformity, but Charles had been careful not to commit himself against his own dream of Episcopal conformity. Meanwhile the Scots believed that they had won the King's goodwill and had obtained all their desire.

47. See C. V. Wedgewood, *op. cit.*, p. 276.

Henderson and Gillespie left London in July to travel back to Scotland in time for the General Assembly. It had opened at St. Andrews on July 20, 1641, but had then been adjourned until the 27th and transferred to Edinburgh so that Henderson might have time to arrive and take its chair as the Moderator. It was at this Assembly that he made his proposals for a Confession of Faith, a Catechism, and a Directory for Church Government and Worship: and his object was to secure formularies which could become binding on the Churches of England and Scotland alike. He was himself asked to draft these formularies; but his other duties stood in the way, and he also saw the necessity of co-operation with the English Divines. "This must be brought to pass by common consent," he told Baillie in April, 1642, "and we are not to conceive that they will embrace our Form, but a new Form must be set down for us all."[48] Henderson asked the Assembly for the sake of his health to move him from Edinburgh to a country parish, but he declined the appointment as Principal of St. Andrews. He was at length released from his duties at Great St. Giles, but he agreed to remain in Edinburgh. Meanwhile Charles had announced that he meant to visit Scotland for the first time since his Coronation eight years before, and his arrival at Holyrood on August 14 was followed by the appointment of Henderson as his chaplain. In this capacity he received a stipend of four thousand marks per annum from the revenues of the Chapel Royal at Holyrood. The King heard him pray and expound morning and evening on Tuesdays, and it was his duty to find preachers for other occasions. Henderson had ample opportunity for private conversation with Charles and there can be no doubt that Charles liked him in a way that was quite new for Scottish preachers. The King felt that he could trust his integrity at a time when it was hard to know in whom to confide, and he listened to his advice in a way that he would never listen to more bitter critics. But there were not wanting those who whispered that Henderson was in the King's pocket, and this moved him at the General Assembly at St. Andrews the next July to voice a long and passionate vindication of his conduct.

48. See David Masson, *op. cit.*, Vol. II, p. 419.

The Reformation in Scotland was Henderson's great work; the Revolution in England went far to wreck his dreams. On August 22, 1642, Charles raised the Royal Standard at Nottingham, and the Civil War broke upon England. Good men north of the Tweed looked on with grave and anxious eyes; their great desire was to keep out of the quarrel and to foster the cause of peace. Henderson exercised all his diplomatic skill in favour of strict neutrality, but his plan for the Queen to come over from Holland to Scotland as a mediator was not acceptable. At the end of February, 1643, he and Loudon were sent by the Privy Council and the Commission of the Assembly to treat with the King at Oxford and to urge peace on the basis of Presbyterian uniformity in England. But they received a cold welcome, and their mission was a failure. Henderson returned to Edinburgh in May and in August was chosen for the third time as the Moderator of the General Assembly. It was just at this time that Sir Harry Vane, Philip Nye and Stephen Marshall had come north as Commissioners for the House of Commons to seek military aid from Scotland, and they also brought a formal request that the General Assembly should send delegates to the Westminster Assembly of Divines. Henderson's sympathies would have made him glad to avoid intervention in the affairs of the Southern Kingdom, but he could not deny that the cause of spiritual freedom was now involved in the military struggle. It was at length agreed only to send Scottish soldiers into England if both countries were joined in a spiritual compact like that of the National Covenant. Thus Henderson and Warriston were called upon to draft the terms of a Solemn League and Covenant. On August 17 this was approved by the General Assembly and the English Commissioners, while Henderson and Gillespie were called upon to set out at once for London to secure its adoption and to attend the Assembly of Divines. Thus, on Saturday, August 19, 1643, Henderson dissolved the Assembly with "a gracious speech and sweet prayer,"[49] and on Wednesday, August 30, he set his face once more towards London, as the ambassador of his church and nation.

49. See J. Pringle Thomson, *op. cit.*, p. 113.

On September 25, 1643, members of the House of Lords and the House of Commons, the Divines from the Westminster Assembly and the Commissioners from Scotland, met in St. Margaret's Church at Westminster. John White led the meeting in prayer and Philip Nye then preached the sermon. Prayer and sermon were each an hour in length, as might befit so august a meeting. This was followed by a speech from Henderson to explain the work in hand, and then the text of the Solemn League and Covenant was read from a roll of parchment. The whole congregation stood with bared heads and hands upraised until the last word had been read. Then two hundred and twenty-two Members of both Houses came forward to subscribe, followed by the Westminster Divines and the Scottish Commissioners. The great meeting was closed with prayer, and the spiritual bond which had been mooted by the Scottish leaders was a reality. It was tendered for subscription in all parts of England on the Sunday and was sponsored by the Puritan ministers throughout the Realm. This great document was "an instrument of impressive power and singular skill"; it was a vow for the abolition of the Episcopal system, but it left the further question of Church Government to be determined "by the example of the best Reformed Churches."[50] Meanwhile its terms were a pledge to preserve the doctrine and worship, the discipline and government, of the Reformed Church of Scotland. It also engaged them to defend the King's person and to uphold the rights of the House of Commons. Thus the National Covenant of Scotland in 1638 had become the basis of the Solemn League and Covenant between the two Kingdoms in 1643. But at best it was a doubtful experiment. Henderson's genius had shown its true instinct in the National Covenant at a grave hour in his own north country; it was in line with the tradition and sentiment of Scotland, and it bound the nation as one man to meet a pressing danger. But his ideal for one uniform religion in both Kingdoms as now proposed in the Solemn League and Covenant was less sure in instinct. Time was to prove that it did not fit in with the history

50. *Dictionary of National Biography*, "Alexander Henderson."

or character of England, and the best that can be said is that it was a splendid vision.

The close of the year found Leslie at the head of twenty thousand Scots who marched into the north of England under the terms of the Solemn League and Covenant. Henderson, however, was to remain at his post in London for some three years as one of the Scottish Commissioners. He was now in regular attendance at the Westminster Assembly and this body of Divines played the part of a grand council to the House of Commons in all matters of religion. They sat daily from Monday to Friday each week for a whole year, and their meetings did not come to an end until they were adjourned in March, 1645. The whole programme which Henderson had suggested to the General Assembly at Edinburgh in 1641 was now carried out in detail. He was himself asked to draft a Directory for Public Worship, and he was at least as active in the preparation of the Confession and Catechisms for which the Westminster Assembly is still famous. Robert Baillie's advice kept him from an open rupture with the Independents, but their growing strength dashed his dream of a uniform settlement for the Church in the two Kingdoms. All the Scottish Commissioners listened more than they spoke; but Baillie observed that ill health kept Henderson virtually silent "for the most part of the last two years."[51] He preached before members of the House of Commons in December, 1643, and before members of the House of Lords in July, 1644, and he never ceased to keep the ideal of the Solemn League and Covenant before his own mind as well as before the mind of others. He was too wise to think that he could force Presbyterianism on the English people against their will; he was not wise enough to see that they were too attached to a moderate Episcopacy to make the change at all. He knew that such a change would have to take place from within, and he thought that the Church as a whole was eager for it. But he had been misled by his English correspondents, and he failed to grasp the lessons of the war as it progressed.[52] Henderson's policy showed up its one fatal weakness when he

51. See R. L. Orr, *op. cit.*, p. 342.
52. See John Buchan, *op. cit.*, p. 147.

refused to make room for toleration; he clung to the Solemn League and Covenant even when the rise of Cromwell and the Independents had so changed the face of things that it had ceased to be practical. But it is only fair to add that he was worn out with disease before that stage was reached; he no longer had the strength of mind or body to meet the new situation.[53]

Henderson seems to have been short and slight in stature, perhaps less than middle height but well formed, with small shapely hands and thoughtful features. There are six original portraits of him in Scotland, and they reveal a face full of courage and calm benevolence. His hair was dark, and he had a short and pointed beard which rested on a huge ruff made of puckered linen and worn above a black gown and cassock. Aiton observed that the sombre colour of his complexion and his apparel gave the canvas the cast of a saint in mourning.[54] He was never robust, and his health may have been undermined as a result of long residence near the Leuchars marshes. He wrote with a crabbed and ragged hand, and walked with a light and easy gait. He had no wife nor child to share his heart or to fix his home in this world, and he left an estate which was valued at a figure which was rather more than £2350 sterling. There were certain personal legacies by the terms of his will, and the balance was set apart for the good of the Church and the cause of education. There was little of the picturesque in his character, and not very much of romance in the external incidents of his career. He was in fact a plain, modest and well-educated man who would have been quite pleased to remain in a country parish to the end of his days. But he had a strength of mind and purpose which taught him how to toil at each new task in the service of God and his generation. He had a vast capacity for the grind of organization, and he combined it with remarkable skill for giving effect to the national sentiment. He was courteous and temperate in conversation, dignified and attractive in bearing, one who combined in no ordinary measure both strength and charm, "a man of whom we would gladly know more than has come down to

53. See R. L. Orr, *op. cit.*, p. 380.
54. See John Aiton, *op. cit.*, p. 611.

us."[55] He had not the daring courage of John Knox who never feared a face of clay, nor had he the sudden sharpness of Andrew Melville who never failed to speak his mind. But he had that splendid elevation of soul and that noble unselfishness of life which made him what he was.

Robert Baillie said that he was "a man truly excellent and divine, famous for all sorts of virtue, but chiefly for piety, learning and prudence."[56] These were the three great qualities which impressed his contemporaries. All those who knew him seem to have been impressed with his deep and genuine piety. Grave, yet modest and affable; firm, yet manly and generous; independent in judgment; considerate in conduct; humble in heart; stainless in life: he won the love as well as the admiration of all who knew him well. Thomas McCrie said that the more intimately his friends knew him, the more devotedly they all loved him.[57] This high tone of moral greatness was the result of a combination of true Christian qualities. "I love you, Sir," so a convert in his Leuchars days once declared, "because I think you are a man in whom I see much of the image of Christ."[58] He was undoubtedly a man of great learning. His life at St. Andrews and at Leuchars had been largely engaged in literature and theology; all the energies of his intellect had been absorbed in the pursuit of truth. The fruit of this was seen when at length he stepped out and took up the burden of the affairs of Church and State. He had trained his own mind as a clear and forceful thinker, and he had the ability to turn his thoughts into words and actions. David Masson said that he was "a man of weight in all respects, able and expert in debate,"[59] with as massive and well-furnished an intellect "as was to be found among the clergy of the three kingdoms."[60] His reputation for prudence was also well founded. Buchan's remark must be observed: "There were few ministers with Henderson's sagacity."[61] He was gifted with an all-round and uniform good

55. R. L. Orr, *op. cit.*, p. vi.
56. See John Aiton, *op. cit.*, p. 610.
57. Thomas McCrie, *op. cit.*, p. 62.
58. John Aiton, *op. cit.*, p. 619.
59. David Masson, *op. cit.*, Vol. I, p. 714.
60. *Ibid.*, Vol. II, p. 191.
61. John Buchan, *op. cit.*, p. 148.

sense which never seemed to fail. "Men . . . felt that he could be trusted as an unselfish, conscientious, incorruptible man; they did trust him in many delicate and difficult affairs, . . . and their trust was never betrayed."[62] This prudence and wisdom were linked with a mildness of temper and a kindness of manner which were rare in those days and which made him the oracle of his party.

Henderson had first emerged from his seclusion in 1637 at the age of fifty-four, and at once became "the most eyed man of the Three Kingdoms."[63] His star knew no decline until Cromwell began to assume the mantle of leadership in 1645 at the age of forty-six and became in turn for years to come the most eyed man of the Three Kingdoms. It was only his strong sense of duty which kept him at work in public affairs, and he literally wore out his life during his last nine years in the service of his Church and country. He it was who led the country during those years of storm, and led it with remarkable skill and courage. But his patriotic feeling was no mean or narrow passion, and he was far from all extremes. He was inspired by a pure and ardent love of freedom, and he made an enduring impression on spiritual and political life in Scotland. The rule that no Churchman should have authority in State affairs was of necessity waived in his case; men of all ranks and walks in life had learned to look to him as new storms and conflicts arose. He was the author, in part or whole, of all his party's papers; he was the leader, alone or with others, in all his party's measures. None of his friends had more real power with the Privy Council or the General Assembly; he was like a Cabinet Minister without office. Yet this was all unsought; it came simply because men saw in him "their most massive and sagacious leader."[64] They saw in him one who joined the moral strength of a great Churchman with the mental power of a great Statesman, and they recognized his place in the succession from John Knox and Andrew Melville in the restoration of the Reformed status of the Church of Scotland. "My researches have

62. G. Webster Thomson, *op. cit.*, p. 106.
63. See John Aiton, *op. cit.*, p. 610.
64. R. L. Orr, *op. cit.*, p. 378.

more and more convinced me," so David Masson declared, "that he was all in all one of the ablest and best men of his age in Britain, and the greatest, the wisest, and most liberal of the Scottish Presbyterians."[65] But no one has better expressed the truth than did Robert Baillie in the General Assembly a year after his death: "This binds it on us and our posterity to account him the fairest ornament, after Mr. John Knox of incomparable memory, that ever the Church of Scotland did enjoy."[66]

On January 10, 1645, the Archbishop of Canterbury was executed on Tower Hill in London as the result of a bill of attainder in the House of Commons; but there is no sign of Henderson's reaction to the fate of the man who more than all others had tried to fasten the yoke of Episcopal authority on the Church of Scotland. He had been named as one of the Commissioners who were to treat with the King at Uxbridge, and the conversations were begun on January 30. Henderson had not seen Charles since his mission to Oxford in 1642, but his personal courtesy and his sincere regret for the King's misfortunes helped to re-establish the old sense of good-will. He took no part in the debates on the Militia or the Irish question, but he was the spokesman for the House of Commons and the General Assembly on the spiritual issues. But the conversations came to nothing, and he was soon back in London. In March the Grand Committee of the Westminster Assembly adjourned for the last time, and in June the Battle of Naseby destroyed the King's last hope. Cromwell and the Independents threw off the mask of deference to the Presbyterians and disclosed their opposition to the Solemn League and Covenant. Henderson was anxious to return to Scotland in October, but affairs in London were in urgent need of his shrewd advice. Baillie went to Scotland instead while friends prevailed on Henderson to stay. He was now the victim of a painful disease with severe and frequent attacks, but his public duties knew no intermission. By the Spring of 1646, the King's fortunes were lost: Bristol had fallen, and Fairfax was marching on Oxford. On April 27 Charles suddenly fled north, and on

65. David Masson, *op. cit.,* Vol. III, p. 16.
66. See John Aiton, *op. cit.,* p. 610.

May 13 he placed himself in the protection of the Scottish army at Newcastle-on-Tyne. This placed the Scots in a very awkward predicament, but they would not compel him to return. Their one hope was to get him to take the oath of loyalty to the Solemn League and Covenant: if they could but convert Charles to their view of things, they might set up a true king in Israel! Charles seemed ready to listen, and expressed a desire to confer with Henderson.

The Scots knew that Charles would plead his honour, his conscience, and his Coronation Oath, but they all longed to save him from hopeless ruin. Robert Baillie said that for this purpose, "no man was so meet as Mr. Henderson," [67] and an express command was laid on him to make his way at once to the Scottish army and to confer with Charles. He was ill and little disposed for a troublesome journey or a delicate mission, but in response to the summons he left London at once. "The Lord be with you," wrote Baillie on May 19, "and help you in this hardest passage."[68] Henderson's interviews with the King had never been like those of Knox with Mary or of Melville with James; he had honest affection for him in his private character, and felt candid sympathy with him in his public afflictions. But this was the "hardest passage" he had yet had to face, and he had to face it alone. The eyes of all were on him as he rode on his way to the north, for all parties in both Kingdoms felt the utmost anxiety as to the outcome of this last journey. He reached Newcastle on May 26 and plunged at once into his task. The King declared that he must be convinced that an Episcopal Church was not of divine institution and that he was not bound by his Coronation Oath to defend the Church of England. There may have been personal interviews, but the debate itself was managed by means of correspondence. Charles wrote the first paper on May 29, and the reply was dated the third of June. His next paper was penned on June 6, and the reply was furnished on June 17. He wrote again on June 22, and was answered on the second of July. He wrote two more papers on the third and sixteenth of July, but the replies were

67. *Ibid.*, p. 586.
68. See J. Pringle Thomson, *op. cit.*, p. 139.

not published so that the last word might lie with the King.[69] The whole correspondence was a mild "encounter of wits and courtesies,"[70] but it achieved little other than a candid and learned exchange of ideas. The King ran the risk of losing his crown, but he was at least as adroit as the Scottish Divine in the skill and logic with which he put his case. Henderson acquitted himself both "modestly and manfully,"[71] and he won the King's praise for "his learning, piety and solidity."[72] But the King would not budge; he was playing for time, and would not yield even to the Queen when she urged him to abandon Episcopacy.

Henderson's health broke down in the midst of this crisis; it was the end result of the mental anxiety and the severe fatigue which he had borne over the years. His health had been precarious ever since 1641 when he had sought release from his public duties; it had quickly become worse since 1645 when illness and melancholy had much reduced his strength. His great plan for uniform government of the Church in the Three Kingdoms had failed, and the last and "hardest passage" in his life's work was to end in disappointment. These things preyed on his mind and increased his weakness. On August 7, Baillie wrote from London to say that "Mr. Henderson is dying most of heartbreak at Newcastle."[73] The rapid progress of complex ailments forced him to give up the controversy with Charles, and he sailed from Newcastle for Leith. On the eleventh of August, he arrived in Edinburgh and on the thirteenth, Baillie wrote to him in farewell: "His Spirit strengthen, comfort and encourage you to the end. I rest in my hearty love and reverence toward you."[74] He had known that his work was done when he sailed for Scotland, but weariness and depression now passed away as clouds before the sun. He had returned as from exile, although it was to die, and he was cheered at the very sight of his home country. His friends found him very frail and reduced in strength, but he was full of joy at the

69. See John Aiton, *op. cit.,* p. 633: 660.
70. David Masson, *op. cit.,* Vol. III, p. 426.
71. R. L. Orr, *op. cit.,* p. 369.
72. See John Aiton, *op. cit.,* p. 592.
73. *Ibid.,* p. 595.
74. *Ibid.,* p. 596.

prospect of a better landing and a brighter welcome on the shore of heaven. "I am near the end of my race, hasting home," he told Sir James Stewart, "and there was never a school-boy more desirous to have the play than I am to have leave of his world."[75] John Livingston paid him several visits, and found him in great peace of mind. It was August 19, 1646 and he was no more than sixty-three years old when he was seized with the last bout of fever. Sir James Stewart and one other friend were standing at the foot of his bed when he opened his eyes and glanced upward: his eyes sparkled like diamonds as if he saw the Son of Man at the right hand of God. It was with that shining look of wonder in his eyes that he died, mercifully taken from the evils at hand.

75. *Ibid.*, p. 597.

BIBLIOGRAPHY

John Aiton, *The Life and Times of Alexander Henderson,* 1836.

Thomas McCrie, *The Life of Alexander Henderson,* 1846.

G. Webster Thomson, *Alexander Henderson* (in *The Evangelical Succession,* Second Series), 1883.

J. Pringle Thomson, *Alexander Henderson: The Covenanter,* 1912.

R. L. Orr, *Alexander Henderson: Churchman and Statesman,* 1919.

Dictionary of National Biography, "Alexander Henderson" (Vol. IX), 1950.

James Melville, *Autobiography and Diary* (Wodrow Society Edition), 1842.

Andrew A. Bonar, ed., *The Letters of Samuel Rutherford,* 1904.

David Masson, *The Life of John Milton* (6 Vols. and Index) 1881.

John Buchan, *Montrose,* 1928.

John Howie, *The Scots Worthies* (ed. by W. H. Carslaw), 1870.

Alexander Smellie, *Men of the Covenant,* 1903.

(*By courtesy of the University of St. Andrews*)

SAMUEL RUTHERFORD

SAMUEL RUTHERFORD
The Saint of the Covenant

1600—1661

A thirst no earthly stream can satisfy:
A hunger that must feed on Christ, or die.

—Andrew Bonar's Preface in
Quaint Sermons of Samuel Rutherford,
p. iv

SAMUEL RUTHERFORD WAS BORN ABOUT the year 1600 in the village of Nisbet, which now belongs to the parish of Crailing in the Presbytery of Jedburgh and the shire of Roxburgh. He was one of three sons who were brought up to the healthy life of a farm in the Scottish Lowlands. Thus he would play by the waters of the Teviot, or would walk the three or four miles to the little town of Jedburgh. A school was held in part of the ancient Abbey, and he must have received all the lessons of his boyhood in its classrooms. But the events of his early life have been lost to view in a haze of obscurity. Very little is known of him until 1617 when he became a student at Edinburgh in the College which was soon to have the status of an independent University. "The Town's College" as it was called[1] had been founded as a direct result of the zeal for education so largely inspired by Andrew Melville, who had studied philosophy under Peter Ramus in the University of Paris and had brought his teaching methods home with him in 1574. On his transfer from Glasgow to St. Andrews in 1580, Melville had come into contact with one of the younger Regents who showed great promise. This was Robert Rollock, who now became one of his most devoted disciples. In 1583 the Town Council of Edinburgh chose Rollock as sole Regent of the newly founded College for a year's trial. A large class of students was soon enrolled and the course of studies was planned for the degree of Master of Arts. In 1585 Rollock was appointed as Principal of the College and four regents began to teach philosophy. Melville's teaching methods were followed by Rollock so that the new college from the outset had its full share in the academic revolt against the authority of Aristotle. This new system involved a discipline of intellect which was of the greatest value in the cultivation of clear thought and language, and it was well fitted to bring out the latent capacities of a man like Samuel Rutherford. Thus in 1621 when he took

1. See Robert Gilmour, *Samuel Rutherford*, p. 25.

his degree as a Master of Arts, his mind had been trained in the most modern school of philosophy.

It was two years later, in 1623, that Rutherford was appointed to the College as Regent of Humanity. This chair was a result of the system which made Latin the one recognized medium for teaching and conversation between the regents and students. It had become necessary in 1597 to provide tutorial help for students in their Latin studies, and the tutor had soon become known as the Regent of Humanity. The Town Council had made it clear that this was an inferior chair to that of the four Regents of Philosophy, but it gave its tenant the right of appointment to the first vacancy in a higher office. The chair was filled by a competitive process and there were four candidates for the appointment. They were allowed some days for the preparation of an Ode of Horace; and then they were required to explain and comment on it for the major part of an hour. Rutherford gained the appointment for "his eminent abilities of mind and virtuous disposition."[2] But in 1625 he was forced to resign as the result of an alleged moral misdemeanor to which the Town Council referred in its records for February 3, 1626.[3] We can hardly doubt that he felt bitter disappointment, for this effectively barred his progress. His subtle and original mind would always have been at home in the schools of philosophy, but this turned him aside from an academic career. Perhaps this was the time of which he wrote in one of his letters: "I know a man who wondered to see any in this life laugh or sport."[4] But it was all allowed of God that he might be led to know the things that are taught by His Spirit.

Very little is known as to this phase of his career, but it seems to have marked the time when he entered into the peace and joy of a saving experience of Christ. There had been no spiritual light to shed its rays on his boyhood in Nisbet, and a letter which was written towards the close of his life makes this plain: "My soul's desire is that the wilderness and that place to which

2. *Ibid.*, p. 28.
3. See *Dictionary of National Biography*, "Samuel Rutherford."
4. Andrew Bonar, *Letters of Samuel Rutherford, with a Sketch of His Life*, Letter 223, p. 435. Hereafter referred to as *Letter*.

I owe my first breathing, in which I fear Christ was scarce named as touching any reality or power of godliness, may blossom as a rose."[5] There are other reminiscent fragments which point to the fact that he had idled away his youth without the grace of God. "I had stood sure," he wrote, "if I had in my youth borrowed Christ to be my bottom; but he that beareth his own weight to heaven shall not fail to slip and sink."[6] But the outstanding reference to his ultimate conversion makes it clear that he had grown to manhood before this great crisis arrived. "Like a fool as I was," so he confessed years later to Robert Stuart of Ayr, "I suffered my sun to be high in the heaven and near afternoon before ever I took the gate by the end."[7] We can still sense the sharp tang of regret in his counsels to young men with regard to the follies of youth. "The old ashes of the sins of my youth are new fire of sorrow to me," he told the young Earlston. ". . . The devil . . . is much to be feared, . . . for in youth he findeth dry sticks, and dry coals, and a hot hearth-stone; and how soon can he with his flint cast fire, and with his bellows blow it up, and fire the house!"[8] But when the great change did take place, it set his feet once and for all on the strait and narrow way which leads to the land that is very far off. Thus sorrow and study were the twin means which it pleased God to use for his spiritual development and he made up his mind from the outset that he would read theology with a view to ordination as a preacher of the Gospel. There had been an independent Chair of Theology in the University of Edinburgh since 1620, and he must have taken up the normal course of reading prescribed for a candidate for the ministry.

Thus in 1627 Rutherford was licensed as a preacher of the Gospel and soon received a call to the little church of Anwoth in the Stewartry of Kirkcudbright. Anwoth was not altogether virgin soil for the seed of the Gospel, for John Welsh had been at Kirkcudbright from 1595 until 1600, when he had moved

5. Letter 344, pp. 679, 680.
6. Letter 240, p. 477.
7. Letter 186, p. 364.
8. Letter 181, p. 349.

to Ayr. This great son-in-law of John Knox was a man of truly Apostolic zeal and labour. He and Robert Bruce of Kinnaird were the most powerful ministers of the time in Scotland. He was "famous in his generation" as one who was mighty in prayer and whose *cri du coeur* found voice in the words: "O God, wilt Thou not give me Scotland? O God, wilt Thou not give me Scotland!"[9] He kept a warm plaid by his bed to wrap round his body when he rose in the night to pray and there were times when his wife would entreat him to desist. But his answer was aye the same: he had that to press him which she had not; he had the souls of three thousand to answer for, and he knew not how it was with many of them.[10] In 1605, he was imprisoned in Blackness Castle and in 1606 he was driven into exile in France. Late in 1621, he was informed that if he chose he might return to London "to be dealt with." He came, and his wife was admitted to an audience with James I. The King asked her who her father had been, and she replied, "John Knox."

"Knox and Welsh!" he exclaimed; "the devil never made sic a match as that!"

"It's right like, Sir," said she, "for we never speired [asked] his advice."

He then asked how many of John Knox's children were still alive, and if they were lads or lasses. She told him that there were three, and that they were all lasses.

"God be thanked," cried the King, lifting up both his hands, "for if they had been three lads, I had never buiked [enjoyed] my three Kingdoms in peace."

She urged the King to let her husband return to Scotland and to give him his native air.

"Give him his native air!" said James; "give him the devil!"

But her wit flashed out with indignation as she rejoined: "Give that to your hungry courtiers!"

The King at last said that he could return if he would first submit to the Bishops. She lifted her apron, held it out,

9. James Young, *Life of John Welsh*, p. 105.
10. *Ibid.*, p. 135, footnote.

and made reply in her father's spirit: "Please Your Majesty, I'd rather kep his head there."[11]

John Welsh died in London in April 1622, and it was long remembered how he had cried on his death-bed in an ecstasy of sweet communion: "Hold, Lord! Enough; I can bear no more."[12]

It was on the invitation of John Gordon of Lochinvar that Rutherford was appointed to the church at Anwoth. He had already invited John Livingston of Torphichen to take the charge, but a delay ensued and he went to Ancrum. "But thereafter," as Livingston observed, "the Lord provided a great deal better for them, for they got that worthy servant of Christ, Mr. Samuel Rutherford."[13] The district of Anwoth had been only a small section of a parish which had two main centres at Kirkmabreck and Kirkdale, and a visit once a fortnight had been paid by William Dalgleish while he was in charge of the whole parish. But a new church had been built in Anwoth, and it was cut off from the rest of the parish under Rutherford's ministry. Thus it was a rural district in the lovely southwest corner of the Lowlands, lapped by the blue waters of the Fleet and sheltered by the soft green hills of Galloway. He loved to speak of it as "fair Anwoth by the Solway,"[14] and it became dearer to him than the country of his birth and boyhood. And if Anwoth itself were only a tiny village with a handful of farmers and peasants living nearby, it was in the heart of country where the landed proprietors and the titled houses were in sympathetic accord with the Reformation faith and doctrines. There were people like the Gordons of Earlston and Knockgray and Cardoness who still revered the name of John Welsh and who were glad to welcome a man of true learning and power as their pastor. John Welsh had once spoken of Nithsdale and Galloway as "this blinded country,"[15] but his labours had been singularly favoured by God. He had gathered in a splendid harvest in the western Lowlands, and some of his converts with their sons and daughters survived to join Samuel

11. *Ibid.*, pp. 403, 404.
12. *Ibid.*, pp. 405; 406, footnote.
13. See Robert Gilmour, *op. cit.*, pp. 32, 33.
14. Mrs. A. R. Cousin, *Last Words* (in Rutherford's Letters, p. 742).
15. James Young, *op. cit.*, p. 86.

Rutherford's flock at Anwoth. Livingston said that Rutherford "was a great strengthener of all the Christians in that country who had been the fruits of the ministry of Mr. John Welsh, the time he had been minister at Kirkcudbright."[16] Thus the mantle of John Welsh was to rest on his shoulders, and men soon felt that a double portion of the Spirit had been poured out on their new friend and guide.

Rutherford's ministry was to invest the village of Anwoth with an immortal interest for the Church of Scotland, for his is a name which men will never let die. There were godly people in the parish who were glad to welcome him with hearts wide open. "Our soules," they said, "were under that miserable extreame femine of the Word that we had onlie the puir help of ane sermone everie second Sabbath."[17] Now they were to be fed with the bread of life at the hand of one who sat daily at the King's own table; for that was the secret of his skill in making the loaves increase as he broke them on behalf of others. His name was to lend a new charm to the whole scene of his labours, and a picturesque interest still clings to its details. There was the house of Bush-o'-bield with the garden and copse between the manse and kirk. There was the great oaken pulpit with a spacious oval window in the background to let the light stream in on his open Bible. Men soon found that he was always praying or preaching, always reading or writing; he was at work by night as well as day, and it was the same in winter as in summer. Those who passed by late at night might have seen the light of a candle shining through his study window, and he was said to rise at three o'clock in the morning to seek that Face and taste that Strength which is divine.[18] He liked to pace up and down the path which was lined with hollies and to pour out his soul in prayer beneath the trees which used to shade the manse. This was the way in which he loved to wait on God as he sought to prepare his heart for the pulpit. It helps us to understand the words of John Livingston. "While Rutherford was at Anwoth," he wrote, "he was the instrument of much good

16. *Ibid.*, p. 88, footnote.
17. See Robert Gilmour, *op. cit.*, pp. 38, 39.
18. See John Howie, *The Scots Worthies* (Edited by W. H. Carslaw), p. 232.

among a poor ignorant people, many of whom he brought to the knowledge and practice of religion."[19] And his ministry soon reached out to people in all parts of Galloway, "the whole country being to him and accounting themselves as his peculiar flock."[20] So might Robert McWard affirm, for the Kirk at Anwoth soon became the spiritual centre of the South of Scotland.

Thus nine years were spent in Anwoth, and the charm of those years may still be felt. There was sorrow, as well as joy, for the shadows of death gathered about his home. In 1630 his wife Eupham died at the end of a long and painful illness, and in 1635 the life of his mother, who was living with him, slowly moved to its close. The two children of his marriage also died in the manse and he learned by experience how hard it is to keep sight of God in a storm. He too fell ill with "a fever tertian" and for three months and more, he could only preach once a week with great difficulty.[21] But the dews of sorrow shone with grace and lustre in the light of God's love and gave him a rich new insight into the hearts of his people. "The great Master Gardener in a wonderful providence with His own hand planted me here," he wrote in 1631, "and here I will abide till the great Master of the Vineyard think fit to transplant me."[22] Anwoth might be obscure and his people scattered, but they were better than a kingdom in his eyes. He would wrestle with the Angel on their behalf, and would not let Him go except He should bless them: and he would call upon the woods and hills to bear witness that he had done all that lay in his power to draw on a fair match between Christ and Anwoth.[23] His early rising, his tireless studies, his constant labours, his patient vigils, all had this goal in view. He was possessed with the Shepherd's watchful eye for those that were in trouble, and the Saviour's tender heart for all who were yet out of the way.[24] The herd-boys were not too humble for him to seek out and instruct; the high-born were not too lofty for him to wait

19. James Young, *op. cit.,* p. 88, footnote.
20. See Robert Gilmour, *op. cit.,* pp. 39, 40.
21. Letter 11, pp. 53, 54.
22. Letter 16, p. 62.
23. Letter 279, pp. 540, 541.
24. See A. Taylor Innes, *Samuel Rutherford* (in *The Evangelical Succession,* Second Series), p. 154.

on and rebuke.[25] He yearned over those who were still unsaved with a love and longing which were akin to the passion for souls that wrung the heart of Christ Himself: "Oh that I could lay my dearest joys, next to Christ my Lord, in the gap betwixt you and eternal destruction!"[26] His thoughts by day and dreams by night were all centred on the needs of his flock, and there were times when sleep fled from his eyes in his anxiety for the lambs of the fold.[27]

Rutherford's ministry while in Anwoth was a noble approach to the splendid ideal of Baxter's Reformed Pastor or Herbert's Country Parson. His first sermon had been based on the text: "And Jesus said, For judgment I am come into this world that they which see not might see, and that they which see might be made blind" (John 9:39). His great desire as a preacher was that he might help those who saw not to see the King and to dwell in His City. Yet it was long before he could convince himself that there was tangible evidence of true and definite conversions. We still hear his wistful lament two years after he had begun his work in the parish: "I see exceeding small fruit of my ministry, and would be glad to know of one soul to be my crown and rejoicing in the day of Christ."[28] That thirst for souls never left him; it consumed his spirit even when in exile. "My witness is above," he cried; "your heaven would be two heavens to me, and the salvation of you all as two salvations to me."[29] Was it so strange that his name should have spread beyond the borders of Anwoth until it rang up and down in all the farms and valleys of the Lowlands? Those were days when men came from far afield in their deep and earnest desire to worship at Anwoth and hear him preach. Marion McNaught, that good and gracious woman to whom so many of his letters were sent, felt no hesitation when she explained why she was one of his hearers: "I go to Anwoth so often," she wrote, "because though other ministers show me the majesty of God and the plague of my own heart, Mr. Samuel

25. Letter 163, p. 305.
26. Letter 225, p. 439.
27. Letter 62, p. 140.
28. Letter 5, p. 43.
29. Letter 225, p. 439.

does both these things, but he also shows me as no other minister ever does the loveliness of Christ."[30] The pure white glow of deep adoration which thrilled her soul when he spoke of the King in His beauty still burns hot on the page of his printed sermons. "What a Flower," he would exclaim, "what a Rose of Light and Love Christ must be!"[31] Marion McNaught and many another felt that they had seen the goings of God in His Sanctuary when they had spent a Sabbath at Anwoth under the spell of his preaching.

The most charming story of his years in Anwoth is told of one who came to the manse in the guise of a passing stranger. He knocked at the door on the eve of the Sabbath and begged for rest and shelter. He was kindly received and took his place in the circle of children and servants at the hour of evening worship. But it so chanced that he was asked how many commandments there be, and he promptly replied that the commandments are eleven in number. "Eleven!" his host exclaimed, in no little surprise that a man of his age and appearance did not know better. Rutherford was early astir in the morning, and soon repaired to his favorite walk to meditate on the duties of the Lord's Day. But as he was threading his way through the copse near the church, he was startled to hear the voice of prayer among the trees. It was the voice of the stranger, and the lofty spirit of his devotions soon told Rutherford that his guest was a man of no common address. He felt that he had housed an angel unawares, and lost no time in asking him to disclose his name. Then the stranger confessed that he was no other than the scholar and divine, one of the most learned and godly men of his age, James Ussher, Archibshop of Armagh and Primate of the Church of Ireland. He was on a journey home from England, and the road to Stranraer led past the gate of the manse in Anwoth. He had paused to visit Rutherford over-night, but had remained incognito so that he might see him in the unstudied privacy of his own home. Rutherford hailed the saintly Primate with unaffected joy and begged him to preach at the

30. Alexander Whyte, *Samuel Rutherford and Some of His Correspondents,* p. 27.
31. Samuel Rutherford, *The Trial and Triumph of Faith,* p. 262.

morning service. So it came to pass that Ussher gave out the text of his sermon from that rustic pulpit in the words of the Lord Jesus: "A *new* commandment I give unto you, that ye love one another" (John 13:34). Rutherford recognized at last the real meaning of the reply which had so surprised him the night before. It is pleasant to think of the evening which would conclude that day when the two men at home in the manse would commune with each other in the presence of their unseen Lord and Master.[32]

One more beautiful anecdote belongs to those years in Anwoth, and it concerns his patron, John Gordon of Lochinvar. Gordon sprang from an old Galloway family and was born in 1599. His youth had been wild and lawless, but while abroad in France, he had been brought to a better mind by John Welsh. On his return, he was friendly to the Presbyterian cause, but was absorbed in his lands and riches. "Sometimes," John Howie says, "he would be filled with a sense of sin which . . . he was scarcely able to hold out against."[33] It was about 1626 that he married Lady Jane Campbell, third daughter of the Earl of Argyll, and they lived at Rusco in the parish of Anwoth during the first two years of Rutherford's ministry. It was a great disappointment for him when they left for England late in September, 1629. "I have received many and divers dashes and heavy strokes since the Lord called me to the ministry," he wrote; "but indeed I esteem your departure from us amongst the weightiest."[34] At the end of 1631 they were back in Scotland at Kenmure Castle some twenty miles from Anwoth. Rutherford was well aware of the weak point in Gordon's character and in April, 1633, he warned his wife: "Madam, stir up your husband to lay hold upon the Covenant and to do good. What hath he to do with the world? It is not his inheritance."[35] The test soon came, for he was made Viscount Kenmure and Lord Gordon of Lochinvar on the visit of Charles I to Edinburgh in June that year. But he withdrew from the city on the pretext of an illness in order to avoid conflict between the King's favour and a tender conscience. A year later he

32. See Robert Gilmour, *op. cit.*, pp. 44-46.
33. John Howie, *op. cit.*, p. 154.
34. Letter 5, p. 43.
35. Letter 28, p. 88.

was struck down with real illness, and was filled with remorse. Rutherford had been away from home, and he broke his journey on the way back to call at the Castle. Kenmure saw the finger of God in this, and in fear of death "drew on a conference with the minister."[36] Peace of mind came for a while, but it was superficial. "Dig deeper," urged the faithful pastor, until at last he got down to the Rock.[37] He was dying, but his farewell words of counsel to friends were not only treasured but were published long afterwards by Rutherford in *The Last Heavenly Speeches and Glorious Departure of John, Viscount Kenmure*. As the sun was setting on September 12, 1634, Rutherford engaged once more in prayer at his request: and as the words of prayer faded into silence, Lord Kenmure passed gently away.

But the pastor of that rural flock at Anwoth was as well a man of action and a maker of history who had his part to play in the mighty events which were taking shape in Scotland. Robert McWard said that he had entered on his work at Anwoth "without giving any engagement to the Bishop";[38] but he foresaw the storm that was at hand while the rising clouds were yet no larger than a man's hand. "Remember Zion!"[39] That had been his watchword as early as 1627, and his early letters show that he was full of apprehension for the troubles ahead. In 1630 he was summoned before the Court of High Commission in Edinburgh on a charge of non-conformity to the Perth Articles; but the charge was brought "by a profligate person" in his parish, and was dismissed when "sea and winds refused to give passage to the Bishop of St. Andrews."[40] In 1634, Thomas Sydserff, an intolerant and unpopular man, was appointed as Bishop of Galloway, and he at once tried to enforce conformity to the Episcopal ceremonies. Rutherford knew that his work was in jeopardy, and in January, 1636 he wrote: "I expect our new prelate shall try my sitting; I hang by a thread, but it is (if I may speak

36. John Howie, *op. cit.*, p. 155.
37. *Ibid.*, p. 159.
38. See Robert Gilmour, *op. cit.*, p. 66.
39. Letter 1, p. 33.
40. Letter 11, p. 53.

so) of Christ's spinning."[41] Then he published his book *Exercitationes Apologeticae pro Divina Gratia,* which was a strong attack on Laud's Arminian theology. It caused a great ferment; Bishop Maxwell of Ross said that he had not thought to find any man in Scotland who had so much learning.[42] Sydserff at once brought him before the Court of High Commission, first in Wigton, then in Edinburgh, on a charge of non-conformity. His real offence was summed up in his own quaint style: "My newly printed book against Arminians was one challenge; not lording the prelates was another."[43]

The trial in Edinburgh took place in July, 1636, and it went on for three days while he was plied with irrelevant questions. He was earnestly supported by the youthful Lord Lorne, the brother of Lady Kenmure, who was soon to become Earl of Argyll and whose speech in defence almost made the scales tip in his favour. But the Court caved in and condemned him when Sydserff swore that he would bring it before the King himself. Thus Rutherford was forbidden on pain of rebellion to preach in any part of Scotland, and was banished to the city and confines of Aberdeen during the King's pleasure.

Rutherford was ordered to proceed to Aberdeen by August 20, and his instinctive reaction was to rejoice that he had been counted worthy to bear the shame of his Master's quarrel. "That honour that I have prayed for these sixteen years, with submission to my Lord's will," so he wrote to Lady Kenmure at the end of July, "my kind Lord hath now bestowed upon me, even to suffer for my royal and princely King Jesus."[44] A week later, on the fourth of August, he subscribed a letter which he wrote at Irvine as one who was on his "journey to Christ's Palace in Aberdeen."[45] But exile and silence were a prospect far from welcome except as a testimony for Christ, and he could not hide the distress which he felt at separation from the flock at Anwoth. He was accompanied by a small and sorrowful retinue of friends as he set out

41. Letter 56, p. 129.
42. See Robert Gilmour, *op. cit.,* p. 74.
43. Letter 60, pp. 135, 136.
44. Letter 61, p. 136.
45. Letter 63, p. 143.

on his way to Aberdeen, and they bade him farewell at last "with great regret at the want of such a pastor, so holie, learned and modest."[46] Rutherford found the atmosphere cold and hostile in this northern city, for it was a noted stronghold of Arminian theology and Episcopal authority. But he was to remain in its confines for some two years, for the date of his last letter from this place of exile was June 11, 1638. It is true that he was neither in stocks nor in prison like Prynne or the elder Leighton; he was free to move to and fro and to join in conversation with the people in the city. It was not as though he had to bare his back for physical suffering, but he had been banished from his congregation and his freedom to preach had been denied. He found that the very Dons and Doctors refused to cross their swords with his after he had worsted Robert Barron of Marischal College in three successive encounters, and he felt that he was held at arm's length by the townsfolk who lived in awe of the authorities. Thus he turned with all the hunger of a lonely heart to dwell in spirit with his flock at Anwoth, and he yearned with all the longing of a tender love for those who were like sheep that now had no shepherd. He was consumed with the fire of God's Word in his spirit;[47] sorrow oppressed his heart because of his silent Sabbaths.[48] "They are dear to my soul," we hear him cry as he called to mind his congregation; "their remembrance breaketh my heart."[49]

He was prepared for the first bleak welcome which he received, but he found that God was more than gracious. Northern love might be cold, but the Lord did not leave him to bear it alone. "I find the townsmen cold and dry in their kindness," he told Robert Gordon, "yet I find a lodging in the heart of many strangers."[50] And his manifest devotion was to win the secret goodwill of some who were afraid to make themselves known in public. "I find folks here kind to me," he told Lady Kenmure

46. See Robert Gilmour, *op. cit.,* p. 76.
47. Letter 73, p. 156.
48. Letter 76, p. 162.
49. Letter 63, p. 143.
50. Letter 66, p. 144.

three months later, "but in the night and under their breath."[51] He would sometimes thread his way through the streets with a sense of friendless solitude and his heart was touched when he heard men speak of him as "the banished minister."[52] But they spoke in whispers and he knew that they were afraid of the frown of those in authority. "But," he owned, "I find Christ neither strange nor unkind, for I have found many faces smile upon me since I came hither."[53] There were times when he thought that the very sparrows which built their nests in God's house at Anwoth were more favoured than he.[54] "But," he said, "I thank God Anwoth is not heaven; preaching is not Christ."[55] He was learning to cast his soul on the love of Christ in a way that he had not known before, and he would not have been without this sweet consolation for all the rough winds of adversity. "He was always kind to my soul," he wrote in March, 1637, "but never so kind as now in my greatest extremities."[56] Such discoveries of Immanuel were enough to suffuse those gray northern skies with the clear sunshine of a better country, and he came to regard himself as a guest in the King's Palace, where the banner over him was a love as strong as death. Nor were his trials without significance for the Church as a whole; they were part of God's plan to shake others out of their sleep. "Oh!" he cried, "blessed hands for evermore that shall help to put the crown upon the head of Christ again in Scotland!"[57] The facts of his exile taught the best men both north and south of the border to watch and pray as they saw the development of the threat to freedom. And they also produced the great majority of those famous letters which were to cheer the heart and steel the nerve of friend and flock alike.

Rutherford's distinction as an author was well known in academic circles in his own day, and the books which he wrote were in constant demand. But he lives by the fame of a volume which

51. Letter 69, p. 149.
52. Letter 70, p. 150.
53. Letter 77, p. 163.
54. Letter 92, p. 195.
55. Letter 96, p. 202.
56. Letter 103, p. 213.
57. Letter 78, p. 165.

he did not write as a book at all, for his letters have long out-lived all his other tomes in popular affection. It was true that he might not preach, but he could write and pray, and he found an outlet for his feelings in an ever growing correspondence. Long and fervent letters went all over Scotland like a breath of fragrant glory from Immanuel's Land. Not one of those letters was meant for the eye of the world at large, but they have long been a fa-vourite manual for the interior life of the soul. They found their way into print in 1664, three years after his death, when the ear-liest collection was published by Robert McWard with the curious title of *Joshua Redivivus*. This was because he had described him-self as one whom God had sent into exile to see the land and try the fords so that like the spies of old he might bring back his re-port as a guide for others.[58] Thus the title pictured him as one who like the son of Nun could lead the godly into a land of rest and riches. Editions multiplied as more letters were brought to light until at length Andrew Bonar gave the world his classical edition with as many letters as the days of the year. Letters in this volume stretch in time from his first year in Anwoth to his last year in St. Andrews, but two out of every three were written during his resi-dence in Aberdeen. Thus the letters may be said to belong espe-cially to his days in exile and they are an unselfconscious revela-tion of the growth of a soul. Few books provide such a perfect window through which we may watch the spiritual development of a saint and servant of God. They show how a profound the-ology finds an outlet for its massive strength in human experience. Richard Baxter was so impressed by this fact that he told William Carstares: "Hold off the Bible, such a book . . . the world never saw."[59] Richard Cecil voiced his judgment in almost equal praise: "Rutherford's Letters is one of my classics; . . . he is a real origi-nal."[60] Alexander Whyte ranked this book among the few on which he had resolved to rest when the shadows of life began to fall: "All good soldiers of Jesus Christ have . . . under their pillow or not far from it . . . Rutherford's Letters, . . . and holding fast by

58. Letter 118, p. 240.
59. Andrew Bonar, *Letters of Samuel Rutherford, with a Sketch of His Life*, p. 25.
60. Josiah Pratt, *Remains of Richard Cecil*, pp. 154, 155.

these . . . they come back into time for a season or pass out into Eternity more than conquerors."[61]

But these letters may not evoke the same spontaneous admiration today; one may need to acquire a taste for them as a result of patient study and sympathetic insight. This is because they are steeped in the style for which Bernard of Clairvaux was famous, and there is much in their language which seems lush and unreal to a modern reader.[62] There are vivid and exotic metaphors which transgress all the limits of a wise man's utterance; there are tender and familiar epithets which neglect all the cautions of a good man's reverence. But we are too prone to forget that these letters were not written for the eye of the world at all; they were in fact written only for friends, often in haste and with never a thought for such points as literary style or canons of taste. His whole soul was on the stretch to find words that would express the strong pent-up feeling of a man who followed hard after God, and we only boggle at his language because we have never followed in his footsteps nor felt all that he felt. David Masson once said that the letters will always command a market because they were the work of a man in whom "the sensuous genius of a poet" was transformed into the radiant holiness of one who had beheld the Face of God.[63] It is not hard to quote from them in a way which will bring out their traits of beauty; and we may see those traits flash like gems in the rays of the sun. But it is a singular fact that quotation is quite inadequate to make us see the full extent of their spontaneous feeling or their soul-subduing passion. Not the only reward of a patient study is to disclose one whose heart was sensitive to the most profound and tender emotion and whose mind was capable of the most vivid and fertile expression. We are rather like men who stand in the shoes of those who eavesdrop as we read them, for we seem to overhear the soft reverie of a heart in love with the Lord Jesus.[64] The Song of Solomon was the sacred lyric in which he found thought and language most in accord with his own deep

---

61. G. F. Barbour, *Life of Alexander Whyte,* p. 641.
62. "The oriental lusciousness of Samuel Rutherford" — See John Buchan, *Montrose,* p. 62.
63. David Masson, *Life of John Milton,* Vol. I, p. 714.
64. J. H. Jowett, *The Passion for Souls,* p. 102.

sense of rapture, and we would need the same glow of sacred passion before we could safely venture to judge him for excess of feeling and fervour. The faults in his letters are of minor account when we bear in mind the surpassing excellence of their merits: their grandeur outweighs their mistakes, and they have brought strength and comfort to a thousand souls in verbal music like the choral harmonies of heaven.

Thus the letters confront us with a man of rich capacity for wide and varied friendship, and still more, with a man of rare humility and penetrating vision. Few things are more beautiful than the sympathy with which he consoles the sad in heart, or the eagerness with which he exhorts the young in years. But the supreme appeal of the letters is his transcendent devotion to the Divine Prince and Saviour. Thus Bishop Moule remarked on "that supreme content and delight in the Lord Jesus which were the light of life to Samuel Rutherford."[65] So too, Alexander Smellie held that "seldom in any country . . . has there been a soul more absolutely enthralled by the . . . surpassing loveliness of Christ."[66] The great burden of the letters was the same in effect as the ruling passion of his whole life: he longed to see the King in His beauty, and to behold the land that is very far off. We can still feel the throb of this master motive in the simple statement of his purpose: he would seek no more to give him everlasting joy than a clear sight of Jesus in His beauty.[67] We can still feel the surge of this desire in his words of loving aspiration: he would be further in upon Christ than His joys, for they but stand on the outer edge of His love; he would wish to be in as a seal on His heart, in where love and mercy have their lodging.[68] This was the great secret which made his life luminous with the afterglow of seraphic devotion and adoring utterance; it was ever apt to absorb his thoughts by day and to suffuse his dreams by night. He longed to speed the time which would hail the morning sky of glory when the Lord would appear, shining as it were through the mist on the mountains; his

65. H. C. G. Moule, Preface to *Lister's Selection from Rutherford's Letters*.

66. Alexander Smellie, Introduction to William Guthrie on *The Christian's Great Interest*, p. xvii.

67. Letter 202, p. 398.

68. Letter 285, p. 556.

thoughts were fixed on the sunrise which would greet the summer day of gladness when the Lord would descend, riding as it were on the arch of the rainbow.[69] All the buried fires of poetry as well as of piety that were latent in his soul seemed to leap into flame when he voiced his heart's desire: "O Thou fair and fairest Sun of Righteousness, arise and shine in Thy Strength . . . Stretch out Thy sceptre as far as the sun shineth . . . Put on Thy glittering crown, O Thou Maker of kings, and make but one stride or one step of the whole earth, and travel in the greatness of Thy Strength."[70]

In March, 1638, public affairs took a sharp turn for the better in the outlook of Church and State, for the National Covenant was drawn up and signed with amazing eagerness throughout Scotland. It was a blow which soon struck the chains of unwilling submission from clergy and people alike, and not even a strong outpost like Aberdeen could ignore its effects in the months which followed. It was in June that Rutherford took advantage of the impending overthrow of the Episcopal regime to risk the law and to leave his place of exile. His last letter from Aberdeen was written on June 11, and the next was written from Anwoth on August 5. He preached in the College Church at Edinburgh and the High Church at Glasgow before the end of June, and was soon home in the manse at Anwoth where he longed to renew those days so like days of heaven on earth. There was neither wife nor child nor mother to share the joy of his return, but his heart was with his flock in Anwoth. There was gladness in the nobleman's hall and the shepherd boy's loft when the chimes of the long silent bell rang out once again and the praise of human lips began to replace the song of birds as the Church filled at the hour of worship.[71] But this reunion was all too brief; the great Master of the Vineyard was about to transplant him to fresh soil. He sat as a member of the great Assembly which met at Glasgow in the month of November, and was vindicated from the protest of the Bishops that he was

69. Samuel Rutherford, *op. cit.*, Dedication, p. 7.
70. Letter 291, p. 584.
71. Letter 206, p. 404.

still under censure from the Church of Scotland. But the Assembly determined to translate Rutherford from Anwoth to St. Andrews as it determined to translate Henderson from Leuchars to Edinburgh. They wished to place him in a sphere where his solid learning would be of the highest service, and he was to fill the Chair of Divinity at St. Mary's College. But he was loath in the extreme to leave Anwoth again, and he could not bear the prospect of a nonpreaching ministry after his "dumb Sabbaths" in Aberdeen.[72] "I trust in God," he said, "this Assembly will never take me from my pastoral charge, for there is a woe unto me if I preach not the Gospel, and I know not who can go betwixt me and that woe."[73] It was referred to the Commission of the Kirk at Edinburgh and the Assembly in August, 1639, confirmed the call. He was compelled to yield, but he could not hide his feelings from a friend like Lady Kenmure. "My removal from my flock is so heavy to me," he wrote, "that . . . I had never such a longing for death."[74]

Thus St. Andrews took the place of Anwoth as the center of his regular ministry and it proved an excellent appointment. He was installed in the Chair of Divinity at St. Mary's College and became the colleague of Robert Blair in the ordinary work of the city pulpit. He was henceforth to stand with the foremost men of the day in their efforts to guide the Church aright and his hands were to help in replacing the crown on Christ's brow in Scotland. He was in a strategic position at St. Andrews for it was the oldest and most brilliant seat of learning in the Kingdom. Sixty years had elapsed since St. Mary's College had been reorganized as a school of Divinity with a Principal and four Professors. Andrew Melville had been Principal from 1580 until his imprisonment in 1607; then came Robert Howie, who still held his office at the time of Rutherford's appointment. Perhaps no one else at the time was so well qualified as Rutherford to take up the work of Melville with young men in their most impressionable years. The strong recollection of his wasted chances in youth had filled

---

72. Letter 98, p. 205.
73. See Robert Gilmour, *op. cit.,* p. 106.
74. Letter 287, p. 567.

him with solicitude for the welfare of those who were just on manhood's threshold. "Oh, what a sweet couple, what a glorious yoke," he told the young Lord Boyd, "are youth and grace, Christ and a young man."[75] There were some who never forgot the great lessons of his saintly character and his lofty scholarship. William Guthrie was one of the students to whom Rutherford's ministry spoke in accents which were full of affectionate authority, and in 1650 Rutherford wrote to him at Fenwick in terms of warm attachment. "Dear Brother," he wrote, "help me, and get me the help of their prayers who are with you."[76] Robert McWard was also a student to whom Rutherford's ministry was as fragrant as the Rose of Sharon, and in 1643 Rutherford took him on his London journey to act as his amanuensis at the Westminster Assembly. McWard could speak of him from the closest knowledge, and his testimony was to inspire Howie's famous statement about his work at St. Andrews: The University "became a Lebanon out of which were taken cedars for building the House of the Lord almost throughout the whole land."[77]

In August, 1643, Rutherford was named as one of the Scottish Commissioners to the Westminster Assembly of Divines in London. The mood in which he faced this task may be gathered from a letter which was written from St. Andrews on the twentieth of October: "I am now called for to England; the government of the Lord's house in England and Ireland is to be handled. My heart beareth me witness and the Lord who is greater knoweth, my faith was never prouder than to be a common rough country barrow man in Anwoth; and that I could not look at the honour of being a mason to lay the foundation for many generations, and to build the waste places of Zion in another kingdom."[78] A month later, on November 20, Rutherford and Baillie were introduced to the Jerusalem Chamber and took their place along with Henderson and Gillespie who had travelled south in August. All that was most vital in the stream of spiritual life and thought in England had poured itself into the

75. Letter 232, p. 461.
76. Letter 330, p. 653.
77. John Howie, *op. cit.*, p. 234.
78. Letter 306, p. 615.

78

veins of the Westminster Assembly. "As far as I am able to judge by the information of all history of that kind," so Richard Baxter wrote, "the Christian world since the days of the Apostles had never a Synod of more excellent Divines than this and the Synod of Dort."[79] Rutherford gave of his best in this Assembly; his work has been described as "the supreme conscious effort" of his life-time.[80] He spared no pains, whether in counsel or debate, and he earned the grateful praise of Robert Baillie: "Mr. Henderson, Mr. Rutherford, and Mr. Gillespie," he said, "all three spoke exceedingly well, with arguments unanswerable."[81] Lightfoot's *Journal* and Baillie's *Letters* both reveal how his store of learning and his skill in speaking compelled men to hear him with the deepest respect. He paid one brief visit to the Epsom Waters with Henderson, whose health had been impaired, but this was his only absence from his post in London in four full years. Often his heart went out to the home and college which he had left in St. Andrews and he would feel tempted to shake himself free from the dust and bustle of London. But the personal sacrifice that was required seemed a small thing in his eyes if he could only help men "to build the waste places of Zion." Thus he outstayed all the Scottish Commissioners, and of them all, he left the most durable impression on the English Divines.

The five Scottish Commissioners put forth their whole strength to promote the aims of the Solemn League and Covenant. They had to match themselves against the most learned Divines of the Independent party on points that dealt with the peculiar polities of the Scottish Reformation. Thus, in September, 1644, Prynne published a pamphlet in which he spoke of "the unhappy divisions touching Church Government" which had been in debate between Rutherford, Nye and others.[82] And Robert Baillie observed: "Had not God sent Mr. Henderson, Mr. Rutherford, and Mr. Gillespie among them, I see not that ever they could agree

---

79. Richard Baxter; *Reliquiae Baxterianae*, p. 72.
80. Robert Gilmour, *op. cit.*, p. 131.
81. *Ibid.*, p. 141.
82. David Masson, *op. cit.*, Vol. III, p. 298.

on any settled government."[83] Milton was so disturbed that he
tried to castigate Rutherford in his famous Sonnet on the New
Forcers of Conscience:

> *Dare ye for this adjure the civil sword*
> *To force our consciences that Christ set free,*
> *And ride us with a Classic Hierarchy,*
> *Taught ye by mere A. S. and Rutherford?*

Milton's first thrust was at Adam Steuart, who — under the
initials A. S. — had been one of the first to rush into print on
behalf of strict Presbytery. Then he rhymed the name of Rutherford with his reference to "the civil sword" as a protest against
the attempt to replace one form of Church tyranny by another.[84]
But had he known the man himself, would he not have found
in him a grandeur of thought and feeling akin to his own?[85] Rutherford at all events learned to honour the giants of the Independent
party as men with whom he felt the ties of true spiritual kinship;
ties which led him to say that "of all that differ from us, they
come nearest to walkers with God."[86] He rubbed shoulders with
them daily on the Assembly floor; he exchanged ideas with them
freely in the committee rooms. He prayed with them in Church
and dined with them at home; he preached before Commons and
Lords and he grasped the worth and vitality of the Puritan
character. "I judge that in England the Lord hath many names,"
he wrote, "and a fair company that shall stand at the side of
Christ when He shall render up the Kingdom to the Father; and
that in that renowned nation, there be men of all ranks, wise,
valorous, generous, noble, heroic, faithful, religious, gracious,
learned."[87]

Rutherford and Gillespie were friends of long standing, as were
Baillie and Henderson. Gillespie was born in 1613 and came
to Kenmure Castle as a tutor to the household during the last
years of Rutherford's ministry in the church at Anwoth. They

83. See Robert Gilmour, *op. cit.*, p. 141.
84. *Ibid.*, p. 148.
85. See Andrew Bonar, *op. cit.*, p. 17.
86. Letter 308, p. 616.
87. See Andrew Bonar, *op. cit.*, p. 17.

were soon drawn together by their scholarly interests and their religious convictions. They read the same deep books and shared the same rich faith; they grappled with the same theological problems and wrestled with the same experimental difficulties. A day came when they rose from their knees in the woods of Kenmure Castle, took each other by the hand, and pledged themselves in a covenant of friendship like that of David and Jonathan. They were to pray for each other in the trials which were then at hand; they were to write to each other on the life of God in their souls.[88] Gillespie was ordained to the charge of Wemyss near St. Andrews in 1638 but was moved to Edinburgh in 1642. He was only thirty when he was called to the Westminster Assembly, but he won a golden reputation for his learning and his powers of debate. Thus Rutherford and Gillespie sat side by side in the Jerusalem Chamber and one beautiful anecdote of their mutual confidence has been preserved. In a debate on Church autonomy, the learned John Selden had delivered a masterly speech in favour of Erastian tenets; his arguments seemed decisive. But Gillespie had been busy with his pen while Selden was on his feet, and as soon as Selden sat down, Rutherford whispered: "Rise George, rise and defend the right of the Lord Jesus Christ to govern the Church which He has purchased with His own blood." Gillespie responded with a speech which utterly demolished his great antagonist. When he sat down, Selden remarked: "That young man by his single speech has swept away the learning and labour of ten years of my life." His friends seized the scrap of paper on which he was supposed to have written his notes; but the only thing they could find was the prayer which he had written again and again: "Da lucem, Domine!" "Give light, O Lord!"[89] Rutherford wrote him a most tender farewell when he was dying in September, 1648: "Reverend and dear brother, I cannot speak to you. The way ye know; the passage is free and not stopped; the print of the footsteps of the Forerunner is clear and manifest; many have

88. Alexander Whyte, *op. cit.*, p. 152.
89. *Ibid.*, pp. 153, 154.

gone before you."[90] And the dying man sent reply: "There is nothing that I have done that can stand the touchstone of God's justice. Christ is my all, and I am nothing."[91]

But the speech of Gillespie in the Jerusalem Chamber was a triumph of the moment, and it fell to Rutherford in those crowded years to bring forth a work which would outlast his age. It was during 1644 that he wrote and published *Lex Rex,* a book which took London and the Westminster Assembly by storm. This book was born of the conflict between King and people, and dealt with the burning issue of the law and the prince; but it belongs to the field of political science, and its significance goes far beyond the times in which it was written. *Lex Rex* was a masterly discussion of the Stuart dogma that the King is above the law, and it provides us with a fine statement of the principles and polities of Puritan government. It was well knit with a convincing argument and great dialectical ability, bound and clamped with the iron bands of proof from Scripture and a mass of syllogisms. It was said by Bishop Guthrie that this new book was "so idolised that whereas Buchanan's treatise *De Jure Regni apud Scotos* was looked upon as an oracle, this coming forth, it was slighted as not anti-monarchial enough, and Rutherford's *Lex Rex* only thought authentic."[92] It was written in the faith that truth to Christ could never be treason to Caesar, and that arbitrary power is a fit garland only for the brow of Eternal Majesty. The true seat of government is the high authority of God, but the present form of government lies in the voluntary choice of nations. No man is born with a diadem on his head or a sceptre in his hand; thus royal power is vested in the people, and the people alone. The authority of the King is only that of a trustee who is empowered to make good laws; and he is in trust to administer the law, not to break it, nor to dispense with it, nor even to interpret it. The duty of interpretation belongs to the magistrates who act as public servants of the Crown, not as private agents of the King. The King is the

90. Letter 324, p. 644.
91. Alexander Whyte, *op. cit.,* p. 160.
92. See Robert Gilmour, *op. cit.,* p. 176.

highest servant of the State, but is a servant always; absolute power would be both irrational and unnatural. The will of the prince can never become the norm of right and wrong, for in such a case it would be with the people worse than if they had no ruler at all.[93]

This brief précis can do no more than hint at the contents of this great work, but its significance can be assessed from the nature of one question which he asks and answers. "Who shall be judge between the King and the people," he asks, "when the people allege that the King is a tyrant?" And the answer is in one of his most pregnant aphorisms. "There is a court of necessity no less than a court of justice," he wrote, "and the fundamental laws will then speak; and it is with the people in this extremity as if they had no ruler."[94] But *Lex Rex* was not his only contribution in the field of literature; he gave the world quite a number of books in the course of his life. Most of them were massive quartos, full of broad dialect, rich in quaint metaphor, now syllogistic, now aphoristic, but so steeped in ancient quarrels that they may daunt all but the most stubborn readers. They brought him fame both at home and abroad, but now they are as good as dead; yet it is in these works that proof is found for the claim that he must rank as the most versatile genius in the whole long line of Scottish theologians. They were largely concerned with the defence of the crown rights of Christ over the Church, and they disclose his most glaring faults side by side with his finest virtues. Taylor Innes described him as an intellectual gladiator who made war with words and ideas in the spirit of constant debate and ruthless logic. His scorn of doubt and ambiguity taught him to pursue every word and dissect every idea, even in "the corner of the corner of an argument."[95] His splendid combination of theological faith and intellectual force made him a controversialist of the highest order. His astute and subtle perception, his adroit and clever argument, his love of system and logic, his scorn of compromise and concession, his courage and candour, with his love of

93. *Ibid.*, pp. 181-190.
94. *Ibid.*, p. 99.
95. A. Taylor Innes, *op. cit.*, p. 137.

country and fear of God, stand out in all his works.[96] But all his fine speculative powers of mind and theology are marred by the narrow thought and bitter tone in which he flayed his antagonists. This is the great reason why so many critics have turned their backs on Rutherford; it is perhaps the chief defect in the mould of his work and character.

But he was a child of his age, and it was not an age in love with the idea of toleration; it was hard for him to tolerate men who would by no means tolerate him. So there is that other side to the picture, even when the worst has been said; and in his case, the worst may be balanced against the best without fear as to the final judgment. His own spiritual elevation shed its clear beams over all his forays into the tangled and trackless maze of controversy. The quaint flash of humorous sallies; the bright glint of picturesque sayings; the rich glow of unconscious eloquence; the true fire of seraphic utterance; the pithy maxims; the pointed proverbs; all ring through the corridors of our memory with power and charm. And once let him away into the fields of pure theology, once let him fix his thoughts on Christ and His glory, and few theologians of any school or any age ever rise to heights more sublime. As for *Lex Rex,* it is beyond doubt one of the ablest pleas in defence of a constitutional form of government which has yet been written, and it still holds its place as one of the few great works on political science that Scotland has produced. Much of it has become part and parcel of the political inheritance of Great Britain, for it hammered out more than one fair stone for the fabric of our British type of monarchy. "A limited and mixed monarchy such as is in Scotland and England," he wrote, "seems to me the best government, when parliaments, with the king, have the good of all the three.[97] This government hath glory, order, unity from a monarch; from the government of the best and wisest it hath safety of counsel, stability and strength; from the influence of the Commons it hath liberty, privileges, promptitude of obedience."[98] When it appeared in 1644, it produced something like a national sensation. It was

96. *Ibid.,* p. 140.
97. "All the three"; i.e., monarchy, aristocracy, and democracy.
98. See Robert Gilmour, *op. cit.,* pp. 190, 191.

soon in the hands of all, and its leading ideas were the talk of the realm. The passion for freedom with which it was inspired was the passion of a Puritan and a patriot, and this passion would make itself felt in spite of all the scholastic argument. It became the political textbook for the Covenanters in Scotland and the Independents in England; it is indeed still fit to serve as a guide for all who live for freedom. Howie declared that Charles I frankly confessed that it was never likely to get an answer; and the only answer which it ever did get was when it was burned at the hands of the hangman.[99]

Thus, from November, 1643, until November, 1647, Rutherford continued his work at the Westminster Assembly; he was in fact the last of the Scottish Commissioners to leave. Henderson left London in May, 1646; Baillie later in the same year; Gillespie in August, 1647; and Rutherford three months later. On November 9, 1647 it was announced in the House of Lords that he was leaving, and the English Divines wrote a gracious letter to the Church of Scotland. "We can not but restore him with ample testimony of his learning, godliness, faithfulness and diligence," they wrote; "and we humbly pray the Father of spirits to encrease the number of such burning and shining lights among you."[100] On his return, he was appointed Principal of St. Mary's College, and in 1651 he became Rector of the University itself. The teaching and preaching in which he was engaged at St. Andrews was the ideal sphere for a man of his talents, and nothing could persuade him to leave his home or country again. In 1648 he declined the Chair of Divinity at Harderwyck in the Netherlands, and in 1649 he refused the Chair of Divinity at the University of Edinburgh. These were flattering proposals, and they were not the last; thus in 1651 he twice declined an invitation to succeed Charles de Matius in the Chair of Divinity at Utrecht. But the death of Henderson in 1646 and of Gillespie in 1648 had left him quite the most eminent minister north of the Tweed, and he could not bear to desert the Ark of Christ's Church in Scotland at such a time. The cause of the Covenanters was in danger

99. *Ibid.*, p. 191.
100. *Ibid.*, p. 167.

through their efforts to save the King, and they could not agree among themselves. Warriston, Livingston, Guthrie and "the milder arguments of Mr. Samuel Rutherford"[101] were against the policy of compromise, and the execution of Charles I in 1649 gave them control. But the Scottish Covenanters and the English Independents had now quarrelled to such a point that the Solemn League and Covenant was all in shreds and the intransigence of the Scottish leaders led to Cromwell's campaign and the crushing defeat of their arms at Dunbar on September 3, 1650. The end of that famous decade had placed the whole Northern Kingdom at the mercy of the English Roundheads; there was nothing which could have saved Scotland from the fate of Ireland if a conquest by arms had been Cromwell's plan of action.

The hand of a strong man ought to have been at the helm to pilot Kirk and Covenant through the stormy waters ahead; but there was no one strong enough, and the waters were strewn with the wreck of hopes and friendships. On January 1, 1651, Charles II was crowned in the Abbey of Scone at the hands of Argyll, and the Scots found themselves pledged to support the King with arms. This led to an attempt to ease the laws which were in force against the Engagers of 1648 so that they might take part in the defence of their country against Cromwell. Certain Resolutions to this effect were brought before the General Assembly which met at St. Andrews in July, 1651, with Robert Douglas as Moderator; but there was strong opposition. Twenty-two ministers led by Rutherford laid a solemn protest on the table, and they challenged the constitution and validity of the whole Assembly. The approach of Lambert's army forced the Assembly to adjourn to Dundee where it endorsed the Resolutions and deposed three of the Remonstrants in spite of Rutherford's protests. But the result of the Resolutions was that persistent Malignants were soon restored to place and power while the Church was racked with schism in its hour of crisis. On September 3, 1651, the first anniversary of the Battle of Dunbar, Cromwell obtained his "crowning mercy" at Worcester[102] and the King's cause was in

101. See David Masson, *op. cit.*, Vol. IV, p. 209.
102. John Buchan; *Oliver Cromwell*, p. 404.

ruins. But in Scotland the breach between Resolutioners and Protesters (or Remonstrants) grew worse. Rutherford did propose a compromise at the General Assembly in 1652, but this was now too late. All Assemblies were disallowed after the Assembly of 1653 was suspended by Cromwell, but the controversy was at white heat. In 1656 both parties appealed to Cromwell, but Lord Broghill secured the defeat of the Protesters. Rutherford was one of the few who would neither bend nor bow, and it was their loyalty to the Covenant which kept alight the torch of faith for men like Hugh McKail and James Renwick. But so bitter was the quarrel that it estranged Rutherford, Livingston and James Guthrie from old friends like Dickson, Baillie and Robert Blair. "I think not much of a cross when all the children of the house weep with me and for me," he wrote, "and to suffer when we enjoy the communion of the saints is not much; but it is hard when saints rejoice in the suffering of saints, and redeemed ones hurt, yea, even go nigh to hate, redeemed ones."[103] He saw that saints misjudge the heirs of life because the saints themselves are not always Christlike, and he feared that they would never be all of one mind until they were all in one heaven.

Rutherford's family life is largely veiled from our eyes, for he seldom refers to his wife or children. We know that he was a man of strong and generous affection, but the finger of death wrote the facts of sorrow into his heart and home. His first wife had died in 1630 as the result of a long and painful illness, and his letters only refer to the loss with touching brevity: "The Lord hath done it; blessed be His name."[104] There had been two children of this marriage, and his mother came to live with them at Anwoth. But the children were not long in this world, and his mother's life was ebbing away when he wrote of her in 1635: "My mother is weak, and I think shall leave me alone; but I am not alone, because Christ's Father is with me."[105] He was married for the second time in 1640 to Jean McMath, who

103. Letter 322, p. 641.
104. Letters 11, p. 53; 8, p. 49.
105. Letter 49, p. 119.

is described as a woman of rare worth and spirit. "I never knew any among men exceed him," wrote one who knew them well, "nor any among women exceed her."[106] Their first two children died while he was in London, and there is a pathetic reference to this sorrow in one of his letters: "I had but two children, and both are dead since I came hither."[107] It was to a childless home that he returned in the year 1647, but five more little ones were born within the next few years. But they were a frail and delicate family, and his daughter Agnes was the only child who survived to cheer his wife when in due time she was left a widow. There were depths of tenderness in his character which won him the trust and love of men and women in all stations of life, and some of the finest names in Scotland are found in the circle of his friendships. Many of his letters were written to strengthen nobles like Loudon and Earlston in their adherence to the Covenant, while not a few of the honourable women of the day, such as Lady Kenmure and Lady Culross, were among his warmest correspondents. It is clear that such strong family affection at home and such tender friendship in a wider circle were part of his essential character; they were personal qualities which found their most transcendent form of expression in his yearning for the love that passeth knowledge.

It is true that we hear all too little of his wife and children whether in the home at Anwoth or the College of St. Andrews; it has even been said that we know more of the birds which sang in the church than of the bairns who played in the manse.[108] But while direct information may be absent, indirect influence could not be hid. All the joys and sorrows of his own heart and home were touched with a glory which his letters reveal in a thousand sayings. It was his own frequent journey at the side of wife or mother, son or daughter, to the dark and troubled waters of death that gave him such superb skill in words of consolation. He never wrote in finer vein than when he wrote for the comfort of the bereaved; it was as though all the springs

106. See Andrew Bonar, *op. cit.*, p. 16.
107. Letter 310, p. 621.
108. Taylor Innes, *op. cit.*, p. 143.

of pity in his own heart found a spontaneous outlet in true fellow feeling with those who mourned. When he heard that his friend David Dickson had lost a child, he called for a pen with the cry: "When one arm is broken off and bleeds, it makes the other bleed with it."[109] Then he sat down to write with his vivid imagery: "Your Lord may gather His roses and shake His apples at what season of the year He pleaseth."[110] Years before he had written to Lady Kenmure, who had been tried with a similar affliction: "He sendeth us to His world as men to a market, wherein some stay many hours, and eat and drink, and buy and sell, and pass through the fair till they be weary; and such are those who live long, and get a heavy fill of this life. And others again come slipping in to the morning market, and do neither sit nor stand, nor buy nor sell, but look about them a little, and pass presently home again; and these are infants and young ones, who end their short market in the morning and get but a short view of the fair."[111] Or from the midst of his toils in London, he took time to write a long and loving letter to one who had lost a young son of great promise in St. Andrews: "Ye are not your own, but bought with a price," he wrote: "and your sorrow is not your own."[112] He gave a new turn to a great saying, and made his point with the finest simplicity. It was out of the depth of his own heart that a noble sentence in one of his sermons was wrung. "I know," he said, "there is a true sorrow that is without tears; and I know there is a real sorrow that is beyond tears."[113]

There is a sense in which Rutherford was as much a paradox in his own eyes as he is now in the eyes of many critics. "I am made of extremes";[114] so he once told David Dickson. No one can fail to be conscious of these extremes when an attempt is made to analyze his life and character. Alexander Whyte has taken pains to point out how these extremes can be traced in detail

109. Letter 298, p. 602 [Editorial Note].
110. *Ibid.*, p. 602.
111. Letter 35, p. 98.
112. Letter 310, p. 620.
113. Samuel Rutherford, *Quaint Sermons*, p. 346.
114. Letter 168, p. 315.

through his books and letters.[115] There were academic extremes which stretched from the splendid heights of imaginative freedom and speculative insight to the ugly depths of acrimonious debate and intolerant tirade. There were literary extremes which ranged from rhapsodies of great beauty and sweetness to paragraphs of plain neglect and nonsense. The strength of an earnest purpose was matched by the warmth of tender feeling; natural sympathies were fused with and fired by heavenly affections. But the supreme point of contrast lies in the gulf between two great extremes: on the one hand there was the stern logic and scholastic style of a volume such as *Lex Rex*; and then there was the rich passion and angelic glow of a book such as his *Letters*. He has suffered devastating criticism on both accounts, but this does not alter the fact that in him such extremes were found. Grosart attacked him for sectarian bitterness in his *Lex Rex*.[116] Buchan referred to "the oriental lusciousness" of his *Letters*.[117] But a searching analysis of this peculiar element of paradox in character has been made by Taylor Innes, and his acute observations are of the first value for all other students. He thought that the reality of these extremes was the outward sign of inward schism; it seemed to him that there were, in fact, two men in Samuel Rutherford,[118] and that they had never really been merged into one strong unit.[119] He held that his life was like a kind of double whirlwind, with an upper and a lower region, and that the swirling currents in each would always revolve in line with their own laws;[120] the storm and the splendour which might at times illumine the heights above were quite independent of the force and fury which would at times agitate the depths below.[121]

Alexander Whyte once remarked that the finest thing which has as yet been written in connection with Rutherford was this

115. Alexander Whyte, *op. cit.*, pp. 11-18.
116. See Robert Gilmour, *op. cit.*, p. 202.
117. John Buchan, *Montrose*, p. 62.
118. Taylor Innes, *op. cit.*, p. 137.
119. *Ibid.*, p. 146.
120. *Ibid.*, p. 138.
121. *Ibid.*, p. 139.

study from the pen of his friend Taylor Innes.[122] It is undoubtedly the most acute and most sympathetic of the many attempts which have been made to understand and interpret one who was both "the saint and the genius of the Covenant"[123] It does full credit to the masculine and masterful strain of logic in a servant of truth and righteousness; and it also does full credit to the feminine and instinctive chord of rapture in a prophet of grace and compassion. Inside his study at St. Andrews, he lived and warred in a world of words and ideas; beyond his study, as in London, he moved and served in a world of facts and affairs. But must this mean that there was the conflict of a dual nature in Rutherford? Or need it mean more than that there were two distinct sides to the one man as a whole? Logical instinct and mystical impulse lie side by side at the bed-rock of all human nature, though the one may develop at the expense of the other in the growth of character. But both these traits seem to have been developed to their maximum in the case of Ruth-erford, and their opposite tendencies were worked out in their most mature form in *Lex Rex* and the *Letters*. That the same man should have been the author of both volumes is the final proof that he was a man of no common mental stature, with rare powers of original thought and accomplishment. He was in fact so far from an unrelated dualism that we are more likely to be correct if we conclude that he was "a very much greater man than even his most sympathetic critics are prepared to allow."[124] He lacked those great personal qualities which made Henderson's leadership so wise and sure, but he stood next to him in true succession to John Knox and Andrew Mel-ville. Moreover it seems probable that the extremes which strike us so forcibly when we turn from the stiff logic of *Lex Rex* to the rich feeling of the *Letters* were not half so apparent to men of his own age. Taylor Innes himself points out how this seem-ing gap was in fact firmly bridged by the man who stands re-vealed in his sermons.[125]

122. Alexander Whyte, *op. cit.*, p. 11.
123. G. F. Barbour, *op. cit.*, p. 650.
124. Robert Gilmour, *op. cit.*, p. 22.
125. Taylor Innes, *op. cit.*, p. 155.

There is a reference in the works of Stephen Charnock to "the excellent speech of a holy man in our neighbor nation";[126] and that holy man was Samuel Rutherford, whose fame as a preacher stood as high in England as it did in Scotland. Preaching was the breath of life for a man such as Rutherford; silence was the hurt which he felt most of all in Aberdeen. "Next to Christ, I had but one joy," he wrote, "to preach Christ my Lord; and they have violently plucked that away from me. It was to me like the poor man's one eye; and they have put out that eye, and quenched my light in the inheritance of the Lord."[127] But the two years spent in exile were the only interruption in a lifetime dedicated to the task of preaching; and his sermons were as continuous as his letters from the early years in Anwoth to the close of his life at St. Andrews. The theology and controversy which were peculiar to the Covenant were packed into all his preaching, and his sermons abound in the kind of teaching which made him so well known as a Divine. But his solid learning did not cumber him with academic isolation from the stirring events of current history. No man could preach with more passionate devotion for the things which are eternal, and yet no man could preach with more impressive directness to the times to which he belonged. The cause of Christ's Crown and Covenant meant everything to Rutherford; all its varied aspects can be reviewed in his life and labours. We see how the thrill of patriotic fervour and the flash of celestial vision in his sermons made the dry bones of scholarship and argument stand up and live. "Would Parliaments begin at Christ, we should not fear that which certainly we have cause to fear," he cried; "one woe is past, and another woe cometh!"[128] He was armed with a tremendous power of rebuke, and he had scant mercy on men who sinned against the light. "If kings would become Christ's tenants," he made bold to say while Charles I was on the throne, "they might be more blessed under Him than under any other

126. Stephen Charnock, *Works,* Vol. V, p. 278.
127. Letter 225, p. 438.
128. Samuel Rutherford, *The Trial and Triumph of Faith,* Dedication. p. 8.

master."[129] His speech before Charles II in 1650 on "the duty of kings" was in Latin,[130] but it would lose nothing on that account in plainness or candour.

But great as was his power of rebuke, his powers of inspiration were greater still. Wodrow spoke of him as one of the most moving preachers ever known in Scotland;[131] and Alexander Whyte declared that for generations the best preaching in all Scotland was inspired by Rutherford.[132] The gales of the stormy age to which he belonged blew on him as hard as on any man; but through five and thirty years of incessant ministry, "the fragrance of heaven" clung to his words.[133] He was always fresh in mental imagery, and his pictures were an index to his own state of mind. "We must think Christ's sense of comforts was ebb and low when He wept . . . and was forsaken of God," he said. "Yet then His faith was doubled, as the cable of an anchor is doubled when the storm is more than ordinary — My God! My God!"[134] It is easy to see that the hand which wrote the sermons was in fact the hand which wrote the letters: for the burning diction and the pictorial oratory which shone through the sermons was forged in the same mould as the glowing language and the poetical imagery which flashed through his letters. No one but the author of the letters would dare to coin such an image for a sermon as this: "Lovely in the womb, the Ancient of Days became young for me."[135] His letters and sermons are both rich in proverbs full of spiritual wisdom. "Prayer is like God's file to stir a rusty heart";[136] "A good conscience is a good soft well-made bed";[137] "The world loves nothing worse than sorrow for sin";[138] these were aphorisms which his hearers would not forget.

129. Samuel Rutherford, *Quaint Sermons*, p. 31.
130. *Dictionary of National Biography*, "Samuel Rutherford."
131. Robert Wodrow, *The History of the Sufferings of the Church of Scotland*, Vol. I, p. 205.
132. G. F. Barbour, *op. cit.*, p. 308.
133. Taylor Innes, *op. cit.*, p. 151.
134. Samuel Rutherford, *The Trial and Triumph of Faith*, p. 316.
135. *Ibid.*, p. 262.
136. Samuel Rutherford, *Quaint Sermons*, p. 134.
137. *Ibid.*, p. 144.
138. *Ibid.*, p. 271.

And in spiritual application, his touch was deft and sure. "A doubting soul is ready to find many faults with God and with Christ";[139] "Humility grows best in winter weather and under storms of affliction";[140] "Once learn this lesson, to think little of thyself; and when it comes to that, thou art within sight of Christ."[141] And the magic of that spiritual poetry which has held men enthralled for three successive centuries flashes like an opal through his sermon to the House of Commons: "O for Eternity's leisure to look on Him, to feast upon a sight of His face! O for the long summer day of endless ages to stand beside Him and enjoy Him! O time, O sin, be removed out of the way! O day, O fairest of days, dawn!"[142]

Rutherford's sermons are a splendid witness to the Covenant message by means of which Scotland was stirred from end to end. No one can read through a volume like *The Trial and Triumph of Faith* without being made to feel the vital glory of that message. His clear exposition of the spiritual life makes him rank with the masters of the Puritan period, for his preaching was the passionate utterance of a man whose soul was deeply versed in the things of God. His masculine strength and aggressive force in the field of logic and argument were balanced by his sensitive touch and delicate grace in the world of feeling and sympathy. No living preacher in either kingdom had so rich a vocabulary or so warm an imagination in consoling the sorrowful or recalling the wanderer. Seamen cannot create the wind, but they can hoist their sails to welcome it; neither can we create the Breath of the Spirit, but are we to miss it when it comes through failure to keep our sails unfurled?[143] Few men knew as he knew how to interpret the dark ways of Providence by the light of Scripture; Providence to his eye was like a special reading in the margin beside the text, written large and clear by the hand of God. Many of his sayings would ring through his hearers' minds long after the sermon had ended. "The devil," he would say, ". . . is twice

139. *Ibid.*, p. 15.
140. *Ibid.*, p. 86.
141. *Ibid.*, p. 243.
142. Andrew Bonar, *op. cit.*, p. 15.
143. Samuel Rutherford, *The Trial and Triumph of Faith*, p. 309.

a devil . . . in his own sphere."[144] "Who is there," he would ask, "that leaves God but they find some fault in Him?"[145] Pithy remarks like these can be found at random in the pages of his printed sermons. "Time fleeth away," he would say, "as swiftly as a weaver's shuttle which leapeth over a thousand threads in a moment."[146] "There be many," he might add, "who will be content to winter Christ that can not be content to summer Him also."[147] And his words would often reflect his own deepest longings: "Ye may know the ardent desire of a soul after Christ can be satisfied with nothing but Himself."[148]

But it was his superb power to set Christ before men in moral splendour and in saving goodness that made him great as an exponent of His Crown and Covenant. We can still imagine the fair and fervent face of the preacher, alight with the beauty of that other world, and we think we know why the English merchant was so enchanted by his sermon on the loveliness of the Rose of Sharon.[149] We can still overhear the shrill and eager voice from the pulpit, intent with the appeal of that better land, and we think we know why the Scottish noble was so uplifted by the sermon on the majesty of the Prince of Zion.[150] Vivid language and rich imagery in this respect were as much a feature of his sermons as they had been of his letters; extracts from each might be copied out and placed side by side, and no critic could tell from which they were taken. Thus he would say that Christ did not die until His hour had come: "He was not like green corn, cut down ere it be half-ripe."[151] Or he would say that the Cross was our summer, but death's winter: "Darkness was in all Judaea when our Lord suffered; and why? Because the Candle that lighted the sun and the moon was blown out."[152] Love, he said,

144. *Ibid.*, p. 58.
145. Samuel Rutherford, *Quaint Sermons*, p. 212.
146. Samuel Rutherford, *The Trial and Triumph of Faith*, Dedication, p. 4.
147. Samuel Rutherford, *Quaint Sermons*, p. 62.
148. *Ibid.*, p. 76.
149. See Robert Gilmour, p. 41.
150. *Ibid.*, p. 42.
151. Samuel Rutherford, *Fourteen Communion Sermons*, p. 123.
152. *Ibid.*, p. 286.

has strong, broad shoulders: "Get love, and no burden Christ will lay on you will be heavy."[153] Love, he said, is a beam from the Eternal Sun of Righteousness: "For love comes not on Christ the day, which was not in Him yesterday."[154] His heart would soar in pure adoration. "Oh, He Himself is an unknown Lover," he would exclaim; "He hath neither brim nor bottom."[155] His voice would swell with true encouragement. "Who has a warm heart to a home-coming sinner," he would inquire, "if Christ have it not?"[156] He spoke with a forceful simplicity from which it was hard to escape: "Thou who art tethered to thy delights, when Christ comes by and cries, Follow Me, if then thou canst break thy tether like a rotten straw rope and gallop after Him, thou hast clear eyes and seest well."[157] The quick upward cast of his eyes when he began to speak of his Divine Master, as if he would pierce the very veil of heaven, was a gesture which served to sum up the whole man. He had made his own heart over to Christ, so that as a preacher, he was himself ever "on tip toe for the sky."[158]

Samuel Rutherford was not faultless in conduct or outlook, but he was a great man. He was often betrayed by hasty temper or bitter reproach, but he was a choice soul. He was not so urbane as Henderson of Leuchars, nor so winsome as Livingston of Ancrum; but he was a standard-bearer in Christ's quarrel worthy to take the field side by side with them both. His own mind had long been made up how to act should he have to choose between his friends and Truth: he would walk with Christ even though the wind were in His face, rather than seek the sunny side of the brae without Him.[159] No one in Scotland ranked so high as preacher or scholar, and it was the home of both. No one in England was his master in theology or controversy, and it was an age of giants. The world has seldom seen a union of scholastic

153. *Ibid.*, p. 186.
154. *Ibid.*, p. 235.
155. Samuel Rutherford, *The Trial and Triumph of Faith*, p. 261.
156. Samuel Rutherford, *Quaint Sermons*, p. 202.
157. *Ibid.*, p. 89.
158. Taylor Innes, *op. cit.*, p. 152.
159. Letter 115, pp. 233, 234.

genius and seraphic devotion equal to that which he displayed. Taylor Innes has summed it up in the happy saying that "it was St. Thomas and St. Francis under one hood."[160] He brought into his own Scottish pulpit all the other-worldly aspirations of an ancient cloister, and he was forever mounting up on wings of glory, "impatient of earth, intolerant of sin," to the contemplation of one bright Face which was as yet unseen.[161] "Oh what love my poor soul hath found in Him," he cried, "in the house of my pilgrimage!"[162] All his waking thoughts were centred on Him; daily he found some new grace or beauty in Him. "Every day," he wrote, "we may see some new thing in Christ; His love hath neither brim nor bottom."[163] Alexander Moody Stuart felt the charm of these words; he liked to quote them, and then would add a single lucid comment in the very spirit of their author: "A few drops from this ocean of love would more than fill our hearts," he would affirm, "and we should be constrained to say, My cup runneth over (Ps. 23:5)."[164]

It could never be said that Rutherford did not take pains with his own soul, for the supreme value of his ministry was due to the lofty spirit of his character. One brief statement in a sermon on The Trial and Triumph of Faith serves to disclose his own clear and candid judgment: "The least faith doth justify; but the Gospel requireth a growth in faith."[165] One short sentence in a letter to a friend and student serves to reveal his own secret for such a growth in faith: "If ye would be a deep divine, I recommend to you sanctification."[166] And a saying on his death-bed shows us that this was the habit of a life-time: "I betake myself to Christ for sanctification as well as justification."[167] He knew the plague of his own heart as few men ever seem to do, and he could lay his finger on the running sores of sin with the most deft and certain touch. Thus he saw how Satan has a friend at

160. Taylor Innes, *op. cit.*, p. 146.
161. *Ibid.*, p. 137.
162. Letter 237, p. 472.
163. Letter 171, p. 323.
164. K. Moody Stuart, *Alexander Moody Stuart*, p. 280.
165. Samuel Rutherford, *The Trial and Triumph of Faith*, p. 212.
166. Letter 82, p. 170.
167. Andrew Bonar, *op. cit.*, p. 21.

court in the heart of youth, and how greed and pride are the two agents which he loves to employ.[168] "Many, alas! too many," he cried, "make a common strumpet of their soul for every lover that cometh to the house."[169] But he knew, too, the power of God's grace as few men ever seem to know it, and he could lead the sinner to the only place of rest with the most kind and gentle hand. Thus he saw that no one can be more humble than a true believer, for it is not pride that prompts a drowning man to stretch out his hand and catch hold of a rock.[170] "Necessity must not blush to beg," he wrote; "your heart is not the compass which Christ saileth by."[171] Experience taught him that many may go to heaven with us, and yet we hear not the sound of their feet in the journey;[172] experience also taught him that many coals make a good fire, and that this is a part of the communion of saints.[173] It would not be unfair to sum up by saying that he was a master in the realm of his own maxim: he was a deep divine, because his was a sanctified spirit.

Rutherford was engaged all through the strife of the fifties in the work which he still loved best of all; books were wrought out in his study, and he was in frequent demand for his help on Communion occasions. There was perhaps no one in all Scotland who was so sought after in the deepest matters of the spirit, for the anxious in heart knew as if by instinct that the secret of the Lord was with him. Howie says that many who had received life for their soul through his ministrations went to heaven before him in those years, and that many others were left after his own going to walk in the same light.[174] But it was a sore trial to be cut off from old friends like Robert Blair and David Dickson with whom he had stood side by side for years; he found himself alone in the Presbytery of St, Andrews in his hostility to the Resolutions, and there were but six like-minded with him in the

168. Letter 142, p. 271.
169. Letter 226, p. 445.
170. Letter 229, p. 455.
171. Letter 181, p. 350.
172. Samuel Rutherford, *The Trial and Triumph of Faith*, p. 271.
173. Letter 286, p. 564.
174. John Howie, *op. cit.*, p. 234.

Synod of Fife.[175] It is pleasant at least to know that his quarrel with Blair was healed before he died, and that Dickson confessed on his death-bed that his friend had been the truer prophet. He had toiled all his life in the interests of Christ's Crown and Covenant and had spent all his strength in the effort to make the Kirk "fair as the moon, clear as the sun, and terrible as an army with banners" (Song of Sol. 6:10). But old friends whom he had dearly loved had now long since gone to a better country and his own thoughts were now ever turning to that land where no wind blows save the soft breath of the Spirit's power and where no sea rolls save the pure stream of the Saviour's love. "Oh, when shall the night be gone, the shadows flee away, and the morning of that long, long day, without cloud or night, dawn?"[176] Coruscations of the old fire still flashed through his letters in those last years; ethereal longings were as strong as ever as he saw the shades of evening loom in the sky. He was like a foot-weary traveller and he leaned hard on the arm of his Guide; for he knew that this was an arm that would not fail until he stood at the gates of glory.[177]

Rutherford's life was not far from sunset at the time when Charles II came home in May, 1660, to claim the crown. And it was his greatest sorrow to see the blue banner of the Covenant trailed in derision at the heels of those who served the Merry Monarch. Nothing could have been more poignant than his lament for the sins of the times only three years before: "The Lord," he cried, "hath removed Scotland's crown, for we owned not His crown."[178] But in spite of seeming failure, his faith in the final triumph of Christ's royal cause never faltered: "The Bush hath been burning about five thousand years," he had once written, "and we never yet saw the ashes of this fire."[179] It was still his hope as late as the last month of his life that the Lord would yet "shine gloriously in the Isle of Britain

175. Robert Gilmour, *op. cit.*, p. 200.
176. Letter 333, p. 662.
177. Letter 275, p. 533.
178. Letter 348, p. 683.
179. Letter 317, p. 634.

as a crowned King."[180] But the last year of his life was darkened
by the frown of tyranny and the threat of martyrdom. He was
bound to incur the strong dislike of the ruling party who could
not forget and would not forgive the fact that he was the author
of that great book, *Lex Rex,* and as early as September, 1660, it
was examined by the Committee of Estates and condemned as a
treasonable writing. It was declared unfit for loyal subjects to read,
and all copies were to be surrendered by October 16; owners
who failed to comply were to be treated as foes to the King and
the peace of the Kingdom. On October 16 the book was burnt
by the common hangman at the Cross of Edinburgh and, a few
days later, at the gates of his own College in St. Andrews. Rutherford was then summoned to appear before the committee, but
three certificates were sent in to excuse him on the ground of
illness and infirmity. His case was then dealt with in his absence
and the cloud of persecution which had so long shadowed
him broke over his head. He was deposed from the ministry, and
dismissed from his Chair at St. Andrews; he was confined to
his own house, and reserved for trial at the ensuing Parliament
on a charge of treason.

The Drunken Parliament, as it was called, met on New Year's
Day in 1661 and sat for six and a half months. It strengthened
the Royal Prerogative, and prepared a new oath of allegiance; it
poured contempt on the Covenant, and forbade its renewal. On
March 28, it passed an Act Rescissory to wipe out the legislation of the last twenty years, and it also took steps to deal with the
four most distinguished men who adhered to the Covenant.
Argyll, Warriston, Guthrie and Rutherford were marked for
the scaffold, and the first two trials were set in motion in the
month of February. On May 27, Argyll knelt down on the platform with his head on the block; on June 1, Guthrie was pushed
off the ladder with a rope round his neck. Warriston was safe
at the time in Europe, but he was to suffer two years later at the
Mercat Cross in Edinburgh. Rutherford also escaped, but not by
his own choice. It was to him a source of deep regret that he
should be denied a martyr's death and martyr's crown; he would

180. Letter 363, p. 703.

like to have stood in the van of those who were to glorify God in the Grassmarket. His enemies were not half so eager to bring him to the scaffold as he was to go; he would have thought it all joy to have been able to seal his life's testimony by thus dying for Christ's Crown and Covenant. "I would think it a more glorious way of going home," he said, "to lay down my life for the cause at the Cross of Edinburgh or St. Andrews; but I submit to my Master's will."[181] He knew that the sands of time were sinking and that his life was near its close.[182] A slow disease had been at work in his wasted body and life's last strength was ebb and low. Thus it was a dying man who at length heard the summons from the Government messengers to come and stand his trial on the charge of treason. He knew that he would soon be called before that Judge whose court is far greater than the greatest earthly assize, and he framed his reply in words which still ring with the accent of noble disdain: "Tell them," he said, ". . . I behove to answer my first summons, and ere your day come, I will be where few kings and great folk come."[183]

Parliament, cheated of its victim, determined not to allow Rutherford to die in his rooms at St. Andrews. But Lord Burleigh at least rose up and lodged a strong protest: "Ye have voted that honest man out of the College," he said, "but ye can not vote him out of heaven."[184] But while the sky grew black as night over Scotland, on that death-bed in St. Andrews there shone the light of a land that is fairer than day. Friends came to take their leave, and he had a word for them all. One was Robert Blair who asked him what he now thought of Christ, and he replied: "I shall live and adore Him. Glory, glory to my . . . Redeemer for ever!"[185] When a remark was made about his work for God, he said: "I disclaim all: the port I would be in at is redemption and forgiveness of sin through His blood."[186] At length the hour arrived when he told his friends that before morning could dawn, he would cast

181. Andrew Bonar, *op. cit.*, p. 20.
182. Letter 147, p. 277.
183. John Howie, *op. cit.*, p. 236.
184. *Ibid.*
185. *Ibid.*, p. 239.
186. Andrew Bonar, *op. cit.*, p. 21.

his anchor in that haven where he so longed to be. And so it came to pass. Early in the morning of March 29, 1661, while it was yet dark in the world around, the tide ran out to sea and he was with Christ on the other side. But the supreme passion of a lifetime was not voiceless in the solemn moment of his dying, and the calm hush of a holy wonder descends upon us still as we linger in thought near his passing spirit. The soft pillow on which his soul reposed was the ancient promise which had inspired all his dreams and desires. "Thine eyes shall see the King in His beauty; they shall behold the land that is very far off" (Isaiah 33:17). But he knew how to turn the words of that promise into the clear vision of faith, and the last words which he was heard to breathe were the exquisite reverie: "Glory, glory dwelleth in Immanuel's Land!"[187] It was as though a glimpse of the distant mountains and the kingly glory were flashed before his eyes; then in the choice phrase of his own beautiful metaphor, he fell asleep on the bosom of the Almighty.[188]

187. *Ibid.*, p. 22.
188. Letter 2, p. 34.

BIBLIOGRAPHY

Andrew Bonar, *Letters of Samuel Rutherford, with a Sketch of His Life,* 1848.

A. Taylor Innes, *Samuel Rutherford* (in *The Evangelical Succession,* Second Series), 1883.

Andrew Thomson, *Samuel Rutherford* (4th edition), 1889.

Alexander Whyte, *Samuel Rutherford and Some of His Correspondents,* 1894.

Robert Gilmour, *Samuel Rutherford,* 1904.

Dictionary of National Biography, "Samuel Rutherford" (Vol. XVII), 1950.

Robert Wodrow, *The History of the Sufferings of the Church of Scotland* (4 Vols.), 1885.

John Howie, *The Scots Worthies* (ed. by W. H. Carslaw), 1870.

Alexander Smellie, *Men of the Covenant,* 1903.

David Masson, *The Life of John Milton* (6 Vols. and Index), 1881.

Samuel Rutherford, *Lex Rex: The Law and the Prince,* 1644.

Samuel Rutherford, *The Trial and Triumph of Faith,* 1646.

Samuel Rutherford, *Fourteen Communion Sermons* (ed. by Andrew Bonar), 1876.

Samuel Rutherford, *Quaint Sermons Hitherto Unpublished* (ed. by Andrew Bonar), 1885.

(From Robert White's pencil drawing, Cracherode Collection, British Museum)

JOHN BUNYAN

JOHN BUNYAN
The Immortal Dreamer

1628 — 1688

Who would true valour see,
 Let him come hither;
One here will constant be,
 Come wind, come weather.
There's no discouragement
Shall make him once relent
His first avow'd intent
 To be a pilgrim.

—John Bunyan, *Works*, Vol. III, p. 235
(edition by George Offor used throughout).

JOHN BUNYAN, THE SON OF THOMAS BUN-
yan and Margaret Bentley, was born in the village of Elstow in
November, 1628. Thus he grew up in that part of England which
had sent the Pilgrim Fathers to the New World and had fostered
men of sturdy independence for the Puritan Succession at home.
Elstow was a little village which lay about a mile to the southwest
of the county seat at Bedford. It had grown up round an ancient
abbey which in Bunyan's day had become the home of Sir Thomas
Hillersdon. This fine old house stood back from the main road
and was approached by a carriage drive which led up to its grace-
ful entrance. It seems to have left in Bunyan's mind the picture
of that "very stately palace the name of which was Beautiful, and
it stood just by the highway side."[1] Bunyan tells us little of his
parents, and perhaps that little ought to be qualified. "For my
descent," he wrote, "it was, as is well known by many, of a low
and inconsiderable generation, my father's house being of the rank
that is meanest and most despised of all the families in the land."[2]
Again he once asked with indignation: "What kind of a YOU
am I? And why is MY rank so mean that the most gracious and
godly among you may not duly and soberly consider of what I
have said?"[3] And once he signed himself as "thine, if thou be not
ashamed to own me because of my low and contemptible descent
in the world."[4] His father is often described as a tinker, and in
his will he is called a "braseyer"[5] — one who worked at the forge by
his cottage or went from farm to farm in the course of his trade.
Bunyan's work on *Christian Behaviour* records a *cri du coeur*:
"The Lord if it be his will convert our poor parents that they
with us may be the children of God!"[6] Poverty but not piety, as

1. *Works*, Vol. III, p. 106.
2. *Ibid.*, Vol. I, p. 6.
3. *Ibid.*, Vol. II, p. 617.
4. *Ibid.*, Vol. III, p. 674.
5. John Brown, *John Bunyan: His Life, Times and Work*, p. 34.
6. *Works*, Vol. II, p. 564.

he judged things, was the mark of that home. But it is now known that the wills of his father and grandfather and his maternal grandfather were all preserved in the District Court of Probate, and this was at a time when the poorest never made wills at all. We may add to this, the fact that the house in which he was born had belonged to his fathers from time immemorial, and thus we may conclude that his parents came of humble stock but were not without independence.

Bunyan's childhood home was on the fringe of Elstow and the bridle path to Bedford ran past the front of the cottage. He could see the spire of St. Paul's Church in Bedford through the elm trees from a nearby hilltop. "Notwithstanding the meanness and inconsiderableness of my parents," he wrote, "it pleased God to put it into their hearts to put me to school to learn both to read and write; the which I also attained according to the rate of other poor men's children; though to my shame I confess I did soon lose that little I learned . . . and that, long before the Lord did work His gracious work of conversion upon my soul."[7] No doubt he had his own experience in mind when he wrote of justification by faith: "It is with many that begin with this doctrine as it is with boys that go to the Latin school: they learn till they have learned the grounds of their grammar, and then go home and forget all."[8] In the *Scriptural Poems* which have been ascribed to him, we read:

> For I'm no poet, nor a poet's son,
> But a mechanic, guided by no rule
> But what I gained in a grammar school
> In my minority.[9]

This seems to indicate that he was educated on the foundation of Sir William Harpur at Bedford; but it is now doubtful whether the lines should be ascribed to him at all. Once when he quotes the phrase *ex carne et sanguine Christi*, he adds a note in the margin: "The Latin I borrow."[10] Again he frankly says: "For my part, I am not ashamed to confess that I neither know the mode

7. *Ibid.*, Vol. I, p. 6.
8. *Ibid.*, Vol. I, p. 618.
9. *Ibid.*, Vol. II, p. 390.
10. *Ibid.*, Vol. III, p. 202.

nor figure of a syllogism, nor scarce which is major or minor."[11] School-days such as they were, in Elstow or Bedford, were short enough. "I never went to school to Aristotle or Plato," he wrote, "but was brought up at my father's house in a very mean condition."[12] Necessity compelled him to leave school and to address his strength to the hammer and forge. Thus school-days were over and the struggle of his teens had begun when he entered upon the year 1644.

This was the year which brought legislation for the abolition of the *Prayer Book* and which proscribed the *Book of Sports*. Wrestling, shooting, bowling, dancing, masques, wakes, and games of all kinds were prohibited on the Lord's Day. Bunyan's mother sickened and died in June, and he followed her bier across the fields to her resting place in Elstow churchyard. This was followed first by the death of his sister in July and then by the second marriage of his father in August. Sorrow and change in such rapid sequence may have helped to estrange the boy from his father and from the home of his childhood. Thus his sixteenth birthday in November brought him to the regulation age for army service at a time when he may not have been loath to get away from home, and he must have spent some months on active service before the Battle of Naseby in June, 1645. Bedford was one of the seven counties from which Parliament drew its main strength, and it did not suffer from the effects of war as did certain others. It was once thought that he served with the King's army, but there is now decisive evidence of an opposite character. There were but few Royalist partisans in the county, and he must have been caught in one of the levies made by Parliament. His only reference to those days was when he mentioned how his life had been spared "when I was a soldier";[13] but he never forgot the things which he saw and heard while in arms. He was in the midst of those fighting and praying captains who were the true originals for his portraits of Great-Heart and others. He may have joined in the salute to Sir Samuel

11. *Ibid.*, Vol. II, p. 661.
12. *Ibid.*, Vol. I, p. 495.
13. *Ibid.*, p. 7.

Luke at Newport Pagnell; he may have fought with Major Ennis on the walls of Leicester against Rupert's assault. Perhaps he would follow Captain Bladwell as he marched to Surrey Downs; perhaps he listened to Captain Hobson as he preached in Lathbury Field. It was all an experience which would do much to stir his mind and to widen his thoughts. Recollections of those days would make his picture of the fight with Apollyon or the siege of Mansoul so much more real and more vivid. Take this picture in the fight for Mansoul: "When they set out for their march, O how the trumpets sounded, their armour glittered, and how the colours waved in the wind . . . ."[14] His dialogue is salted with the talk of Roundhead captains as when he quotes the rough soldier saying: "Blood up to the ears."[15] When he has to describe fighting, it is with sword rather than with musket, and his pictures are full of life and strong vitality.[16]

The army was disbanded in 1646, and he must have gone home to work as a tinker. It was no doubt during the next three years that his life was stained with the sins which he thought were of a crimson pattern. He was to sketch his own moral state in bold and vivid colours, bolder and more vivid perhaps than a detached judgment would have required. But he knew the plague of his own heart, and he was bowed by a burden which seemed beyond his power to bear. It was this searching self-knowledge that made him write the words that flash and flame through his writings and that gave him such a hold on the hearts of his readers. He could always enforce his most awful diagnosis by an appeal which no one could deny; and that appeal was as blunt as it was direct: "I know what I say."[17] Thus he reproached himself for the sins which had scarred his life as he grew up into manhood. They were not sins of an immoral character so much as the sins of a man who had no fear of God before his eyes. He was not a drunkard, and in after years he passionately denied that he had been unchaste. But we can trace in the weakness of his youth the reverse of what became the strength of his developed

14. *Ibid.*, Vol. III, p. 285.
15. *Ibid.*, I, p. 661.
16. *Ibid.*, Vol. III, pp. 113, 358.
17. See, for example, *Works*, Vol. I, p. 489.

character. He who beyond most men was to strive for spiritual reality and to stand with awe in his heart before eternal verities began with the guilt of flagrant outrage against the reverence and sanctity of truth.[18] His story was very like that of John Newton a hundred years later, and each man thought himself first and foremost in the godless society in which he moved. Thus John Bunyan declared: "I had but few equals . . . for cursing, swearing, lying and blaspheming the holy Name of God."[19] He could not bear reproof and tried to smother the voice of conscience: "Heaven and hell," he wrote, "were both out of sight and mind, and as for saving and damning, they were least in my thoughts."[20] When he looked back across the years, he could observe with an unaffected sincerity: "There must go a great deal to the making of a man a Christian: for as to that, every man is a fool; yea, the greatest fool, the most unconcerned fool, the most self-willed fool of all fools; yea, one that will not be turned from his folly but by the breaking of his heart. David was one of these fools . . . and so was I — and that, the biggest of all."[21] Thus it was with Bunyan until he came to "the state of marriage";[22] then the struggle which was to break his heart began.

In 1649 John Bunyan was married, but we do not even know the bride's name. He spoke of her father as one who was now dead, but who had been "counted godly."[23] It is clear that his wife had no dowry to bring with her. "This woman and I," he wrote, ". . . came together as poor as poor might be, not having so much household stuff as a dish or spoon betwixt us both."[24] But this marriage gave him a home which was brightened with love such as he had not known since his mother's death in 1644. His first child was baptized with the name of Mary in July, 1650, and her blindness evoked the most tender love on his part until her death. The first four years of his marriage were those in which he passed through the mighty conflict which was to issue in

18. See John Brown, *op. cit.*, p. 59.
19. *Works*, Vol. I, p. 6.
20. *Ibid.*, p. 7.
21. *Ibid.*, p. 704.
22. *Ibid.*, p. 6.
23. *Ibid.*, Vol. I, p. 7.
24. *Ibid.*

his conversion. His wife had brought him a better dowry than gold in the form of two small and homely books which had been left to her by her father. Bunyan's heart was softened by her gentle nature and he began to stir up a skill for reading aloud which had almost perished. "In these two books," he wrote, "I should sometimes read with her, wherein I also found some things that were somewhat pleasing to me."[25] These books awoke in him a new hunger for clean speech and a good conscience, but there was no tremendous conviction of sin. He fell in with the times and went to church "twice a day, and that too with the foremost."[26] But he was still far from any real change of heart, any cry from the depths. "Come, come," he wrote in the light of his own experience, "conversion to God is not so easy and so smooth a thing as some would have men believe it is. Why is man's heart compared to fallow ground, God's Word to a plough, and His ministers to ploughmen if the heart indeed has no need of breaking in order to the receiving of the seed of God unto eternal life? Who knows not that the fallow ground must be ploughed, and ploughed too before the husbandmen will venture his seed; yea, and after that, oft soundly harrowed, or else he will have but a slender harvest?"[27] The plough was soon driven across his heart. "And at that time, I felt what guilt was, though never before that I can remember; but then I was for the present greatly loaden therewith and so went home when the sermon was ended with a great burden upon my spirit."[28] This was only the first furrow, and it was not yet deep enough. He went home, ate his meal, shook the sermon out of his mind, and went back to the games of which he was so fond.

A series of struggles was to ensue, and Bunyan was soon in the grip of a fierce conflict over those games. It was after lunch on the same day that he was playing a game of cat somewhere on the green round the old Market Cross of Elstow. He had struck once and was about to strike again when a challenge flashed through his mind: "Wilt thou leave thy sins and go to

25. *Ibid.*
26. *Ibid.*
27. *Ibid.*, p. 720.
28. *Ibid.*, p. 8.

heaven, or have thy sins and go to hell?"[29] He stood stock-still, conscience stricken, looking up as if he saw the very face of Jesus. There were other players on the field, but he said nothing to them. "Suppose that there be a hell in very deed," he was to ask others: "not that I do question it any more than I do whether there be a sun to shine."[30] And on the green that day, he felt his heart sink in despair as if it were too late to change, and he turned back to play in an effort to rid himself of the voice of conscience altogether: "For, thought I, if the case be thus, my state is surely miserable: miserable if I leave my sins, and but miserable if I follow them; I can not but be damned, and if I must be so, I had as good be damned for many sins as to be damned for few."[31] This self-induced despair gained such control that he began to think that there could be no more comfort for him except in the pursuit of sin: "For heaven was gone already, so that on that I must not think."[32] Thus he proposed to rush headlong into the path of sin lest he should die before he had had his desire: "In these things," he wrote, "I protest before God, I lie not, neither do I feign this sort of speech: these were really, strongly, and with all my heart, my desires. The good Lord Whose mercy is unsearchable forgive me my transgressions."[33] But he could not escape from the grip of conscience quite so smoothly. His own experience taught him at length to write: "Be afraid of sins: they are like blood-hounds at the heels."[34] A month later, he was standing outside a shop window, swearing and cursing to excess, when a loose and godless woman told him that she trembled to hear his oaths and that he was spoiling the youth of the whole town. He fell silent, hanging his head in shame, longing with all his heart that he might be a child again, "that my father might learn me to speak without this wicked way of swearing."[35] It was the end of such swearing: whereas he had not been able to speak with-

29. *Ibid.*
30. *Ibid.,* Vol. III, p .592.
31. *Ibid.,* Vol. I, p. 8.
32. *Ibid.,* p. 9.
33. *Ibid.*
34. *Ibid.,* p. 742.
35. *Ibid.,* p. 9.

out an oath, he now began to speak better and with a more pleasant spirit than he had ever known. But he never forgot the blight which had poisoned his life and made him a by-word for all kinds of reckless folly. "I speak by experience," he wrote; "I was one of these great sin-breeders; I infected all the youth of the town where I was born with all manner of youthful vanities. The neighbors counted me so; my practice proved me so; wherefore Christ Jesus took me first."[36]

This great outward reformation in his life and manners lasted for the better part of a year, and he thought that he pleased God as well as any man in England. And yet "all this while I knew not Jesus Christ, neither did I leave my sports and plays."[37] Thus while neighbours marvelled at the change in his life, his heart was still in a state which he was later to describe as "unweldable."[38] He borrowed the image from his own trade as a blacksmith, recognizing that grace alone can weld the heart to Christ. It was not long before he found himself in the throes of further conflict. The first point at issue was the pastime of bell-ringing, which he began to think was wrong. He turned away from the belfry with a leaden heart, no longer daring to act as one of the ringers. The love of bells remained with him throughout his life and was to ring through the pages of his books as long as he lived. We need only recall how the bells of heaven rang in welcome for the pilgrims who had crossed the river. Nor was that all indeed, for in his dream he saw them pass within the gates and "all the bells in the city rang again for joy."[39] Meanwhile Bunyan still came and leaned against the old door-post, looking on with wistful eyes while others tugged at the ropes. But at heart he knew that he was not yet in sight of that far-off golden city, and a tender conscience made him wonder what would become of him should the bells or belfry over his head collapse. Such a vivid apprehension was like the dreams which had haunted him in childhood. When he described the House of the Interpreter, he spoke of the man who shook and trembled. That man had

36. *Ibid.*, p. 79.
37. *Ibid.*, p. 9.
38. *Ibid.*, p. 216.
39. *Ibid.*, Vol. III, p. 166.

just dreamt that he was under the eye of the Judge of mankind, and he had tried in vain to hide. "My sins also came into my mind," he said, "and my conscience did accuse me on every side."[40] We can hardly doubt that Bunyan painted that scene from the haunting recollection of his own dreams. At all events, that swift sense of apprehension put an end to all his visits to the belfry. But hard as it was to give up the bells, it was even harder to renounce his dancing on the village green or in the Moot Hall. "I was a full year before I could quite leave that";[41] so he confessed. And when he did leave it, he thought that there could be no one who pleased God more than he. But God's hour was at hand, and he was soon to strain his eyes to catch a glimpse of the distant shining light and the narrow wicket gate.

God, who had led Bunyan by a way that he knew not, was about to shake him free from the last hold of self-complacency. He has described the scene in a famous passage. "Upon a day, the good providence of God did cast me to Bedford to work on my calling; and in one of the streets of that town, I came where there were three or four poor women sitting at a door in the sun and talking about the things of God; and being now willing to hear them discourse, I drew near to hear what they said, for I was now a brisk talker also myself in the matters of religion, but now, I may say, I heard but I understood not; for they were far above me, out of my reach; for their talk was about a new birth, the work of God on their hearts."[42] Bunyan fancied himself in the role of his own character Talkative, but the talk of those poor godly women was quite out of his depth and he had to remain silent. "And methought they spake as if joy made them speak; they spake with such pleasantness of Scripture language and with such appearance of grace in all they said, that they were to me as if they had found a new world, as if they were people that dwelt alone and were not to be reckoned among their neighbours."[43] He was humbled and yet fascinated by what he heard; for he knew that he was still a stranger to that new world of which they spoke. "I felt my

40. *Ibid.*, p. 102.
41. *Ibid.*, Vol. I, p. 10.
42. *Ibid.*
43. *Ibid.*

own heart began to shake as mistrusting my condition to be nought; for I saw that in all my thoughts about religion and salvation, the new birth did never enter into my mind."[44] Bunyan left them and went about his chores as a tinker; but their conversation would not leave him, for he was now convinced that he lacked the experience of the new birth. He was compelled by this sense of painful anxiety to seek out those women time and again; he could not stay away from those who had found the secret of God. The more he went, the more he was forced to question the state of his own soul, and there soon came over him "a very great softness and tenderness of heart" and a constant inclination towards godly meditation.[45] "A soft, a tender, and a broken heart," he learned to say, "is a fit place for the grace of fear to thrive in."[46] "I know what I say in this matter, and also where I had been long ago . . . had it not been for the fear of God."[47] But he was still to pass through a long and searching struggle before he could sit with those poor women in the sunshine of God's love and favour.

Bunyan was now on fire with longing to find the way to heaven, and his thoughts were fixed on eternity. This taught him to read the Bible with new understanding. But there was still darkness as well as light in his experience. Glimmers of hope would be followed by the terrors of one who could not find the way. He was afraid lest he had missed God's time of grace, and he could not reproach himself enough because he had not turned before. He was harassed by "that grim-faced one, the Captain Past-Hope," whose blood-red standard was carried by his Ensign Despair.[48] At length he was so vexed with fear that he scarcely knew what to do, until the voice of Christ broke in upon his soul, saying "yet there is room" (Luke 14:22). "These words were sweet words to me; for truly I thought that by them I saw there was place enough in heaven for me."[49] If the Lord would only make His call clear,

44. *Ibid.*
45. *Ibid.*, p. 11.
46. *Ibid.*, p. 486.
47. *Ibid.*, p. 489.
48. *Ibid.*, Vol. III, p. 346.
49. *Ibid.*, Vol. I, p. 14.

he would not be denied. "I can not now express with what long-ings and breakings in my soul I cried to Christ to call me."[50] He was all in a flame to hear that call and it ruled his thoughts by day and his dreams by night. "I could seldom read of any that Christ did call but I presently wished, Would I had been in their clothes! Would I had been born Peter! Would I had been born John! Or would I had been by and had heard Him when He called them! How would I have cried, O Lord, call me also!"[51] And while he sought the face of God, he had never been so tender on the subject of sin. "Oh!" he cried, "how gingerly did I then go in all I did or said!"[52] And yet, "sin would as naturally bubble out of my heart as water would bubble out of a fountain."[53] This sense of his own sin drove him close to despair, for he could not think how such a man could be in a state of grace. "And yet God was so far off from rejecting of me, as I found afterwards, that there was music and dancing in His house for me, and for joy that I was come home unto Him."[54] It was then that he heard someone preach on the text: "Behold, thou art fair, my love; behold, thou art fair" (Song of Sol. 4:1). As he went home, those words kindled a new warmth in his soul, and he kept on hearing a voice within: "Thou art my love; thou art my love!" "Now was my heart filled full of comfort and hope, and now I could believe that my sins should be forgiven me; yea I was now so taken with the love and mercy of God that I remember I could not tell how to contain till I got home; I thought I could have spoken of His love and of His mercy to me even to the very crows that sat upon the ploughed lands before me."[55]

Meanwhile he had opened his heart to those godly women, and they mentioned his need to John Gifford, who had become their pastor in 1650. Bunyan talked things over with him and soon joined his congregation. His doctrine and teaching were by God's grace much used for his stability, and he was led from truth to

50. *Ibid.*
51. *Ibid.*, p. 15.
52. *Ibid.*
53. *Ibid.*, p. 16.
54. *Ibid.*, p. 80.
55. *Ibid.*, p. 17.

truth by God. But he oscillated from one extreme to the other. When he came to look back on the experience of those years, it was not always easy to be sure of the right sequence of his trials and mercies. "Temptations followed me very hard," he wrote, "and especially such temptations as did tend to the making me question the very way of salvation; viz., whether Jesus Christ was the Saviour or no; and whether I had best to venture my soul upon His blood for salvation or take some other course."[56] This was to last for "a year and upwards" before he could feel that he had any sound proof of his personal interest in that glorious salvation.[57] Sometimes he was tempted on a point of doctrine, as when he was troubled to know whether the Lord Jesus was both Man as well as God and God as well as Man. This was resolved when he pondered the verse: "And I beheld, and lo, in the midst of the Throne and of the four beasts, and in the midst of the Elders, stood a Lamb" (Rev. 5:6). " 'In the midst of the throne,' thought I, there is His Godhead; 'in the midst of the elders,' there is His Manhood. . . . It was a goodly touch and gave me sweet satisfaction."[58] But his trials were mostly on the question of his own share in God's grace and goodness, and he longed to compare his own experience with that of some great man of God. At length an old book came into his hands, "so old that it was ready to fall piece from piece if I did but turn it over."[59] This was Luther's *Commentary on the Epistle to the Galatians,* and its pages were a mirror of the struggle in his own heart. "I do prefer this book of Martin Luther," he wrote, ". . . before all the books that ever I have seen as most fit for a wounded conscience."[60] Bunyan read that book and thought that in it "he heard the voice of a man" who had gone before.[61] He was to need all the comfort of that very voice as he now entered the dark valley which held his most terrible temptation.

Bunyan was tempted to "sell and part with the blessed Christ,

56. *Ibid.,* p. 549.
57. *Ibid.*
58. *Ibid.,* p. 21.
59. *Ibid.,* p. 22.
60. *Ibid.*
61. *Ibid.,* Vol. III, p. 115.

to exchange Him for the things of this life, for anything."[62] This thought followed him night and day for a whole year, and he could not stoop for a pin without hearing the dark whisper: "Sell Christ for this or sell Christ for that; sell Him; sell Him."[63] He would literally throw out his hands as if to ward off the tempter while he answered: "I will not; I will not; I will not; no, not for thousands, thousands, thousands of worlds."[64] But the time came when he thought that he had succumbed. "And down fell I as a bird that is shot from the top of a tree."[65] He saw himself to be guilty and he was in profound despair; and that despair was to last for two years before God brought him out. His sin was a momentary consent to give up Christ, and to him that was worse than all the sins of the redeemed. He was assailed by foes that "cared not for his sword,"[66] and like Pilgrim, he could only fall back on the weapon of prayer. "My case being desperate, I thought with myself, I can but die; and if it must be so, it shall once be said that such an one died at the foot of Christ in prayer."[67] It was in this frame of mind that he walked across the fields one day and sat down on a bench in one of the streets. It was as if the sun refused to shine for him; he thought that the very stones seemed to cry out in protest. "O how happy now was every creature over I was; for they stood fast and kept their station, but I was gone and lost."[68] He felt that his was a wound that no hand could heal, for what comfort had God for a sinner such as he was? But God's comfort was just at hand, for as if in answer to his own self-reproach, he heard a voice saying, "This sin is not unto death."[69] He was amazed at the fitness of this sentence; it made him feel that he stood on the same ground as other sinners. It meant that he had the same right as they had to the means of grace in the Word of God and in prayer, and as he sought the Lord's face the next day, he heard God say as an echo to his

62. *Ibid.*, Vol. I, p. 22.
63. *Ibid.*
64. *Ibid.*, p. 23.
65. *Ibid.*
66. *Ibid.*, Vol. III, p. 115.
67. *Ibid.*, Vol. I, p. 28.
68. *Ibid.*, p. 30.
69. *Ibid.*

longing: "I have loved thee with an everlasting love" (Jer. 31:3). He went to bed with a quiet mind and found this truth still fresh in his spirit when he awoke in the morning. And thus at last, with much trembling, he found comfort, now here, now there, until God brought home to his heart the words: "My grace is sufficient" (2 Cor. 12:9). Yet for some two months his peace came and went twenty times a day because he heard not the words, "for thee." At last one day he was in a meeting of God's people, thinking that he was as far from grace as ever, when God's voice came to him. "These words did with great power suddenly break in upon me, My grace is sufficient for thee, My grace is sufficient for thee, My grace is sufficient for thee, three times together; and oh, methought that every word was a mighty word unto me."[70]

There was battle before Bunyan yet, but he found grace in the words of invitation: "Him that cometh to me I will in no wise cast out" (John 6:37). "Oh, the comfort that I have had from this word, 'In no wise!' "[71] So he exclaimed; but there was a severe conflict before he could feel sure that it was meant for him. "Him that comes," he would think; "HIM; any him; him that cometh . . . I will in no wise cast out."[72] He would wrestle for that promise as Jacob once wrestled with the angel for his blessing. "If ever Satan and I did strive for any word of God in all my life, it was for this good word of Christ; he at one end, and I at the other."[73] As time went on, Bunyan was led to consider prayerfully some of those dark words of Scripture which had held him in such torment; and he "found their visage changed, for they looked not so grimly on me as before I thought."[74] But his former fear and anguish had been so sore and real that he was like one who had been alarmed by an outbreak of fire. "I thought every voice was Fire, fire! every little touch would hurt my tender conscience."[75] But the end was sudden relief. He was crossing a field, still with some fear at heart, when a sentence flashed

70. *Ibid.*, pp. 32, 33.
71. *Ibid.*, p. 33.
72. *Ibid.*
73. *Ibid.*, p. 34.
74. *Ibid.*
75. *Ibid.*, p. 35.

through his mind: "Thy righteousness is in heaven." "Methought withal that I saw with the eyes of my soul Jesus Christ at God's right hand: there, I say, as my righteousness . . . . I also saw that it was not my good frame of heart that made my righteousness better, nor yet my bad frame that made my righteousness worse; for my righteousness was Jesus Christ Himself, the same yesterday and today and forever."[76] His chains fell off just as Pilgrim's burden fell off and rolled away as he stood by the Cross. He went home with a heart full of joy and began to search for that sentence. But he could not find it and his heart sank again until he got the words: "Who of God is made unto us wisdom and righteousness and sanctification and redemption" (1 Cor. 1:30). That told him that the first sentence was true, even if it were not in the Bible. "Oh, methought, Christ! Christ! there was nothing but Christ that was before my eyes. . . . Now I could look from myself to Him and reckon that all those graces of God that now were green in me were yet but like those cracked groats and fourpence half-pennies that rich men carry in their purses when their gold is in their trunks at home. Oh, I saw my gold was in my trunk at home! In Christ my Lord and Saviour! Now Christ was all; all my wisdom, all my righteousness, all my sanctification, and all my redemption!"[77]

This long night of sombre conflict dragged on for a little more than two years, but the daybreak came at last and filled his heart with song and sunshine. "What is a Christian?" he was to ask, and to furnish his own reply: "One that is born again, a new creature; one that sits at Jesus' feet to hear His word; one that hath his heart purified and sanctified by faith which is in Christ."[78] This was now his experience, and the world seemed to wear a new face in his eyes. He had been in frequent consultation with John Gifford like Pilgrim with Evangelist, and had been a regular adherent of his congregation since 1651 or 1652. He joined the church during 1653 and his name stands nineteenth on its roll of members. Gifford was soon aware that he was no ordinary convert, for the change in his life caused no

76. *Ibid.*, pp. 35, 36.
77. *Ibid.*, p. 36.
78. *Ibid.*, Vol. II, p. 676.

little stir among his neighbours. "I have been vile myself," Bunyan confessed, "but have obtained mercy; and I would have my companions in sin partake of mercy too."[79] Many began to walk over from Elstow to Bedford to hear Gifford preach for themselves, for they could not close their eyes to God's work of grace in one who had been so well known as a "Jerusalem sinner."[80] "When I went out to seek the Bread of Life," Bunyan wrote, "some of them would follow and the rest be put into a muse at home. Yea, almost the town at first at times would go out to hear at the place where I found good; yea, young and old for a while had some reformation upon them; also some of them perceiving that God had mercy upon me, came crying to Him for mercy too."[81] In 1654 or 1655, Bunyan moved from Elstow to a house in Bedford, but the prolonged conflict had left its mark on his health and fitness. He went through a phase of weakness in which he lost all his natural bouyancy and looked for a time in the face of death. But it was transient; he soon became well in mind and body at once. He was sitting by the fire at home when he was seized by the thought that he must go to Jesus, and the glories of His Kingdom were swept before his view. His mind was filled with the vision which is described in the twelfth chapter of the Epistle to the Hebrews (12:22-24). "And then," he cried, "with joy I told my wife, O now I know, I know! That night was a good night to me, I never had but few better; I longed for the company of some of God's people that I might have imparted unto them what God had showed me. Christ was a precious Christ to my soul that night: I could scarce lie in my bed for joy and peace and triumph."[82]

Bunyan was to experience sorrow and loss during the year 1655, but it was to fit him for his career as preacher and author. The first shadow was the death of his wife who had shared all his trials, and who left him to care for four little children. This sorrow was heightened by the death of Gifford, who sent a most moving farewell to his congregation, begging them to walk in

79. *Ibid.,* Vol. I, p. 68.
80. *Ibid.,* p. 70.
81. *Ibid.,* p. 79.
82. *Ibid.,* p. 40.

love even as Christ had loved them. It was in these circumstances that some of the brethren whom he counted the most able first urged him to speak a word of exhortation at one of the meetings. He was dismayed, but he spoke with fear and trembling once or twice in private. His hearers were solemnly affected and gave thanks to the God of all mercy for the grace which they saw in him. Soon he began to go out with others who were to preach in the country, and he would add his word. The call of God slowly became clear to himself as to others, and he was set apart with the rites of prayer and fasting for the proclamation of the Gospel. Once the country knew that poor John Bunyan had turned preacher, "they came in to hear the Word by hundreds, and that from all parts."[83] And his preaching was not without the seal of God: "For I had not preached long before some began to be touched by the Word and to be greatly afflicted in their minds at the apprehension of the greatness of their sin and of their need of Jesus Christ."[84] It was almost a year later when his preaching brought him into controversy with the Quakers and his first book appeared. But while preaching led to writing, it was not in controversy that his best work was to be done. He was to touch men's hearts both as preacher and as author by his skill in bringing the love of Christ to bear on the lost and sinful, and he was still feeling his way when his second work was announced with a wicked advertisement in an issue of the *Commonwealth Mercury.* Cromwell's death was listed in this paper and was at once followed by the statement: "There is lately published A Few Sighs From Hell or The Groans of a Damned Soul, by John Bunyan."[85] But he was on firmer ground in 1659 when he published a book on *The Doctrine of Law and Grace,* for it is marked by a strong faith and a clear view of Christ. It marked the end of the years of apprenticeship for a man whose call was from God and who had all the signs of grace.

Bunyan had thus proclaimed the love of Christ for some five

83. *Ibid.,* p. 41.
84. *Ibid.*
85. See John Brown, *op. cit.,* p. 118, footnote.

years while he carried on his trade to earn a living.[86] But his right to preach was often called in question and he had to surmount varied forms of opposition. He came into conflict, now with Ranters, now with Quakers, with Gownsmen from Cambridge and Clergy from Bedford. Once at least, in 1658, the arm of the law was invoked at his expense and the church at Bedford was in prayer for "counsaile what to doe with respect to the indictment against brother Bunyan at the Assizes for preaching at Eaton."[87] Bunyan did not so much mind these frontal attacks, but he also had to contend with the voice of slander. It was one thing to be called a witch or a Jesuit: "these things upon mine own account trouble me not; no, though they were twenty times more than they are."[88] He knew that he was but dust and ashes; he was only what sin had left, and had something of the smutch and smear of sin yet upon him.[89] But there was one line of attack which provoked the most indignant piece of writing in all his works, and that was the vulgar report that he had his "misses," two wives at once, and other like rumours. Was he to chide, or to flatter, or to entreat such men to hold their tongues? Not John Bunyan. "When they have used to the utmost of their endeavours and made the fullest inquiry that they can to prove against me truly that there is any woman in heaven or earth or hell that can say I have at any time in any place by day or night so much as attempted to be naught [naughty] with them; and speak I thus to beg mine enemies into a good esteem of me? No, not I. I will in this beg relief of no man; believe or disbelieve me in this, all is a case to me."[90] He may have had this in mind when he wrote of those who think that they may sin and sin again because Christ will save them. "If I were to point out one that was under the power of the devil and going posthaste to hell, for my life I would look no farther for such a man than to him that would make such a use as this of the grace of God. What, because Christ is a Saviour, thou wilt be a sinner? Because His grace abounds, there-

86. *Works,* Vol. II, p. 201.
87. See John Brown, *op. cit.,* p. 120.
88. *Works,* Vol. I, p. 45.
89. *Ibid.,* p. 167.
90. *Ibid.,* p. 46.

fore thou wilt abound in sin? O wicked wretch! rake hell all over, and surely I think thy fellow will scarce be found."[91] But he went yet further in self-defence. "My foes have missed their mark in this their shooting at me. I am not the man. I wish that they themselves be guiltless. If all the fornicators and adulterers in England were hanged by the neck till they be dead, John Bunyan . . . would be still alive and well."[92] But he refused to take credit for a life which had been blameless in this respect, and his refutation of the slander ends with an ascription of praise to God: "Not that I have been thus kept because of any goodness in me more than any other, but God has been merciful to me and has kept me: to Whom I pray that He will keep me still, not only from this, but from every evil way and work, and preserve me to His heavenly Kingdom. Amen."[93]

"The very grave person" who was pictured in the Interpreter's House will stand in the eye of our minds for ever. "It had eyes lifted up to heaven, the best of books in his hand, the law of truth was written upon his lips, the world was behind his back. It stood as if it pleaded with men, and a crown of gold did hang over its head."[94] Bunyan may have had John Gifford in view when he drew this picture, but it is clear that it was an unconscious self-portrait. Preaching was to prove the master passion of his life and labours. He stands before us still as the preacher who felt than an angel of God stood at his back.[95] He had no book learning on which to draw, but he knew the Bible as few men do. He knew that he could not always claim to be right, but at least he had not "fished in other men's waters."[96] His sound common sense was second only to his knowledge of the Bible and made him an acute judge of what a preacher should say and do. He chose plain and simple words that would hit the mark where more learned ones would only pierce the air; and he argued that the preacher who strives to

91. *Ibid.*, p. 554.
92. *Ibid.*, p. 46.
93. *Ibid.*
94. *Ibid.*, Vol. III, p. 98.
95. *Ibid.*, Vol. I, p. 42.
96. *Ibid.*, Vol. III, p. 464.

be learned often fails to be understood either by his hearers or by himself.[97] He was careful in his preparation and drew up his material in notes. Thus he could tell the Clerk of the Peace in 1661 that to avoid prejudice or misgiving, he was ready to give all his sermon notes to any man who asked for them in private.[98] Notes would help him when he lacked a sense of freedom, for there were times when he was so straitened in speech that he felt as if his head were in a bag.[99] But he often found a freedom which would carry him far beyond his notes, and he knew that it was often a word cast in by the way which wrought more than all that he had thought to say. "Sometimes when I have thought I did no good, then I did the most of all; and at other times when I thought I should catch them I have fished for nothing."[100] His own experience had made him a master of the human heart and all its feelings. The City of Mansoul had no nook or lane to which he was a stranger, and well he knew the sound of the Enemy's Drum. He could speak to any congregation as one who had scaled the heights and plumbed the depths of human need and sorrow. He preached what he felt, and felt what he preached; to those who were in chains he came as one who had himself been bound. He was in pains to bring souls to the birth, and he could not remain content unless children were brought forth in the name of Christ. But there was at times a going of God on his spirit when God had work for him to do, and he preached as a man who had Eternity before his eyes.

The Restoration of Charles II in May, 1660, was to provoke a vast change in Bunyan's life at Bedford and the autumn months were gray with threats of interference. The Declaration of Breda proved of little value and he was the first to suffer for the cause of conscience in the new reign. In October, 1660, the Magistrates for Bedfordshire made an order in the Quarter Sessions held at Bedford for the restoration of the Book of Common Prayer in public worship. Bunyan was a vigorous opponent of

97. *Ibid.,* p. 398.
98. *Ibid.,* Vol. I, p. 59.
99. *Ibid.,* p. 44.
100. *Ibid.,* p. 43.

all attempts to force the Prayer Book on congregations, and his dislike for all written forms of prayer was increased by the attitude of their advocates. He was distressed "by the ignorance, profaneness, and spirit of envy that reign in the hearts of those men that are so hot for the forms and not the power of praying. Scarce one of forty among them know what it is to be born again, to have communion with the Father through the Son."[101] On November 12, he set out to hold a service in a farmhouse at Lower Samsell, near Harlington and about thirteen miles from Bedford. But the congregation had been informed that a neighbouring magistrate, Francis Wingate, had a warrant for his arrest should he attempt to preach. They were alarmed for his safety and urged him to desist, but he faced the situation calmly. "No, by no means," he said; "I will not stir, neither will I have the meeting dismissed for this. Come, be of good cheer, let us not be daunted; our cause is good, we need not be ashamed."[102] There were a few minutes to spare and he left the house to walk in the field, where he paced beneath the now leafless elm trees and tried to think out his duty. If he were to make his escape, would not all his converts surmise that he was strong in word but not in fact? Besides, if God meant him to be the first in a firm stand for the freedom of the Gospel, how could he turn and flee? Therefore, although there was an hour to spare, he went back to the house: "For blessed be the Lord, I knew of no evil that I had said or done."[103] Meanwhile the rest of the congregation had come across the fields, and it was time for the meeting to start. Bunyan began with prayer and was about to preach on the subject of faith in Christ.[104] He was standing with the Bible in hand, when the appearance of a constable brought things to a climax. He was only able to speak a few words of counsel before he was forced to submit. He was taken to the home of Francis Wingate, only to find that the magistrate had gone away; and he was then released on the promise of a friend that he would appear in the morning.

101. *Ibid.*, p. 625.
102. *Ibid.*, p. 51.
103. *Ibid.*
104. *Ibid.*, Vol. II, p.593.

Thus John Bunyan, his friend, and the constable, all went in the morning to wait on the magistrate. Wingate wanted to know what the people had done when the arrest took place, hinting that they had come in arms. But the constable insisted that he had found only a few people who had come to hear the preacher, and that there was no sign of anything sinister. The magistrate was frustrated: "He could not well tell what to say."[105] No new law had been passed and no overt act had occurred when the warrant had been issued. The order in Bedford at the Quarter Sessions a month before did no more than provide for the restoration of the Prayer Book in church worship, and the Act of Uniformity had not yet been framed or approved. But this did not deter Wingate who now began to ask Bunyan why he had gone to the meeting and why he did not stick to his calling. Bunyan said that he had gone to proclaim the Word of God; he thought that he could do this and follow his calling too. Wingate swore that he would break the neck of all such meetings, but he only evoked the quiet reply: "It may be so."[106] Wingate refused to allow bail unless Bunyan would promise to give up his preaching. Bunyan replied that such a demand was quite useless; he would not be silent for the sake of freedom. Such a decisive utterance was too much for Wingate, who gave orders that he should lie in gaol until the next Quarter Sessions. Thus Bunyan left the house to proceed to gaol, but met two friends on the way who assured him that he would be set free if only he would repeat certain words in Wingate's presence. Bunyan turned an earnest look on his friends and said that if the words could be spoken in good conscience, he would speak them; not else. So they retraced their steps while he lifted up his heart to pray that he might be kept from all that would dishonour God or discourage the Church. It was now late on that November afternoon, and a candle threw its light on the scene as he engaged in a new and fruitless conversation. The time for words had gone and there was no alternative to his imprisonment. "And verily," he wrote, "as I was going forth of the doors, I had much ado to

105. *Ibid.*, Vol. I, p. 51.
106. *Ibid.*

forebear saying to them that I carried the peace of God along with me: but I held my peace, and blessed be the Lord, went away to prison with God's comfort in my poor soul."[107]

It was next day when John Bunyan crossed the bridge at Bedford in the constable's custody and passed through the old gate of the County Prison. His friends approached the Justice at Elstow in an attempt to bail him out until the next Quarter Sessions. This Justice knew Bunyan, but he was much perplexed. There had been no other arrest for mere preaching, and he declined to take action lest some fact of a more serious character should lie behind the charge. Bunyan was not dismayed; he would lie in prison with the comfort that not one hair of his head could fall to the ground without the will of his Father. It was two months later when the January Quarter Sessions began, and he appeared before a bench of five County Magistrates under Sir John Kelynge. Bunyan had this notorious justice in view when he drew his picture of Lord Hategood in the trial of Faithful at Vanity Fair; indeed all the trial scenes in the Pilgrim's Progress and the Holy War are drawn from his own immediate experience. He had now to face an accusation on the ground that he did not go to Church, but was taking part in extra-legal conventicles. Kelynge entered into a long altercation with him because he made it clear that he would not attend a Church where the Prayer Book had been restored to use. The dialogue was nothing if not spirited, and one of the magistrates thought it was too dangerous. Kelynge would not desist, vindicating himself with rash statements: "He can do no harm: we know the Common Prayer Book hath been ever since the Apostles' time."[108] Bunyan's replies were too direct for one of the five who asked if his God were Beelzebub and who said that he must have a devil. "All which sayings," he wrote, "I passed over; the Lord forgive them."[109] Kelynge accused him of pedlar's French and canting, and began to engage him in facetious argument from the Scriptures; but he could not out-wit Bunyan and soon declared that he was not so well versed in Scripture as to dispute. He had to stop and ask point-blank if

107. *Ibid.*, p. 54.
108. *Ibid.*, p. 55.
109. *Ibid.*, p. 56.

he confessed the charge or not. It was only then that Bunyan knew that he was arraigned and he replied that all he could confess was that he and his friends had met often enough to pray and preach and that they had known the presence of God in their meetings. "Then, said he, hear your judgment. You must be had back again to prison, and there lie for three months following; and at three months' end, if you do not submit to go to Church to hear Divine Service, and leave your preaching, you must be banished the realm; and if after such a day . . . you shall be found in this realm, . . . you must stretch by the neck for it."[110] The gaoler was ordered to have him back to gaol; but as he went, he gave the justice one last thrust: "I told him as to this matter, I was at a point with him; for if I was out of prison to-day, I would preach the Gospel again to-morrow by the help of God."[111]

For three more months Bunyan was kept in prison, "not knowing what they intended to do with me."[112] Then, on April 3, 1661, he received a semi-official visit from a Mr. Cobb, Clerk of the Peace. Cobb had been sent by the magistrates to demand his return to the Church of England and to extract from him a pledge that he would give up his preaching. But neither persuasive argument nor prospective penalty could touch Bunyan's spirit; it might fare worse with him at the Quarter Sessions, as Cobb hinted, but he would not submit. Three weeks later, on April 23, Charles II was crowned and the coronation was marked by the release of hundreds from prison. But a recommendation had to be made by the local authorities, and this had been denied to John Bunyan. Therefore he remained in prison from April till August when a further assize was held. Bunyan thought that he ought to try by all lawful means to secure release and he began to hope that his case might now be heard in open court. A petition was presented three times at the hands of his wife to the Judge of Assize. The first time she gave it to Sir Matthew Hale, who was in Bedford that year. He received her kindly, telling her that he would do what he could, but he feared that it would be little. The

110. *Ibid.*
111. *Ibid.*, p. 57.
112. *Ibid.*

next morning she threw another petition into Twisden's coach as he was passing through St. Paul's Square, but he tartly replied that her husband would not be released until he gave a promise to desist from preaching. She approached Sir Matthew Hale a second time as he sat in court, but he would not listen when Sir Henry Chester told him that her husband had been lawfully convicted. She turned away, but the Sheriff had seen her and now spoke the one word of encouragement she was to hear. He told her that there would be one more chance to speak to the Judges if she went to the Swan Chamber when the Assize came to an end. Thither she went, and her appeal is a classic in the annals of that troubled decade. Once more with a trembling heart she approached Sir Matthew Hale to plead as only a wife can plead. Twisden and Chester were very severe, but she applied herself to Hale. She had been to London and had spoken to some Peers at the House of Lords; they had advised her to commit the case for judgment at the next Assize, and she was now acting on their advice. "My Lord," she said, "I have four small children that cannot help themselves — of which one is blind — and have nothing to live upon but the charity of good people."[113] Sir Matthew Hale was touched by the pathos of her appeal, but his colleague Twisden grew more angry every moment. When she said that God had owned his preaching, he could hardly contain himself. "God!" said he; "his doctrine is the doctrine of the devil!"[114] So with sorrow in her heart and tears in her eyes, she left them and went home to her lonely cottage while he remained in the cheerless prison. And there, without further charge or sentence, in defiance of Habeas Corpus, he was to spend the next twelve years.[115]

But the years of imprisonment in the County Gaol of Bedford were to vary greatly in their severity. After the August Assize in 1661, he was allowed a certain measure of freedom, and on various occasions he seems to have left the gaol to visit his home and to exhort his flock to stand fast in the faith. Once he ventured to take the road which runs south to London, but the journey became

113. *Ibid.*, p. 61.
114. *Ibid.*
115. See John Brown, *op. cit.*, p. 154.

known and almost cost the friendly gaoler his post. "Whereupon," he wrote, "my liberty was more straitened than it was before: so that I must not look out of the door."[116] All that winter he was strictly confined, but in January, 1662, he made every effort to secure a hearing before the new assize. But the Clerk of the Peace removed his name from the list of cases which were to come before the court: "And thus was I hindered and prevented at that time also from appearing before the judge and left in prison."[117] Bunyan's name does not once occur in the records of Church meetings from October 28, 1661 to October 9, 1668, but it was to appear from time to time during the next four years. It is said that he was released for a few weeks during 1666 "by the intercession of some in trust and power that took pity of his sufferings."[118] But he was soon under arrest once more, although for what offence or in what place, we are not told. It must have been in the County jurisdiction since he went back to the County Gaol in Bedford. There for six more years he was to remain, although we know much less of this second term of imprisonment than of the first. It may have been from this experience that he was to describe how Giant Despair thrust the Pilgrims "into a very dark dungeon, nasty and stinking to the spirits of these two men."[119] But we are told that the gaoler "took such pity of his rigorous sufferings that he did as the Egyptian jailer did to Joseph, put all the care and trust into his hands."[120] Bunyan had made his choice and he was too manly to shrink from the consequences. "I have determined," so he was to write in 1672, "the Almighty God being my help and shield, yet to suffer, if frail life might continue so long, even till the moss shall grow on mine eyebrows rather than thus to violate my faith and principles."[121] But while his lot varied in rigour and hardship, we can never forget that twelve years of imprisonment which had begun at the age of thirty-two and lasted into middle life were a trial of the greatest severity for a man of action such as he was.

116. *Works,* Vol. I, p. 62.
117. *Ibid.*
118. *Ibid.,* p. 64.
119. *Works,* Vol. III, p. 140.
120. *Ibid.,* Vol. I, p. 64.
121. *Ibid.,* Vol. II, p. 594.

"Before I came to prison," Bunyan wrote, "I saw what was a-coming and had especially two considerations warm upon my heart: the first was how to be able to endure, should my imprisonment be long and tedious; the second was how to be able to encounter death, should that be here my portion."[122] He sought and found comfort in the thought that he would live by faith in God who is invisible; but when the time came which he had foreseen, it was far from easy. "I found myself a man, and compassed with infirmities: the parting with my wife and poor children hath oft been to me in this place as the pulling the flesh from my bones."[123] His blind daughter, Mary, now lay nearer his heart than all he had besides, and he grieved at the thought of the hardship she would incur. "But yet, recalling myself, thought I, I must venture you all with God, though it goeth to the quick to leave you. O I saw in this condition I was as a man who was pulling down his house upon the head of his wife and children; yet thought I, I must do it, I must do it."[124] But if he had to venture them for God, he would now engage God to care for them. "I have seen men," he wrote, "take most care of and best provide for those of their children that have been most infirm and helpless, and our Advocate shall gather His lambs with His arms and carry them in His bosom."[125] And the other trial was no less severe. In his early days in prison, he was beset by doubt and fear. He had heard the threat of transportation or death if he would not conform. This threat still hung over his head. Satan strove to beat him out of heart when he thought how he might yet end up on the gallows. He saw himself as if he were on the ladder with the rope round his neck, and he could not resist the fear that he would make but "a scrabbling shift" to climb the scaffold.[126] It would be to his shame if he were to shake and tremble when he was called to die for such a cause as this. "Wherefore," he wrote, "I prayed to God that He would comfort me and give me strength to do and suffer

122. *Ibid.*, Vol. I, p. 47.
123. *Ibid.*, p. 48.
124. *Ibid.*
125. *Ibid.*, p. 168.
126. *Ibid.*, p. 49.

what He should call me to; yet no comfort appeared."[127] But at length he resolved to commit the future into the hands of God, whether he had comfort or not: "If God doth not come in, thought I, I will leap off the ladder even blindfold into eternity, sink or swim, come heaven, come hell; Lord Jesus, if Thou wilt catch me, do; if not, I will venture for Thy Name."[128] And from that time onward, gallows, ladder, scaffold, halter lost all power to dismay. Bunyan had now faced the worst that men could threaten, and he was not appalled.

Thus for twelve years Bunyan was kept in the County Gaol of Bedford: but the iron gates could not shut out the rich compensations of God. He found work for his hands, making hundreds of long lace tags, which would meet the necessities of his home and himself, and his sky was brightened with the vision of that city not made with hands and with dreams of glory that now live for ever.[129] His fame as a spiritual guide brought men and women in search of his counsel,[130] and there were times when he could preach to a gaol which had been crowded with men who loved the truth.[131] He had few books apart from the Bible,[132] but he soon made himself master of God's message of Grace; and the truth which he found in the Bible was applied and tested in the experience of his own heart. "I never had in all my life so great an inlet into the Word of God as now," he wrote; ". . . Jesus Christ also was never more real . . . than now: here I have seen Him and felt Him indeed."[133] Bunyan had not much to offer in the way of human learning and would not place himself in debt even for a thread or a shoe-latchet to the scholars of his own age;[134] yet he arrived at a remarkable knowledge of Truth by his study of the Scriptures with much prayer and meditation. "Expositors I reverence, but must live by mine own faith," he wrote; "God hath nowhere bound Himself to them more than to others with

127. *Ibid.*
128. *Ibid.*
129. See *Works*, Vol. III, p. 397.
130. *Ibid.*, p. 610.
131. See John Brown, *op. cit.*, p. 170.
132. See *Works*, Vol. III, p. 464.
133. *Works*, Vol. I, p. 47.
134. *Ibid.*, Vol. III, p. 398.

respect to the revelation of His mind in His Word."[135] "I honour the godly as Christians," he said, "but I prefer the Bible before them; and having that still with me, I count myself far better furnished than if I had without it all the libraries of the two Universities. Besides I am for drinking water out of my own cistern; what God makes mine by the evidence of His Word and Spirit, that I dare make bold with."[136] This close study of the Bible furnished him with a store of things both new and old with which his own writings were to shine and sparkle. It is interesting to note that in one book alone, *The Saints' Knowledge of Christ's Love,* there are nearly 440 distinct quotations from or references to the Scriptures.[137] Each word had been weighed and valued by him like grains of gold. "I tell thee, friend," he wrote, "there are some promises that the Lord hath helped me to lay hold of Jesus Christ through and by, that I would not have out of the Bible for as much gold and silver as can lie between York and London piled up to the stars; because through them Christ is pleased by His Spirit to convey comfort to my soul."[138]

Sometimes Bunyan's sermons in prison grew into manuscripts and found their way to Francis Smith near Temple Bar, who published them for the world at large. There were nine books which saw the light during the first six years. Few things in his writings are more lovely than this picture in one of these early volumes: "Christians are like the several flowers in a garden that have upon each of them the dew of heaven, which being shaken with the wind, they let fall their dew at each other's roots whereby they are jointly nourished and become nourishers of one another."[139] In the second term of six years, he seems only to have published two books. Was this because it was growing more difficult to get his books licensed? Was it because he was growing less elastic in mind as the years still dragged by? But the classic of these years in prison was a moving account of his own long inner conflict. This was published in 1666 under the title of

135. *Ibid.,* Vol. II, p. 624.
136. *Ibid.,* Vol. III, p. 398.
137. See *Works,* Vol. II, p. 1.
138. *Ibid.,* Vol. III, p. 721.
139. *Ibid.,* Vol. II, p. 570; see also p. 550.

Grace Abounding to the Chief of Sinners. It will always retain its place as one of the finest records of a profound spiritual experience. It is the first of his three great books which owe "their brilliance and originality to the one indelible experience out of which they are written. Christian and Mansoul go through the same depths of affliction and conflict as Bunyan himself, and reach the same peace and reconciliation. But volume by volume there is a difference. The writer looks back from time to time upon the scene of the conflict, but each time from a higher and happier level. The memory of what he went through is ineffaceable, but it is no longer his only memory; it is enriched with others; he has a larger, a more varied, and a more restful mind."[140] Bunyan had to battle through wind and storm before he found the rock on which his faith could stand, and the soul made great by the storm had to dwell in sunshine and peace before it could produce its best.[141] Thus the narrative of *Grace Abounding* drew its materials from his own life and its inspiration from his vivid recollection of God's mercies. It was phrased in language which owed its strength to the English Bible and its sense of reality to his gift for living through those days of struggle again.[142] It was written, "now in fire, now in dew," with all the strength of stark simplicity and truth.[143] There are times when the book whirls us on "with clouds and tempest, with winds of earth and fires of heaven";[144] yet its alternations were a faithful transcript of his experience, and the book must be read in all its parts if we would know him both in his strength and weakness.[145]

On April 11, 1670, the Conventicle Act was re-enacted and a sustained effort was made to put down all unauthorised meetings. The district from Bedford to Cambridge was under close watch, and a system of spies was in constant operation. Bunyan was to reflect this new phase of trouble in the pages of *Mr. Badman* when he made the scoundrel act as an informer against his wife, and when

140. T. R. Glover, *Poets and Puritans*, p. 116.
141. See Elvet Lewis, Introduction to Everyman's Edition of *The Pilgrim's Progress*, p. ix.
142. See Glover, *op. cit.*, p. 117.
143. Elvet Lewis, *op. cit.*, p. vii.
144. *Ibid.*, p. viii.
145. See Brown, *op. cit.*, pp. 181, 182.

he told the story of William Swinton who roamed the woods and hid in the tree-tops to spy on such meetings. But when Parliament was prorogued in April, 1671, there was a mild relief and the Bedford congregation began to think of a settled pastor. They had never liked the necessity of an exhortation by the brethren who had to take their turn, and their thoughts were now fixed on John Bunyan although he was still in prison. Thus on November 24, "the church was minded to seeke God about the choice of Brother Bunyan to the office of an Elder."[146] His long imprisonment had proved him strong in faith; his books were proof of his maturity in doctrine and experience. *Grace Abounding* had laid bare the work of God in his heart; his letters to brethren in need, his counsel to seekers for truth, his gifts as a preacher, all marked him out as the true heir of John Gifford's mantle. Thus at a full Assembly of the Church on January 21, 1672, we read: "After much seeking God by prayer, and sober conference formerly had, the congregation did at this meeting with joynt consent, signifyed by solemne lifting up of their hands, call forth and appoint our brother John Bunyan to the pastoral office or eldership. And he accepting thereof gave up himself to serve Christ and His Church in that charge, and received of the Elders the right hand of fellowship."[147] Within two months, on March 15, the King issued his Declaration of Religious Indulgence whose chief effect was to suspend execution of all penal laws against Non-Conformists, whether Protestant or Catholic. On May 8, a Petition came before the King-in-Council from Bunyan and five fellow prisoners, and on September 13 their names were listed in the General Pardon which was published. Bunyan may have been set free as early as May; at least he was allowed freedom to come and go from his prison quarters from May onward. On May 9 he was duly licensed as a preacher, and a barn which belonged to Josias Ruffhead was licensed as a place of worship "for the use of such as doe not conforme to the Church of England who are of the Perswasion commonly called Congregationall."[148]

146. *Ibid.,* p. 227.
147. *Ibid.,* p. 228.
148. *Ibid.,* pp. 188-229.

Thus the twelve years' imprisonment came to an end and John Bunyan at the age of forty-three found himself pastor of the congregation which had been brought into being by John Gifford twenty-five years before. It was a Church which had always avowed its desire to receive saints as saints and so to avoid all dispute on baptismal issues. Early members had been baptised and had had their children baptised in the Church of England. John Gifford had appealed to the brethren from his death-bed not to divide the Church on such questions. There are only four slight references to the *Act Book of the Church* from the time of its foundation until after the death of John Bunyan. In the *Baptismal Register* for the Parish Church of Elstow, there are entries for the baptism of his daughters Mary, in July, 1650, and Elizabeth, in April, 1654; and in that for the Church of St. Cuthbert in Bedford, there is an entry for the baptism of his son, Joseph, in November, 1672. The last entry is of singular interest, for it proves that he had no strong feelings on the subject. His books imply — rather than they assert — that he was a Baptist. He defends "the godly in the land that are not of our persuasion."[149] And he goes on to say: "I own water baptism to be God's ordinance, but I make no idol of it."[150] In the posthumous work, *The Heavenly Footman,* he put the case much more plainly: "Here is one runs a-quaking; another a-ranting; one again runs after the Baptism and another after the Independency. Here is one for Free-will and another for Presbytery; and yet possibly most of all these sects run quite the wrong way, and yet every one is for his life, his soul, either for heaven or hell. . . . Keep company with the soundest Christians that have most experience of Christ, and be sure thou have a care of Quakers, Ranters, Free-willers; also do not have too much company with some Anabaptists, though I go under that name myself."[151] But it was the practice of the Church with regard to true Christian fellowship which gave him real concern, and he defined his views on this subject in the Confession of Faith which he published in the last year of his imprisonment. It was written with a view to winning freedom

149. *Works,* Vol. II, p. 640.
150. *Ibid.,* p. 641.
151. *Ibid.,* Vol. III, p. 383.

and it declares that his aim was to live at peace with all who seek true faith and holiness. He could not consent to hold communion with the ungodly and profane, nor could he refuse to hold communion with saints from whom he might differ on some questions. This led him to touch on Baptism and the terms of Communion, and he made it clear that he would meet all true saints in fellowship. He drew a distinction between the doctrine and practice of Baptism: a man might have the thing signified though he wanted the sign or the outward circumstance.[152] "A failure in such a circumstance as water doth not unchristian us. This must needs be granted . . . for that thousands of thousands that could not consent thereto as we have, more gloriously than we are like to do, acquitted themselves and their Christianity before men and are now with the innumerable company of angels and the spirits of just men made perfect."[153] "Strange!" he wrote; "Take two Christians equal in all points but this, nay, let one go beyond the other far, for grace and holiness; yet this circumstance of water shall drown and sweep away all his excellencies, not counting him worthy of that reception that with hand and heart shall be given to a novice in religion because he consents to water."[154]

Bunyan's views were roughly handled. The most learned of the Baptists took them up in controversy and one pamphlet denounced him as a devil. A great meeting was planned by the London Baptists who hoped to swamp him with numbers. Three men published a joint reply in which they heaped scurrilous ridicule on one who had written while in prison.[155] Thus in 1673, Bunyan went to London, not to dispute, but to publish his book, *Differences in Judgment about Water Baptism No Bar to Communion*. He had no great liking for the controversy and would never have written this particular book were it not for the fact that the more rigid brethren had for so long menaced the peace of the Church at Bedford. "All I say is," he declared, "that the Church of Christ hath not warrant to keep out of their communion the Christian that is discovered

152. *Ibid.*, Vol. II, p. 609.
153. *Ibid.*, p. 611.
154. *Ibid.*, p. 613.
155. *Ibid.*, p. 592.

to be a visible saint by the Word, the Christian that walketh according to his light with God."[156] These more rigid Baptists had sent for him to try if they might yet persuade him to break communion with his brethren. "Also," he observed, "with many others they have often tampered, if haply their seeds of division might take."[157] Bunyan argued the whole case with convincing thoroughness and proved himself a most able antagonist. "That Christ, not Baptism, is the way to the sheepfold is apparent: and that the person who thus enters, in mine argument, is entitled to all these, to wit, Christ, grace, and all the things of the Kingdom of Christ in the Church is . . . as evident."[158] This work provoked a short reply and he returned to the attack in 1674 with his *Peacable Principles and True*. "I have denied," he wrote, "that Baptism was ever ordained of God to be a wall of division between the holy and the holy: the holy that are, and the holy that are not, so baptised with water as we."[159] They had asked with fescennine intention how long it was since he had become a Baptist, and he replied with unperturbed dignity: "I must tell you . . . I know none to whom that title is so proper as to the disciples of John. And since you would know by what name I would be distinguished from others, I tell you I would be and hope I am a Christian."[160] They jibed at him because he had been promised a commendation for his book by the great, the grave, "the sober Dr. Owen," but he had withdrawn. "And perhaps," said Bunyan, "it was more for the glory of God that truth should go naked into the world than as seconded by so mighty an armour-bearer as he."[161] There is no sign that he ever returned to this dispute, but he never ceased to lament the breach among those who ought to have been brethren in the Father's Household. Thus, in 1684, in *A Holy Life the Beauty of Christianity*, he wrote: "It is strange to see at this day how, notwithstanding all the threatenings of God, men are wedded to their own opinions beyond what the law of grace and

156. *Ibid.*, p. 617.
157. *Ibid.*, p. 618.
158. *Ibid.*, p. 634.
159. *Ibid.*, p. 648.
160. *Ibid.*, p. 648.
161. *Ibid.*, p. 649.

love will admit. Here is a Presbyter, here is an Independent, and a Baptist, so joined each man to his own opinion that they can not have that communion one with another as by the testament of the Lord Jesus they are commanded and enjoined. What is the cause? Is the truth? No! God is the author of no confusion in the Church of God. It is because every man makes too much of his own opinion."[162] Bunyan's Church at Bedford, Congregational in name, Anabaptist in rite, was ecumenical in the fellowship of saints and the communion of love.[163]

The barn which Bunyan secured in May, 1672, became the home for his congregation and the church in which he proclaimed the Word of God until his death. There is a short account by the hand of a friend which may refer to the initial interest which was displayed when he was first licensed to preach: "The first time he appeared there to edify, the place was so thronged that many were constrained to stay without, though the house was very spacious, every one striving to partake of his instructions that were of his persuasion and show their good-will towards him by being present at the opening of the place."[164] He soon became known as "Bishop Bunyan," for he began to organize the whole district from Bedford to the outskirts of London. He had applied for a license for twenty-five other preachers and for thirty other buildings in his own or in the neighbour counties. It might be a room, a barn, a hall, a malt-house, a garden, an orchard, a chamber in a ruined monastery or a cellar in an ancient castle: and the church at Bedford drew its members from as far as Ashwell in Herts and Gamlingay in Cambridgeshire. "And here he lived in much peace and quiet of mind, contenting himself with that little God had bestowed upon him and sequestering himself from all secular employments to follow that of his call to the ministry."[165] Sometimes he would visit London where his preaching to the Non-Conformist congregation was to their "great good liking."[166]

162. *Ibid.*, p. 538.
163. And so it continued. Offor noted that the minister in his time baptised infants and received help from a neighbouring Baptist pastor for the baptism of adults. See *Works,* Vol. III, p. lxvi.
164. *Works,* Vol. I, p. 63.
165. *Ibid.*
166. *Ibid.*

Sometimes he was busy with a new work such as *Light for Them That Sit in Darkness* which came out in 1675. "Reader," he began, "let me beseech thee to hear me patiently. I have presented thee with that which I have received from God. I know it to be the way of salvation. I have ventured my own soul thereon with gladness; and if all the souls in the world were mine as mine own soul is, I would through God's grace venture every one of them there."[167] There is meagre information as to his work during those years, but the tradition of his preaching tours is strong on all sides and his converts spread far and wide. Then those years of freedom came to an end with "another short affliction which was an imprisonment of half a year."[168] This is confirmed in the Preface to his *Instruction for the Ignorant* which appeared in 1675 as from one who had been driven from his flock and on whom the Lord had laid new bonds.[169] It was during this year that the Declaration of Indulgence was withdrawn and a new Test Act came into operation. The King's License which so many preachers had received in 1672 had been revoked. Bunyan could not protect himself against the work of informers and was soon once more sent to gaol.

It was during those six months in prison on the bridge at Bedford, for the offence of preaching within the borough, that the first part of the *Pilgrim's Progress* took its shape in his dreams. It was not a book which he had meditated; it was only begun as a kind of relaxation from *The Strait Gate* which came out in 1676. He fell into allegory almost before he was aware and his thoughts grew as fast as the sparks which fly from the fire. At first he thrust aside the bright fancies which were lighting up his prison quarters, but the work was finished at length and then he was eager to know what his friends thought of it:

> *Some said, John, print it; others said, Not so:*
> *Some said, It might do good: others said, No.*[170]

167. *Ibid.*, p. 392.
168. *Ibid.*, p. 64.
169. *Ibid.*, Vol. II, p. 675.
170. *Ibid.*, Vol. III, p. 85.

He was perplexed until his own sturdy sense came to the rescue and he resolved to print. Thus the winter months of 1676 had seen him start to write: "As I walked through the wilderness of this world, I lighted on a certain place where was a den."[171] Bunyan explained the word "den" as "the jail" in a marginal reference in the third edition. There was a break in the story when the Pilgrim left the Delectable Mountains. It was at this point that Bunyan awoke from his dream, and before he went on, he added the note: "I slept and dreamed again."[172] This means that he had been released from his imprisonment and was left to finish the First Part in freedom. Bishop Barlow, who was preferred to the See of Lincoln in June, 1675, was moved by Dr. Owen's intercession and helped to secure Bunyan's release.

The book was placed in the hands of Nathaniel Ponder late in 1677 and was published in the early part of 1678. But the work still grew in Bunyan's mind and there were various additions in the reprints of 1678 and 1679. Any doubt as to the wisdom of its publication vanished and the second reprint within a year proved that it had won the heart of England. Critics then declared that Bunyan could not have been the real author, and he wrote in reply that no other hand had added so much as five words or half a line to his work.

> For none in all the world without a lie
> Can say that this is mine, excepting I.[173]

Such was the birth of an allegory which is now a classic in our literature and has become a favourite for translation in the language of all peoples. Bunyan knew by instinct how to meet the love of parable and metaphor which is part and parcel of our nature, and no other writer before or since has been able to present the ideal of a pilgrim life with the same vivid simplicity. *Pilgrim's Progress* shares with *Paradise Lost* the creative quality and dramatic unity which mark them out as two great books produced on the forge of Puritan genius: and this dream stands alone in this

171. *Ibid.*, p. 89.
172. *Ibid.*, p. 146.
173. *Ibid.*, p. 374.

class of literature, for in every language in which it speaks, it has the tone of a friend and brother.[174]

There are numerous qualities which have contributed to the unique hold which *Pilgrim's Progress* has won in so many quarters. Scholars find in it a classic of clear Saxon language; preachers find in it a record of true spiritual experience; children find in it a pageant of most exciting adventure; missionaries, psychologists, readers of all varieties, find in it a mirror of our universal humanity.[175] It was the dream of an authentic genius, one whose clear-eyed vision saw great spiritual issues in picture forms. It is alive with the artless simplicity and the spontaneous freedom of life itself: it lives and grows with a development which is realistic and quite unforced. The dialogue and narrative alike are drawn from the common speech of the age, and, if sometimes crude or rustic, they are always plain and direct. Bunyan wrote page after page with short two-syllable words and always said just what he wished to say with faultless instinct. Pathos, grandeur, sympathy, vehemence, are all expressed in this terse style: no poet or preacher or spokesman or divine could improve the effect. It is full of homely touches and of kindly humour which make us feel that we are called to watch living figures as they tread the pilgrim way to Zion. A strong human appeal runs through the tale and grips the mind, due in part to successive adventures and in part to character interests. Spiritual experience, true to psychology and to theology, is told in a way that throws fresh understanding on the reader's own heart. Situations and the *dramatis personae* are sketched with rapid strokes and vivid colours. Bunyan poured all his own burning recollections into scenes such as the conflict with Apollyon or the trial of Faithful, and he called on undying memories when he drew a man like Evangelist, or the man whose picture hung in the House of the Interpreter. Sometimes we learn a world of truth simply from the names which he coins, be it of the place where Pilgrim sustains some new experience or the people whom he meets on the way. Who can ever forget the clear

174. H. Elvet Lewis, *op. cit.*, p. x.
175. *Ibid.*

mental image which such names will create? Who does not at once know the kind of man Bunyan has in mind when he hears what he is called? He could visualize the man and then place him before us with photographic accuracy. He could often identify himself with them or else relate his own experience to theirs. "He had himself been Ignorance, for he too was a 'brisk talker.' He had looked down the street where Atheist lived. Worldly Wiseman had tried to let him a house in the village of Morality where (as he very justly remarked in 1678) houses stood empty and were to be had at very reasonable rates. By-Ends — and that half-brother of his mother's, the Mr. Two-Tongues who was 'the parson of our Parish,' holding on in spite of the Uniformity Act — the old gentleman Mr. Legality, and the 'pretty young Man,' his son Civility, with the 'simpering looks' — Bunyan had known them all."[176] This is one of the most charming features of his Allegory; it is all so full of ease and so true to life.

Bunyan saw in his dream "a man clothed with rags, standing in a certain place, with his face from his own home, a book in his hand and a great burden upon his back."[177] Evangelist pointed out the shining light and wicket gate far across the field, and he began to run with all his might, crying Life, Life, Eternal Life! Rescued from the Slough of Despond and the frowning Hill of the Law, he turned back to the way "like one that was all the while treading on forbidden ground and could by no means think himself safe till again he was got into the way which he left."[178] He passed through the wicket gate and saw the narrow way that stretched on ahead. Both sunshine and shadow shone on that way as he found in the House of the Interpreter. The great burden fell off his back and rolled away when he came to the Cross, and three Shining Ones gave him a roll with a seal on it which he was to look on as he ran and to hand in at the gate of the Celestial City. The two men who tumbled over the wall show how men still love to avoid the Gate, but they left him when they came to a hill: for "the narrow way lay right up the hill and the name

176. Glover, *op. cit.*, p. 133.
177. *Works*, Vol. III, p. 89.
178. *Ibid.*, p. 96.

of the going up the side of the hill is called Difficulty."[179] He
had to climb its steep ascent on hands and knees, and it was dark
before he reached "the very stately Palace . . . the name of which
was Beautiful."[180] He passed the lions because he kept to the
midst of the path: they were chained, though he saw not the
chains; he heard them roar, but they did no harm. That night
he heard talk of the Lord of the Hill and he slept in the room
called Peace "whose window opened toward the sun rising."[181] In
the morning from the top of the house he saw Immanuel's Land
and from thence he was told he would see the gate of the City.
He left with the warning that "it is a hard matter for a man to go
down into the Valley of Humiliation . . . and to catch no slip by
the way."[182] It was there that he fought and overcame Apollyon,
and no man could conceive "unless he had seen and heard as I
did" how fierce was that conflict.[183] He got through the Valley
of the Shadow of Death and joined Faithful, with whom he went
on in loving conversation until they found themselves in Vanity
Fair. Faithful was put to death, "and was carried up through
the clouds with sound of trumpet the nearest way to the Celestial
Gate."[184] But the Pilgrim was not left to go on alone, for he was
now joined by Hopeful. They met By-Ends whose grandfather
was a water-man "looking one way and rowing another" and who
always had the luck to jump with the times;[185] but when By-Ends
went over to Demas, "this I observed, that they never were seen
again in the way."[186] The account of By-Path Meadow where
the going was soft, and then of their imprisonment in the cells
of Doubting Castle by Giant Despair is told with a power and a
verve which are overwhelming. They came to the Shepherds on
the Delectable Mountains which they had seen from the Palace
called Beautiful and which were within sight of the City. But

179. *Ibid.*, p. 104.
180. *Ibid.*, p. 106.
181. *Ibid.*, p. 109.
182. *Ibid.*, p. 111.
183. *Ibid.*, p. 113.
184. *Ibid.*, p. 132.
185. *Ibid.*
186. *Ibid.*, p. 137.

their hands shook and they could not look steadily through the glass which the Shepherds gave them: "yet they thought they saw something like the gate, and also some of the glory of the place."[187]

The Four Shepherds sent them on their way with warning as well as with encouragement. They met Ignorance, "a very brisk lad," but were not deceived.[188] They met Flatterer whose back was covered "with a very light robe," and were soon caught in his net.[189] They got over the Enchanted Ground by talking of God's grace in their hearts. They came into the country of Beulah "whose air was very sweet and pleasant, the way lying directly through it."[190] Here they were within sight of the City they were going to; also "here met them some of the inhabitants thereof: for in this land the Shining Ones commonly walked because it was upon the borders of heaven."[191] There were only two more difficulties ahead, and they had to meet them by their own faith. "Now I saw that betwixt them and the gate was a river, but there was no bridge to go over."[192] It was quite true that the river was not all the same depth; they would in fact find it now deep or now shallow, as they believed in the King of the Place. Thus they addressed themselves to the water. Christian soon began to sink and cried out in alarm. Hopeful heard his cry and replied: "Be of good cheer, my brother: I feel the bottom, and it is good."[193] Nevertheless Hopeful had much ado to keep his head above water until he heard the word: "When thou passest through the waters, I will be with thee: and through the rivers, they shall not overflow thee" (Isa. 43:2). He soon felt ground beneath his feet, and crossed the rest of the way in shallow water. Bunyan's account of their approach to the City and their glorious reception ranks with the most famous scenes in literature: it is the crown of all his work, and "no man

187. *Ibid.*, p. 145.
188. *Ibid.*, p. 146.
189. *Ibid.*, p. 150.
190. *Ibid.*, p. 161.
191. *Ibid.*
192. *Ibid.*, p. 163.
193. *Ibid.*

may give it but Bunyan himself."[194] They were met on the bank of the river by two men in raiment that shone like gold. They saw that the City crowned the summit of a very high hill, but they went up with ease. As they approached the gate, they were met by a host of the Shining Ones and by several of the King's trumpeters who compassed them about and sounded the trumpets "so that the very sight was to them that could behold it as if heaven itself were come down to meet them."[195] They now had the City in view and thought that they "heard all the bells therein to ring, to welcome them thereto."[196] So they arrived before the gate and gave in their certificate. Bunyan saw in his dream how they both went in through the gate and were clothed in golden raiment like that of the Angels. His mind was full of the chime of the bells which he had loved as a lad in Elstow, and he heard in his dream how all the bells of the City rang yet again for joy. And as the gates swung clear to let them in, he looked after them and beheld how the City shone like the sun; the streets also were paved with gold, and in them walked many who were crowned with joy and gladness. "And after that, they shut up the gates; which when I had seen, I wished myself among them."[197]

Was not that a glorious conclusion? And yet with all its chaste and perfect feeling, Bunyan did not end there. He had something more still to tell, and there follows the bleak account of the fate of Ignorance. It has its own literary strength and purpose. He had crossed the river with ease; he was ferried across by a boatman known as Vain Hope. But there were no Shining Ones to escort him home and he had no certificate to hand in at the gate: he could only fumble in his bosom for what he knew that he did not possess. So they took him, bound him hand and foot, and had him away. "Then I saw that there was a way to hell even from the gates of heaven as well as from

194. John Brown, p. 272.
195. *Works*, Vol. III, p. 165.
196. *Ibid.*
197. *Ibid.*, p. 166.

the City of Destruction. So I awoke, and behold it was a dream."[198]

Bunyan thought that the right sequel for the *Pilgrim's Progress* would be to place it in contrast with a bad man's story, and in 1680 he brought out *The Life and Death of Mr. Badman*. It was a book in which homely proverbs abound, but it failed in its real purpose. He was to see that a better sequel would be to back up the account of his Pilgrim with the story of his wife and children. Thus early in 1684 he brought out the second part of *Pilgrim's Progress,* and it began with an explanation: he had exchanged his "den" in the prison for his house in a "wood" about a mile away; and as he slept, he dreamed again.[199] It has been said that the result is an inferior composition: the incongruous and mediocre are more frequent, and the allegory is less finely sustained.[200] The new pilgrims were to follow the route marked out before, and were to find that their predecessor was well known all along the way. They met the same people, and passed the same land-marks, and came at last to the gates of the same golden City. But we soon feel the charm of true creative artistry in the fresh and lovely touches that are quite new. There may be less adventure, but there is more dialogue; not less experience but more theology. There are laughter and music on the part of those who would be merry; there are riddles and proverbs for the sake of those who would be learners. The first Pilgrim set out alone, and his only fellow pilgrims were Faithful and Hopeful; but this part gives us a growing band of men and women who all journey under the escort of Great-Heart. The First Part is rich in exciting narrative, while the Second Part excels in character creation. There were many variations in the experience of the pilgrims, and this allowed Bunyan to draw some of his most memorable pictures. Christiana may reflect his second wife Elizabeth in her vigorous strength of character, while the gentle Mercy may be a heart reminiscence of the wife of his youth.[201] She was encouraged to start on her journey

198. *Ibid.*
199. *Ibid.*, p. 171.
200. See John Brown, p. 281.
201. *Ibid.*, p. 276.

with the assurance: "They will all be glad when they shall hear the sound of thy feet step over thy Father's threshold."[202] There were sights in the House of the Interpreter which we hear of for the first time, such as the man with the muck-rake and the garden with its variety of flowers. It was the Interpreter who called for Great-Heart and told him to conduct the women and children through the dangers of the journey. Mercy was thrilled in the palace called Beautiful with "music in the house, music in the heart, and music also in heaven for joy that we are here."[203] They passed through the Valley of Humiliation and found its green beauty full of comfort. They heard the song of the shepherd lad as he went about his work:

> *He that is down needs fear no fall:*
> *He that is low, no pride;*
> *He that is humble ever shall*
> *Have God to be his guide.*

"I will dare to say," quoth Great-Heart, "that this boy lives a merrier life and wears more of that herb called Heart's-Ease in his bosom than he that is clad in silk and velvet."[204] The Lord of the pilgrims loved this Valley, and Mercy had never felt so well in her life. "So the family moves on together to the Celestial City, meeting kindly faces and leaving pleasant memories . . . . They do not have Christian's troubles . . . for such troubles belong chiefly to spiritual solitude, and here was a group of people, bound by ties of blood, and a common purpose and experience."[205]

Apart from Christiana and Mercy, characters of two distinct types were introduced. First of all there were those like Mr. Fearing and Mr. Feeble-Mind, Mr. Ready-to-Halt and Miss Much-Afaid. Bunyan's heart went out to those who were like reeds bruised in the storm, and he took pains to show how well they fared in the darkest passage of all. Thus, Mr. Fearing was "a man that had the root of the matter in him, but he was one of the most troublesome pilgrims."[206] He was not baulked by the

202. *Works*, Vol. III, p. 174.
203. *Ibid.*, p. 198.
204. *Ibid.*, p. 206.
205. T. R. Glover, *op. cit.*, p. 140.
206. *Works*, Vol. III, p. 212.

Hill called Difficulty, nor did he quail before the lions: for his trouble was not with the perils of the journey but with what would happen when he had to ford the river. At last he reached its banks, and we are told that the water had sunk lower at that time "than ever I saw it in all my life."[207] Miss Much-Afraid was to cross the river singing, though none knew what she sang.[208] But then there were others who might have been drawn straight from the ranks of Cromwell's Ironsides, men who could fight or preach as the hour might require. There was Great-Heart who slew Giant Despair and destroyed Doubting Castle: he went with the Pilgrims as far as the river and then returned to his post in the House of the Interpreter. There was Old Honest, a good man who came from the town of Stupidity which "lieth about four degrees beyond the City of Destruction"; he had not much intelligence, but was stout of heart and sturdy of limb and "would have fought as long as breath had been in" him.[209] When he heard the call to cross the river, it was overflowing its banks, but Good Conscience lent him a hand and so he got over.[210] There was Valiant-for-Truth whom the pilgrims found with "his sword drawn and his face all bloody";[211] he had just fought a long three-hour battle single-handed and had repulsed his foes. Great-Heart took the sword in his hand "and looked thereon a while"; then he pronounced it a "right Jerusalem blade."[212] Valiant-for-Truth gladly joined in conversation as they went on their way and they were all thrilled when he sang "The Song of a Pilgrim."[213] When the summons came for him to cross the river, he left his sword for him that should succeed him in his pilgrimage and his courage and skill to him that could get it. Many went down with him to the river and heard him cry as he went in: "O Death, where is thy sting?" As he went down deeper, his voice rang out: "O Grave, where

207. *Ibid.*, p. 214.
203. *Ibid.*, p. 242.
209. *Ibid.*, pp. 211, 212.
210. *Ibid.*, p. 242.
211. *Ibid.*, p. 232.
212. *Ibid.*, p. 233.
213. *Ibid.*, p. 235.

is thy victory?" (I Cor. 15:55). "So he passed over, and all the trumpets sounded for him on the other side."[214] But the finest of them all was Mr. Standfast, "a right good pilgrim" whom they found on the Enchanted Ground.[215] "Behold, they saw as they thought a man upon his knees with eyes and hands lift up, and speaking as they thought earnestly to one that was above."[216] When the time came for him to pass over, he went down to the bank of the river. "Now there was a great calm at that time in the river: wherefore Mr. Standfast when he was about half-way in stood a while and talked to his companions that had waited upon him thither."[217] But while he was yet speaking, his face changed and he ceased to be seen of them. "But glorious it was to see how the open region was filled with horses and chariots, with trumpeters and pipers, with singers and players on stringed instruments, to welcome the Pilgrims as they went up and followed one another in at the beautiful gate of the City."[218]

Bunyan's release from his second term of imprisonment was on the eve of the troubled years which saw the Popish Plot in 1678 and the death of Charles II in 1685. He could not tell if the storm would pass him by or would blow him back on to the rocks of fresh persecution. But he carried on his preaching and gave himself up to his books. Thus, in 1678, he brought out his *Come and Welcome to Jesus Christ,* a winning appeal with music in its title which grew from a sermon on the words which had once helped to heal his own wounds (John 6:37). And in 1680 he brought out *The Life and Death of Mr. Badman,* which had a good deal of searching material and which revealed his keen insight into man's heart; but it falls far below *Pilgrim's Progress,* and its moralizing is so long that we lose the thread of the story. Then, in 1682, came *The Holy War,* which ranks next to *Grace Abounding* and *Pilgrim's Progress* in spiritual renown. It was both more ambitious and more intricate than his

214. *Ibid.,* p. 243.
215. *Ibid.,* p. 238.
216. *Ibid.*
217. *Ibid.,* p. 243.
218. *Ibid.,* p. 244.

other allegories and it shows an astonishing insight into all the subtle maze of thoughts and motives which twist and turn within the heart. We may at once agree that it does not compare with the *Pilgrim's Progress* as an epic which lays its hold on the simple instincts of the heart for ever. We may also agree that its Captains in camp or in battle are but shadows by the side of men like Great-Heart and Standfast. But no allegory before had tried to deal with the inner conflict which is waged in Mansoul. It is a more elaborate study than the *Pilgrim's Progress* and it demands a more mature understanding. There is meat for the mind in its penetrating psychology as it describes how the Diabolonian offspring lurk in the walls or walk in the streets as prayer is made or withheld. There is no end to the war in Mansoul as there is to the life of the Pilgrim: Emmanuel recaptures the city, but War still hangs about its coasts; and the epic of that prolonged war should enthrall all who love a right good story. And John Bunyan identified himself closely with what he wrote, for the City of Mansoul was his own heart:

> For my part, I myself was in the town,
> Both when 'twas set up, and when pulling down;
> I saw Diabolus in his possession,
> And Mansoul under his oppression.
> Yea, I was there when she own'd him for lord
> And to him did submit with one accord.[219]

And he described Emmanuel's advance for its relief in words which could only refer to his own case:

> What is here in view
> Of mine own knowledge I dare say is true.
> I saw the Prince's armed men come down,
> By troops, by thousands, to besiege the town.
> I saw the captains, heard the trumpets sound,
> And how his forces covered all the ground.
> Yea, how they set themselves in battle-ray
> I shall remember to my dying day.[220]

219. *Ibid.*, p. 253.
220. *Ibid.*

Bunyan's picture of the Councils of Diabolus or Emmanuel may not be so convincing as we might wish, but he was on sure ground when he came to describe the City of Mansoul. He drew its gates and walls, its streets and lanes, its keep and tower, from the recollection of Newport Pagnell or Newarke at Leicester. His keen observation of all that went on, his retentive memory and his fertile imagination are all here on display. The army of Shaddai, with captains and soldiers marching, wheeling, handling arms and blowing trumpets; the siege of the City with the ensigns and the weapons and the alarms of war, were all reminiscent of what he had seen in the New Model Army under Cromwell. The actions of Diabolus when he captured Mansoul, ousting the mayor and his officebearers for magistrates and aldermen of his own choice, spoiling the old law-books for the sake of his own regulations, were all reminiscent of what he had seen in the Bedford Corporation under Charles II. The four captains whom the King sent against Mansoul were "very stout and rough-hewn men, men that were fit to break the ice and to make their way by dint of sword; and their men were like themselves."[221] The siege went on with sling and shot, and one shot cut down six of the City Aldermen.[222] Captain Anything proved "a brisk man in the broil, but both sides were against him because he was true to none."[223] One old Diabolonian is drawn in his best style: "His name was Mr. Loth-to-Stoop, a stiff man in his way, and a great doer for Diabolus."[224] We read how a breach was made at Ear-gate where the guard of Deaf Men had been posted: "Then did the Prince's trumpets sound, the Captains shout, the town shake, and Diabolus retreat to his hold."[225] The rebels of Mansoul went forth to stand before the Prince with ropes round their necks and nothing but mercy to plead; but they returned with pardon for Mansoul and all the bells of the City began to ring.[226] Bunyan had no use for men like Mr. Haughty, a burgess of Man-

221. *Ibid.*, p. 270.
222. *Ibid.*, p. 278.
223. *Ibid.*, p. 282.
224. *Ibid.*, p. 289.
225. *Ibid.*, p. 294.
226. *Ibid.*, p. 305.

soul who cared not in what cause he fought so long as he fought like a man and came off as victor. Mr. Haughty was put to death by the men of Mansoul.[227] But when Mr. Godly-Fear was made keeper of the Castle gates, he remarked: "I have wished sometimes that that man had had the whole rule of the town of Mansoul."[228] The four Captains had their orders from the King to prepare for the final battle and the trumpets were to sound with "the best music that heart could invent."[229] But the trumpets awoke Diabolus with a start, and he asked: "What can be the meaning of this? They neither sound boot and saddle, nor horse and away, nor a charge. What do these mad men mean that yet they should be so merry and glad?"[230] And the answer came back: "This is for joy that their Prince Emmanuel is coming to relieve the town of Mansoul."[231] Captain Credence looked up in the heat of battle, and saw: "And behold, Emmanuel came, and he came with colours flying, trumpets sounding, and the feet of his men scarce touched the ground, they hasted with that celerity towards the Captains that were engaged."[232] Emmanuel's speech ends the book on a fine note: "Remember O my Mansoul that thou art beloved of me; as I have therefore taught thee to watch, to fight, to pray, and to make war against my foes, so now I command thee to believe that my love is constant to thee. O my Mansoul, how have I set my heart, my love, upon thee; watch. Behold, I lay none other burden upon thee than what thou hast already. Hold fast till I come."[233]

The last years of the reign were to consign Bedford to a state of constant ferment as a result of forced changes in her Corporation and the execution of Lord William Russell. Bunyan had never been indifferent in such matters. One of his very first books had spoken out against the social evils of 1658 in words that burn with strong moral feeling: "O what red lines will those

227. *Ibid.*, p. 315.
228. *Ibid.*, p. 351.
229. *Ibid.*, p. 357.
230. *Ibid.*
231. *Ibid.*
232. *Ibid.*, p. 359.
233. *Ibid.*, p. 373.

be against all those rich ungodly landlords that so keep under their poor tenants that they dare not go out to hear the Word for fear their rent should be raised or they turned out of their houses. What sayest thou, landlord? . . . Will it not give thee an eternal wound in thy heart . . . to be accused of the ruin of thy neighbour's soul, thy servant's soul, thy wife's soul, together with the ruin of thy own?"[234] Patriotic indignation turned his words in another direction when in 1680 he poured out his lament at the sins which had made England shake and totter. "Wickedness . . . is like to drown our English world," he wrote. " . . . It has almost swallowed up all; our youth, middle age, old age, and all, are almost carried away of this flood. O debauchery, debauchery, what hast thou done in England? . . . O that I could mourn for England, and for the sins that are committed therein!"[235] Debauchery he described as "one of the most reigning sins in our day."[236] This deep concern did not grow less as the years passed by and his words still rang out in warning. Thus, in 1683, he made a strong appeal for men to count the cost of true discipleship: "For following of Me is not like following of some other masters; the wind sits always on My face."[237] And what of those other masters? "He that feeds his own soul with ashes will scarce feed thine with the bread of life; wherefore take heed of such an one; and many such there are in the world."[238] Then in 1684 he had yet more to say: "Repentance is rare this day, and yet without doubt, that without which things will grow worse and worse. . . . That which is most of all to be lamented is that sin through custom is become no sin."[239] There were home truths for all members of the community, not least for the clergy: "Alas, alas, there is a company of half-priests in the world, and they can not, they dare not, teach the people the whole counsel of God, because in so doing they will condemn themselves and their manner of living in the world; where is that minister now to be found that dare say to his people, Look on me, and walk

234. *Ibid.*, p. 699.
235. *Ibid.*, pp. 592, 593.
236. *Ibid.*, p. 610.
237. *Ibid.*, Vol. I, p. 105.
238. *Ibid.*, p. 143.
239. *Ibid.*, Vol. II, p. 509.

as you have me for an example."[240] There were shrewd thrusts at the nominal profession of so many: "For my part, I doubt of the faith of many and fear that it will prove no better at the day of God than will the faith of devils, for that it standeth in bare speculation and is without life and soul to that which is good. Where is the man that walketh with his cross upon his shoulders? Where is the man that is zealous of moral holiness?"[241] This keen spirit of observation and admonition was to remain undiminished. There were further words written by Bunyan in 1684 which were no less timely. "I have often thought that the best Christians are found in the worst of times: and I have thought again that one reason why we are no better is because God purges us no more. I know these things are against the grain of the flesh, but they are not against the graces of the Spirit. Noah and Lot, who so holy as they in the day of their affliction? Noah and Lot, who so idle as they in the day of their prosperity?"[242] And those words were written as fresh storms burst on the Non-Conformists, who were driven from home, ruined by fines, or locked up in prison. "Persecution of the godly was of God never intended for their destruction, but for their glory, and to make them shine the more when they are beyond this valley of the shadow of death."[243]

It was the King himself who in February, 1685, entered the dark valley, and James II came to the throne. But the new reign brought the Catholic policy to a climax and the Protestant reaction was to have far-reaching effects for Churchmen and Non-Conformists alike. Three years of grave misrule drove James in sheer desperation to court Non-Conformist support so as to stave off his threatened ruin. Thus in January, 1688, a fresh attempt was made to change the whole composition of the Bedford Corporation by an Order of the King in Council. Six or seven of the new Aldermen or Councillors were from Bunyan's congregation and a direct attempt was made to win Bunyan's support by the offer of a minor place of trust in Government employment.

240. *Ibid.*, p. 520.
241. *Ibid.*, p. 545.
242. *Ibid.*, p. 707.
243. *Ibid.*, p. 736.

But he would have none of it and would not so much as see the man who was sent to make the offer. He was convinced that it would cause further trouble and he tried to save his congregation from being misled and imposed upon.[244] Then in April the King published a new Declaration of Indulgence which led to the arrest and trial of the seven bishops. On June 30 the bells from a hundred steeples rang with joy on the news of their release and the ebb-tide of that short reign set in with great rapidity. Bunyan had drawn up a deed of gift in 1685 in which he had described himself as a "brazier," and this may mean that he had been compelled in those troubled times to return to his old trade.[245] But such work could only have been occasional, for he carried on his calling as preacher and author without ceasing. Thus he produced six new books in the last year of his life, and left sixteen unprinted manuscripts behind him when he died. Among his works were some in rhyme and with poetical intent; they have many attractive similes which were ever spreading like fresh ripples over his mind. It may be true that his muse was clad in russet and spoke with a country accent; but there was pith and point in his rudest rhyming, and a certain dash of beauty in his best lines.[246] The songs in the Second Part of *Pilgrim's Progress* are in varied metres which lend themselves to rhythm and music, and the Pilgrim Song which follows the talk with Valiant has a certain sparkle of soul and a lyric note which English verse was in danger of losing.[247] Nor did his prose lose the power of incisive utterance; for he cultivated plainness of speech to the end of his days. What could be more direct than his question: "Didst thou never learn for to outshoot the devil in his own bow and to cut off his head with his own sword as David served Goliath?"[248] What could be more telling than the statement concerning Solomon's Temple: "All sons are servants to assist in building this spiritual edifice, but all servants are not sons to inherit a

244. *Works*, Vol. I, p. 63.
245. John Brown, *op. cit.*, pp. 350, 352.
246. *Ibid.*, p. 40.
247. T. R. Glover, *op. cit.*, p. 140.
248. *Works*, Vol. I, p. 572.

place in it."[249] When he was asked for his advice as to whether women should meet for prayer "without their men,"[250] his verdict was against all such practice; and his reasons were clinched with the surprising argument, "Have you not in your flock a male?" (Mal. 1:14).[251] Was this conscious humor or a far-fetched allegory? We can not say; but we are thrilled by the passion of the preacher which rings through his mighty summons. "Let the Angels make a lane and let all men give place that the Jerusalem sinner may come to Jesus Christ for mercy."[252]

Bunyan was twice married and his home was known as a strict school of prayer and exhortation.[253] But that was not the whole picture and his own words must be allowed to speak as well: "I love to play the child with little children, and I have learned something by so doing."[254] He had two sons and two daughters by his first wife, who had died in 1655; and then two more children, son and daughter, by his second wife, who died in 1691. Bunyan knew and loved the noble ideal of true Puritan womanhood, and the Second Part of *Pilgrim's Progress* affords proof of his clear insight into feminine character in its strength and weakness. His long imprisonment must have been a grievous disadvantage for his children and the blindness of his eldest daughter was for him a source of the most tender concern. His great friend John Wilson said that he was grave and composed in looks and in manner and was ever likely to strike something of awe into those who lacked God's fear in their hearts.[255] Dr. George Cokayn said that he was stern and rugged to look upon but was mild and gentle in his conversation. He was not a ready talker unless he had somewhat to say, but he loved to foster friendship with all. He was tall, strong of limb, fresh-faced, with a moustache after the old British fashion; his hair had been reddish, but was sprinkled with gray; he had a good forehead, a well-set nose and a large mouth, and his eyes were full of sparkle. He

249. *Ibid.*, Vol. III, p. 462; see p. 467.
250. *Ibid.*, Vol. II, p. 659.
251. *Ibid.*, p. 674.
252. *Ibid.*, Vol. I, p. 90.
253. *Ibid.*, p. 64.
254. *Ibid.*, p. 674.
255. John Brown, *op. cit.*, p. 399.

had little of this world's goods, and his dress was always plain and modest. But with that quick sharp eye, he was no fool; he could observe the facts and then discern the truth with as shrewd a wit as any man in England.[256] Bunyan's finest trait was perhaps his deep and true humility. " 'I am the high and lofty One, I inhabit eternity.' Verily this consideration is enough to make the broken-hearted man creep into a mouse-hole to hide himself from such a majesty . . . . There is room in this man's heart for God to dwell!"[257] His own spiritual experience which had carried him down to the gates of hell and lifted him up to the gates of heaven has been told in ever memorable language. The calm resolution with which he faced a long imprisonment and was ready, had need required, to face transportation or death is a glowing testimony to his faith and courage. Few have ever equalled him in command of plain nervous English with its Saxon flavour and its direct appeal. He drew words and imagery from the army or the law-courts with an ease and accuracy which bear witness to his remarkable powers of observation.[258] His was not the mind of a trained theologian, but he clothed the truths of Puritan theology with charm and appeal. *Pilgrim's Progress* has had a vogue second only to that of the Bible and has made the strait gate and the narrow way a reality in the lives of thousands. Bunyan's name will be known and his work loved as long as the Puritan heritage endures.

Political change and revolution were in the air as he entered the last year of his life, but he did not live to see the abdication of James II and the dawn of a new freedom. His own eyes were towards another sun-rising, and his faith was expressed in firm objective reference to the grain of corn as a true figure of the resurrection: "It is sown a dead corn; it is raised a living one. It is sown dry, and without comeliness; it riseth green and beautiful. It is sown a single corn; it riseth a full ear. It is sown in its husk, but in its rising it leaveth that husk behind it. Further, though the kernel thus die; be buried, and meet with all this change and alteration in these things, yet none of them can cause

256. *Works*, Vol. I, pp. 64, 65.
257. *Ibid.*, pp. 690, 691.
258. See, for example, *Works*, Vol. I, p. 151.

the nature of the kernel to cease — it is wheat still. Wheat was sown and wheat ariseth; only it was sown dead, dry, and barren wheat; and riseth living, beautiful and fruitful wheat."[259] We know little of his last days apart from the books which were still being produced. When the month of August arrived, he set out on his last journey, taking with him one more book for publication. He had often been in London on such errands and was well-known to the Non-Conformist congregations in the city. His fame as a result of his imprisonment and the *Pilgrim's Progress* used to attract many who were impressed with his "worth and knowledge" and went away asking whence had this man these things.[260] Charles Doe says that when he preached in London, "if there were but one day's notice given, there would be more people come together to hear him preach than the meeting house would hold. I have seen to hear him preach by my computation about twelve-hundred at a morning lecture by seven o'clock on a working day in the dark winter time."[261] The great Dr. John Owen took every opportunity to hear him preach and told Charles II that he would gladly give all his learning in exchange for the tinker's skill in touching the heart.[262] "Thus he was no stranger to the City to which he was setting out once more in the month of August, 1688."[263] He travelled on horseback and rode first of all to Reading in order to reconcile a son with his father. Then he took the road for London, forty miles from Reading, and was drenched with driving rain all the way. Wet and weary, he reached the home of his friend John Strudwick at the Star on Snowhill, and on August 19 he preached for the last time at a meeting near Whitechapel. Two days later he was seized with a high fever, and for ten days more he lingered in the Land of Beulah before his summons came. He seems to have known that the end was at hand, and he composed his mind to die. His last sayings were all brief and succinct and full of the spiritual wisdom for which he was famous. "No sin against God can be

259. *Works,* Vol. II, p. 91.
260. *Ibid.,* Vol. I, p. 63.
261. *Ibid.,* Vol. III, p. 766.
262. *Ibid.,* p. lxx.
263. John Brown, *op. cit.,* p. 386.

little," he said, "because it is against the great God of heaven and earth; but if the sinner can find out a little God, it may be easy to find out little sins."[264] Again, "when thou prayest, rather let thy heart be without words than thy words without a heart."[265] Then on Friday, August 31, 1688, not as yet quite sixty years old, but having now followed his own Pilgrim from the City of Destruction to the swellings of that bridgeless river, John Bunyan passed over while all the trumpets were sounding for him on the other side.

264. *Works*, Vol. I, p. 65.
265. *Ibid.*

BIBLIOGRAPHY

John Brown, *John Bunyan: His Life, Times and Work*, 1885.

T. R. Glover, *Poets and Puritans* (3rd edition), 1923.

E. A. Knox, *John Bunyan in Relation to His Times*, 1928.

H. Elvet Lewis, Introduction to *Pilgrim's Progress* (Everyman's Library edition), 1929.

George Offor, *The Works of John Bunyan*, with Notes and Introductions (3 Vcls.), 1858.

(From the painting in 'Dr. Williams' library)

RICHARD BAXTER

RICHARD BAXTER
A Mere Non-Conformist

1615-1691

He preach'd, as never sure to preach again,
And as a dying man to dying men.

—Richard Baxter: *Poetical Fragments*, p. 30.

RICHARD BAXTER WAS THE ONLY CHILD TO
bless the marriage between his father and Beatrice Adeney, and
he was born in her home at Rowton on Sunday, November 12,
1615. He would derive from his parents the strength of the yeo-
man stock of England, and his inheritance was to consist of an
estate that was small, but enough. "I was born," he wrote in
1691, "but to five tenements of free hold as my patrimony"; but
he never took a farthing from any of them for himself, as poor
kinsmen needed it all and as much more as he could spare.[1] He
and his future wife were born within four miles of each other, but
she belonged to one of the chief Houses in Shropshire.[2] He pointed
the contrast more than once in his own fashion: "I had been bred
among plain mean [humble] people, and I thought that so much
washing of stairs and rooms . . . and so much ado about cleanli-
ness and trifles was a sinful curiosity and expense of servants'
time who might that while have been reading some good book.
But she that was otherwise bred had somewhat other thoughts."[3]
Nevertheless, he was "called a Gentleman for his ancestors' sake,"[4]
for his grandfather's grandfather had married the eldest daughter
and co-heiress of the Lord of Leighton in the reign of Henry
VIII.[5] Baxter's social affinities were those of the landed gentry,
and men of rank received him as one who belonged to their own
class. But there is not a grain of pride in his writings and
the reference to his ancestors was in a brief parenthesis. It seems
that his father's estate had become burdened with gambling
debts and other difficulties, and the result was that he lived in
his grandfather's house at Rowton until he was "near ten years"

1. *Poor Husbandman's Advocate*, p. 213.
2. J. T. Wilkinson, *Richard Baxter and Margaret Charlton: A Love
Story [The Breviate]*, p. 67.
3. *Ibid.*, p. 137.
4. *Ibid.*, p. 67.
5. Frederick J. Powicke, *A Life of the Rev. Richard Baxter*, Vol. I,
p. 289.

old.[6] But it pleased God so to touch and change his father by the reading of the Scriptures that his life was reclaimed for God. This took place by "the bare reading" of the Bible, without the guidance of preacher or friend,[7] and the Bible which was henceforth to lie on his table became his most treasured volume. Thus the ten-year-old lad left the home at Rowton for the ancestral residence of the Baxters at Eaton Constantine, and there, as he liked to recall, he was in the heart of Shropshire, only a mile from the Wrekin and half a mile from the Severn.[8] It was a kind dispensation that brought peace and stability into the life of that home as he now entered his teens, for he would need the strength of a steady home life to fit him for that age of storm and trial. He was to grow up under the first James, to see Charles I lose his head, and to reach his prime under the iron rule of Cromwell; he was to grow old under the next Charles, to see James II lose his crown, and to end his days under the new House of Orange. Thus his life would span the strenuous century in which men of Puritan character made a lasting impact on the life of England, and he was to "stand forth as one of the supreme figures" in a movement akin to that of the Reformation.[9]

Baxter was to be a witness to the growth of Dissent from the Church of England, for the disordered character of the times could not be concealed. There was very little preaching in the Shropshire of his childhood and the moral standards of the County clergy were just as lax as in mediaeval England. The church at High Ercall where he had been baptised was served by four readers while he lived at Rowton: all were ignorant; two were immoral. The church in his father's village had a reader who was old and blind, who read the prayers by heart and did not preach at all. He was compelled to leave the rest of his duties in the hands of others who came and went in a disgraceful succession. "We changed them oft," Baxter observed,[10] because they were fonder of the tavern than of books or sermons; yet such were

6. J. M. Lloyd Thomas, *The Autobiography of Richard Baxter, [Relinquiae Baxterianae]*, p. 3.

7. *Ibid.*, p. 4.

8. *Ibid.*, p. 3.

9. J. T. Wilkinson, *op. cit.*, p. 17.

10. J. M. Lloyd Thomas, *op. cit.*, p. 4.

the masters who were responsible for his education in mind and soul until he was fourteen years old. "I was in my childhood first bred up under the school and church teaching of eight several men, of whom only two preached once a month and the rest were but Readers of the Liturgy and most of very scandalous lives."[11] It left a scar on his boyhood which time could not remove and which he found hard to forgive: "These were the school masters of my youth," he wrote, "who read Common Prayer on Sundays and Holy Days, and taught school and tippled on the week-days, and whipped the boys, when they were drunk."[12] Things were better during the year or two in his middle teens which he spent at the free school in Donnington or Wroxeter: he was grateful to the master under whom he acquired his knowledge of Latin and he became the head boy of his form. There were other troubles as well which left their mark on his boyhood. The Book of Sports which was published with the sanction of Church and Crown had changed the whole spirit of the village life of England. Thus his home was disturbed on the Lord's day by the noisy revels of the morris dancers who could play as long as they liked once the morning service was at an end. Sometimes they came into the church in their scarfs and antic dresses, with the jingling of the bells on their feet:[13] and as soon as the old man had read the prayers they hurried out to dance and play "till dark night almost."[14] The large maypole on the village green was not a hundred yards from his door, and the narrow street was choked with hilarious noise and shouting. Baxter's father could not read the Scriptures, nor sing a Psalm, nor join in prayer for the noise of pipe and tabor outside. "Many times my mind was inclined to be among them, and sometimes I broke loose from conscience and joined with them."[15] But he was cured from the love of Sunday frolics when he heard his father being scoffed at as a Puritan or a Precisian: "For I considered my father's exercise of reading the Scripture was better than theirs,

11. Frederick J. Powicke, *op. cit.*, Vol. I, pp. 15, 16, footnote.
12. J. M. Lloyd Thomas, *op. cit.*, p. 4.
13. See J. M. Lloyd Thomas, *op. cit.*, p. 279.
14. J. M. Lloyd Thomas, *op. cit.*, p. 6.
15. *Ibid.*, p. 6.

and would surely be better thought on by all men at last."[16] He was indeed about fifteen years old when he began to yield beneath the touch of the Divine Finger: "yet whether sincere conversion began now, or before, or after, I was never able to this day to know."[17]

Baxter's schooldays came to an end when he was about sixteen years old, and his dearest desire was to enroll at Oxford or Cambridge; "but," he wrote, "my master drew me into another way which kept me thence where were my vehement desires."[18] He was induced to take up a course of private reading with the chaplain to the Council at Ludlow who was eager to coach "a scholar fit for the University."[19] Baxter was told that this would be better than Oxford or Cambridge for him, and it pleased his parents who were glad to have him so close to home. But the chaplain failed him as a tutor and he was left very largely to his own ends. "He never read to me nor used any savoury discourse of godliness; only he loved me and allowed me books and time enough."[20] He spent eighteen months at Ludlow Castle and then returned home for some months, thankful to have been kept unscathed in the midst of men who were "much given to tippling and excess."[21] Meanwhile the chaplain at Ludlow had been very pressing for him to lay aside thought and preparation for the Christian ministry and had urged him to go up to London where he might get a place at court as "the only rising way."[22] "I had no mind of his counsel who had helped me no better before; yet because that they knew that he loved me and they had no great inclination to my being a minister, my parents accepted of his motion."[23] Baxter says that this was "about the eighteenth year" of his age,[24] but his later remarks on "the greatest snow that hath

16. *Ibid.*
17. *Ibid.*, p. 7.
18. *Ibid.*
19. *Ibid.*
20. *Ibid.*
21. *Ibid.*, pp. 7, 8.
22. *Ibid.*, p. 12.
23. *Ibid.*
24. *Ibid.*

been in this age"[25] make it clear that it was late in the year 1634.[26] Thus the lad of nineteen left his home in Shropshire for the Court of Charles I in Whitehall where he was a guest in the house of Sir Henry Herbert, the Master of Revels: but the experiment was to end in failure. He must have heard of George Herbert during his stay in Sir Henry's household; it is certain that he knew and loved his poems in the years that followed. But George Herbert had sipped the sweets of a court life for years before he gave them up to be ordained, and his death had occurred only the year before Baxter came to Whitehall. Baxter had no need of years to make up his mind; a month was all that he required. "When I saw a stage-play instead of a sermon on the Lord's days in the afternoon, and saw what course was there in fashion, and heard little preaching but what was as to one part against the Puritans, I was glad to be gone."[27] He was away and home before Christmas, 1634, in time for a winter of great severity. He found his mother in a state of extreme pain and weakness, and her life ebbed away in May, 1635. Baxter remained at home with his father, and furthered his studies by a course of private reading. This meant that he had no academic status in the ordinary sense of the word, and this was for him the cause of life-long regret. "As to myself," he wrote with dignified and beautiful simplicity, "my faults are no disgrace to any University, for I was of none.... Weakness and pain helped me to study how to die; that set me on studying how to live; and that on studying the doctrine from which I must fetch my motives and comforts."[28]

It was because he felt conscious of a strong thirst for the souls of others that his thoughts now turned to ordination. "I resolved," he wrote, "that if one or two souls only might be won to God, it would easily recompense all the dishonour which for want of titles I might undergo from men."[29] The issues of Conformity held no difficulties for him as yet, for his teachers and books kept his scruples at bay. He was ordained as a Deacon by the Bishop

25. *Ibid.*, p. 13.
26. *Ibid.*, Note, p. 280.
27. *Ibid.*, p. 12.
28. William Orme, *The Practical Works of the Rev. Richard Baxter,* Vol. I, p. 9.
29. J. M. Lloyd Thomas, *op. cit.*, p. 15.

of Worcester in December, 1638, and was licensed as an usher in a school at Dudley. "I thought it not an inconvenient condition for my entrance," he wrote, "because I might also preach up and down in places that were most ignorant before I presumed to take a pastoral charge."[30] His first sermon was preached in the upper parish church and after this he often preached in surrounding villages. He was forced to make a closer study of the problems raised by Non-Conformists and he modified his first opinions: but the censorious spirit of the Non-Conformists seemed to him as great an offence against the law of Christian charity on the one side as was persecution on the other. Meanwhile the poor nailers and scithe smiths of Dudley crowded the church even to the windows, and there were so many conversions that their reverence for him upheld the honor of Conformity among the best people. Then in 1639, after less than a "twelve month" at Dudley, he was "by God's very gracious providence" called to Bridgnorth which he described as "the second town of Shropshire."[31] Here he remained for a little less than two years, preaching to large congregations at the full height of his early fervour. Indeed his passion for preaching had full scope in Bridgnorth, and he observed that he never elsewhere preached with a more intense desire to win the souls of men.[32] He was also free to declare himself on the points at issue between Laud and Non-Conformists, and the Et Cetera Oath, in 1640, had a decisive influence on the development of his thinking: "We that thought it best to follow our business and live in quietness and let the Bishops alone were roused by the terrors of an oath to look about us and understand what we did."[33] He would not take the Oath, nor use the Sign of the Cross in Baptism, nor put on a surplice, and he began to doubt whether the English pattern of episcopal work were lawful. But his freedom to preach was a freedom which he valued as "a very great mercy . . . in those troublesome times."[34] Then in April, 1641, a call came from the long neglected congregation

30. *Ibid.*, p. 16.
31. *Ibid.*, p. 18.
32. *Ibid.*
33. *Ibid.*, p. 19.
34. *Ibid.*, p. 21.

of St. Mary's Kidderminster, where the Vicar used to haunt the taverns and was content to preach only once a quarter. It was arranged that the Vicar should retain his office and read the prayers, but that he would allow sixty pounds per annum for a preacher instead of a curate. Baxter had longed for an untried parish 'where he could work as in fresh soil, and this thriving township of three thousand people in the Western Midlands was just the place to suit his frame of mind. "My mind was much to the place as soon as it was described to me, because it was a full congregation and most convenient temple," he wrote; "an ignorant rude and revelling people for the greater part, who had need of preaching, and yet had among them a small company of converts who were humble, godly, and of good conversations."[35] His appointment as Lecturer was by unanimous consent of those responsible, and he took up the task at once. "Thus I was brought by the gracious providence of God to that place which had the chiefest of my labours and yielded me the greatest fruits of comfort."[36]

"I have these forty years been sensible of the sin of losing time; I could not spare an hour."[37] Baxter wrote those words in 1681 and the forty years to which he referred would take his thoughts back to his first year in Kidderminster. One of the first demands on his time was for his studies, and he pursued this aim with a singleminded love for learning which the crowded years could never abate. "The whole man and the whole time," he thought, "is all too little in so great a work."[38] An Oxford or Cambridge background might have added to the polish of his training but they had nothing to add to the vigour of his thinking. The want of a degee could not restrict his breadth of mind, and his love for books did more for him than college tutors could have ever hoped to achieve. Books were the one pleasure in life which he deemed a necessity, and he spared no money in their purchase. He had formed a friendship while at Whitehall with a godly bookseller's apprentice from whom he could always

35. *Ibid.*, pp. 24, 25.
36. *Ibid.*, p. 25.
37. J. T. Wilkinson, *op. cit.*, p. 136.
38. *Ibid.*, p. 55.

obtain information about new books and get them as he wished.[39] Shelves lined the walls of his upstairs room in Kidderminster, and books lay on the floor and were piled on the chairs. Once as he sat in his study, the weight of his largest folio volumes broke down three or four shelves and they crashed down around his chair: "the place, the weight and greatness of the books was such, and my head just under them, that it was a wonder they had not beaten out my brains."[40] Nothing grieved him more in the Great Fire of 1666 than the half burnt leaves of books which the winds scattered miles from London: "The loss of books was an exceeding great detriment to the interest of piety and learning."[41] This love of books was to survive all the vicissitudes of the future. "When I die," he wrote in 1683, "I must leave my library and turn over those pleasant books no more."[42] We do not know when he found time to read in view of his other labours, "all which," he said, "leaveth me but little time to study which hath been the greatest external personal affliction of all my life."[43] We must suppose that he read far into the night when the streets were still and silent. He read the old and the new with equal ardour, and he must have read with rapid eye and retentive memory. He pored over old and musty volumes in a tireless effort to wring from them all their treasures, and he amassed a vast store of knowledge on all kinds of subjects. He made himself at home with Fathers and Schoolmen, and though he had not the tongue of any foreign country, he read French and Dutch and German Divines in English translations.[44] He toiled through vast tomes on mediaeval philosophy, mastered the chief authorities on metaphysics and dialectics, and took up the study of fresh subjects like pharmacy and medicine. The long list of authors who were part and parcel of his daily reading form an amazing catalogue of names. Scotus and Okam, Vives and Hutton, Scaliger and Erasmus, Aquinas and Durandus, Casaubon and Bradwardine: these are a few of the men who

39. J. M. Lloyd Thomas, *op. cit.*, p. 13.
40. *Ibid.*, p. 77.
41. *Ibid.*, p. 198.
42. William Orme, *op. cit.*, Vol. XVIII, p. 313.
43. J. M. Lloyd Thomas, *op. cit.*, p. 78.
44. *Ibid.*, Note, p. 286.

were more familiar to him than Julius Caesar to a modern school-boy. He could quote from hundreds of books and there were marginal allusions to more than a hundred authors, even in such a work as the second edition of *The Saints' Rest*. It was not for nothing that he gave his advice with regard to marriage: "So great are the matters of our studies and labours, requiring our total and most serious thoughts that I earnestly advise all that can to live single."[45]

Baxter could not tolerate confusion in his studies, and he was as independent in his thinking as he was omnivorous in his reading. "I had the unhappiness from my youth to be inclined to strict definition . . . and to abhor confused harangues: and therefore the now despised Schoolmen were my pleasant study next to the Bible and practical Divinity."[46] So he wrote in 1691. It was in the loving wisdom of God that the Bible meant more to him than a hundred authors of mere human standing: "I found that my hearty love of the Word of God . . . was not without some love to Himself."[47] This was the true background of the mental vision and the moral grandeur which were to distinguish his ministry. It taught him the supreme authority of the Lord God of Truth, and no better discipline could have been found for his restless intellect. It was with this Book in hand that he set out to explore the whole field of moral science and it gave a new edge to his power for subtle thinking. Thus he turned to logic and to metaphysics, and read all the Schoolmen whose works he could obtain: "for next practical divinity, no books so suited with my disposition as Aquinas, Scotus, Durandus, Ockam, and their disciples."[48] All his skill and insight were brought to bear as he strove to find his way through trackless deserts of argument and opinion. He was just as eager to secure a definition of each obscure doctrine as he was to provide a diagnosis for some abstruse difficulty, and his assault on every kind of problem brought with it the pursuit of every shade of meaning. There were times when his thoughts followed paths where few can

45. J. T. Wilkinson, *op. cit.*, p. 55.
46. J. M. Lloyd Thomas, *op. cit.*, Note, p. 284.
47. *Ibid.*, p. 11.
48. *Ibid.*, p. 9.

tread with safety, for he never refused a clash with doubt or unbelief. He did in fact reach an impasse which forced him to think out the most basic questions, and he could not lay the spectre of doubt until he had found a rational foundation on which his faith could stand: and this he did "that so my faith might be indeed my own."[49] He had gone down into the dark abyss where faith is not, and had touched its bottom; and he had then returned to the upper air where faith has its home and felt assured of the ability of the intellect to answer the questions of the intellect.[50] He could freely admit that of the things which he believed to be true, some were more certain than others,[51] and he was to subscribe himself late in life as one "who by God's blessing on long and hard studies hath learned to know that he knoweth but little, and to suspend his judgment on uncertainties."[52] Thus he did find a path through the arid wastes of mediaeval speculation and the relief which he then felt is well expressed in his own quaint saying: "The jingling of too much and too false philosophy . . . often drowns the noise of Aaron's bells; I feel myself much better in Herbert's Temple."[53] He rebuked the folly of those who affect to despise learning, because they know not what it is, but he felt a profound satisfaction as he left the Schoolmen for the simplicities of the Gospel: "I would not dissuade my reader from the perusal of Aquinas, Scotus, Ockam, Arminiensis, Durandus, or any such writer, for much good may be gotten from them: but I would persuade him to study and live upon the essential doctrines of Christianity and godliness incomparably above them all."[54]

Baxter's work in Kidderminster had been carried on for barely fifteen months when the Civil War forced him to review the whole situation. In July, 1642, the Royal Standard was unfurled at Nottingham and the "Damn-me's" — as the common soldiers of the King were called — took up arms against Parliament.[55] It

49. *Ibid.*, pp. 26, 27.
50. *Ibid.*, p. xxx.
51. *Ibid.*, pp. 110, 111.
52. *Ibid.*, Note p. 285.
53. William Orme, *op. cit.*, Vol. XV, p. 16.
54. J. M. Lloyd Thomas, *op. cit.*, p. 109.
55. *Ibid.*, p. 36.

was not long before the King's Declaration was read in the market place at Kidderminster, and the shout of traitor was raised against Baxter as he chanced to pass by. There was not "a syllable of reason" to justify the shout, but the streets soon rang with the cry, "Down with the Roundheads."[56] Baxter was advised "to withdraw a while from home,"[57] but no sooner had he gone to Gloucester than it was said that he must be afraid or else against the King. He was back in Kidderminster at the end of a month, but the fury of the rabble as well as of the King's soldiers convinced him that there would be no safety at home. Thus he withdrew to a village ten miles east of Worcester and, on September 23, he saw the fight at Powick Bridge when a party of Roundheads was ambushed by Prince Rupert. He spent the next month in Worcester, where the Earl of Essex was in command until the King's army drew him into the field. On Sunday, October 23, Baxter heard none of the sounds of battle as he preached at Alcester on the appropriate saying: "The Kingdom of Heaven suffereth violence" (Matt. 11:12): but the congregation who heard him preach could not quite close their ears to the distant roar of guns at Edgehill. On the Monday morning he went out to see the sodden scarp where Essex was still facing the King's army: they were about a mile apart and a thousand bodies lay in the fields between.[58] Baxter was now in a difficult position, without money or friends, and hemmed in by soldiers from both armies; but he went to Coventry, where it was his intention to stay until peace was restored: "For so wise in matters of war was I, and all the country besides," he wrote, "that we commonly supposed that a very few days or weeks by one other battle would end the wars."[59] A month passed by, and there was still no sign of peace. Thus his circumstances disposed him to accept a warm invitation to lodge with the Governor and preach to the garrison of the city. Here he preached twice a week, on a week-day to the soldiers and on Sundays to the towns-folk,

56. *Ibid.,* p. 39.
57. *Ibid.,* p. 42.
58. *Ibid.,* p. 42.
59. *Ibid.,* p. 43.

and followed his studies with as much quiet as in a time of peace. A year passed by, and then he left Coventry for two months with a troop which had various skirmishes near Nantwich and Longford. On his return to the Coventry garrison he followed his studies again, until his health gave fresh cause for anxiety. It was probably in October, 1644, that he took the road for London, where he "was long under the cure of Sir Theodore Mayerne."[60] On his recovery he settled down again with the Coventry garrison: but like a man in a dry house who hears the sounds of storm without, so he daily heard news of fresh battles.[61] At length, in June, 1645, the Battle of Naseby was fought and he was told of the total rout of the King's army. Two days later he went by the field of battle to the army which was then at Leicester to see or ask about his friends: and this was a journey which brought him face to face with a problem which put an end to all his quiet studies for months to come.

Baxter had thought that the war would only last a matter of months and had identified himself with those who hoped for a purified monarchy. "We took the true happiness of king and people, Church and state, to be our end, and so we understood the Covenant."[62] But when he reached Cromwell's camp at Leicester, he was dismayed at the state of affairs. There were many good and sober men who followed Cromwell, but they were not a match for the "hot-headed sectaries."[63] The best preachers in all England would have found it hard to reclaim such men, and he began to blame himself for his choice of a quiet retreat when he might have become chaplain to the original Ironsides. He now recalled that when Cromwell "lay at Cambridge long before with that famous troop which he began his army with," he had declined such an invitation.[64] This must have been during the first year of the war while he was at Coventry: and he had heard no more of it until now when he met Cromwell by chance and was reproached for his failure to join him at

60. *Ibid.*, p. 45.
61. *Ibid.*
62. *Ibid.*, p. 49.
63. *Ibid.*
64. *Ibid.*, p. 50.

Cambridge. That cold reproach was now driven home by the keen regret which was born of self-blame and close observation. "These very men that then invited me to be their pastor," he wrote, "were the men that afterwards headed much of the army . . . which made me wish that I had gone among them however it had been interpreted; for then all the fire was in one spark."[65] Thus when Colonel Whalley now asked him to become chaplain to his regiment, said to be "the most religious, most valiant, most successful of all the army," conscience would not allow him to refuse and he hurried back to consult his friends in Coventry.[66] They all agreed when they heard his plans and motives, although he fell foul of Colonel Purefoy, who voiced the threat: "If Nol Cromwell should hear any soldier speak but such a word, he would cleave his crown."[67] Purefoy queered his pitch with Cromwell before he could even join the army, and his hopes were thus foiled from the outset. "Cromwell coldly bid me welcome," he wrote, "and never spake one word to me more while I was there. . . . But Colonel Whalley welcomed me and was the worse thought on for it by the rest of the Cabal."[68]

Thus for eighteen months he marched to and fro with the army while he strove to make all men weigh the things of time on the scales of eternity. He loathed the hard fare of camp life and the crude speech of rough men; he loathed still more the sights and sounds of battle and bloodshed. But he braved what he loathed that he might preach to the living and pray with the dying. Thus in July, 1645, he was with the army when the fight at Langport took place: "The dust was so extreme," he wrote, ". . . that they that were in it coud scarce see each other; but I that stood over them upon the brow of the hill saw all."[69] During the next two months he was present at the siege of Sherborne Castle and the fall of Bristol City. He spent some six weeks in winter quarters where he engaged in a day-long debate with certain sectaries: "And I alone disputed against them from morning until almost night,"

65. *Ibid.*
66. *Ibid.*
67. *Ibid.*, p. 51.
68. *Ibid.*, p. 52.
69. *Ibid.*, p. 53.

he wrote, ". . . I stayed it out till they first rose and went away."[70] He saw Worcester fall in July, 1646, and he hurried away to see friends and flock in Kidderminster. They hoped that he would now return, and he resolved to seek advice from friends in Coventry. He told them that the day for which he had laboured had yet to come, and he believed that "the greatest service with the greatest hazard" was still ahead.[71] Thus they advised him to remain with the army.

But a sudden collapse in health was to bring Baxter's army days to an end. He had been subject to pain and illness from his childhood and had been drugged and bled at the hands of numerous physicians. He had fallen ill in the midst of the siege of Bristol and had been close to death when it pleased God to raise him up.[72] Therefore when he made up his mind to stay in the army after his visit to Kidderminster, he left Whalley's men in camp at Worcester and went up to London to consult Sir Theodore Mayerne about his health. He was sent for a short visit to Tunbridge Wells and then returned to his regiment. He found that his quarters were in the home of Sir Thomas and Lady Rous, about twelve miles east of Worcester. He had never before been to their home at Rous Lench Court, but they received him as a son. "The Lady Rous was a godly, grave, understanding woman, and entertained me not as a soldier, but a friend."[73] It must have been late in 1646 that he left this home and came to "Major Swallow's quarters at Sir John Cook's house at Melbourn . . . in a cold and snowy season."[74] It was here that his health broke down, and he was so reduced in looks and strength that friends hardly knew him. But in Melbourn he was among strangers and did not know how to get home. He was confined to his room for three weeks and then moved to Kirkby Mallory "where with great kindness I was entertained three weeks."[75] Meanwhile Lady Rous had by some means heard

70. *Ibid.*, p. 56.
71. *Ibid.*, p. 58.
72. *Ibid.*, p. 54.
73. *Ibid.*, p. 58.
74. *Ibid.*
75. *Ibid.*, p. 59.

of his illness, and she at once sent a servant to look for him. The man failed in his search and went back to report that he could not be found. She sent him off again with strict orders to find out where he was and bring him back to Rous Lench Court. "And in great weakness, thither I made shift to get, where I was entertained with the greatest care and tenderness."[76] He had been close enough to the margin of things unseen before, but now it seemed as though there could be no return. He lay in the shadow of death for some weeks and he seldom awoke without thinking that dawn had come for the last time. He felt that die he must; yet he prayed that it might be in the will of God for him to be restored. He could not know that he was still so far from the pilgrim's last bourne, though he was in fact to lead a long life before the end would be in sight. Meanwhile his prayers were heard. "Blessed be that mercy which heard my groans in the day of my distress, and granted my desires, and wrought my deliverance when men and means failed."[77] Slowly, gently, with unfailing sympathy and unwearied devotion, he was nursed back to health. Rous Lench was an ideal retreat where he could drink in the tonic of fresh country air as winter yielded to spring. Five months of such care and convalescence allowed him at last to return home to Kidderminster. This was in June, 1647, and the kindness of his hosts still followed him in abundance. But he was still in great weakness, and he seldom spent an hour that was free from pain.[78]

Baxter once said that while he was in health he had never thought of writing books or trying to serve God in any other way than preaching.[79] But he did not return from the gates of death until with long look and rapt gaze he had viewed the land where is the rest that remains for the people of God. He had no books but his Bible and concordance, but his heart burned within him as he mused on that theme. He began to transcribe his thoughts while at Kirkby Mallory, and his notes grew during the five months which he spent at Rous Lench Court. The whole task

76. *Ibid.*
77. *Ibid.*, p. 75.
78. *Ibid.*, p. 76.
79. *Ibid.*, p. 94.

was finished shortly after his return to Kidderminster, and the marginal citations were filled in when he came home to his books.[80] Thus he brought out a large volume with the title of *The Saints' Everlasting Rest*. It was his first attempt to write a book, and its success would mark it out as a worthy parent of "all those which after followed."[81] It had the ring of a maturity of understanding and experience which could not be denied, and it taught him that "the transcript of the heart hath the greatest force on the hearts of others."[82] It is at once a dirge on the sufferings of a fugitive life in this world and a psalm on the hope of glory in the world to come. We can still watch by the bed where he lay racked with pain and fever, wishing by night that it were morning and wishing by day that it were evening.[83] We can still catch the shrill sound of controversy in camp or field and we can hear voices that throb now with party passions, now with lofty ideals. "I know the best are but negligent loiterers and spend not their time according to its worth; but yet he that hath a hundred years' time and loseth it all, lives not so long as he that hath but twenty and bestows it well. It is too soon to go to hell at a hundred years old, and not too soon to go to heaven at twenty."[84] The woes of earth are but a foil for the joys of heaven, and hope kindles into rapture at the thought of the rest of the saints in glory. "Yonder twinkling stars, that shining moon, the radiant sun, are all but as the lanterns hanged out at thy Father's house to light thee while thou walkest in the dark streets of the earth. But little dost thou know, ah, little indeed, the glory and blessed mirth that is within!"[85] The human trust that answers to divine love shines through an exclamation that is also rich in humility: "Though I can not say as Thy Apostle, Thou knowest that I love Thee, yet can I say, Lord, Thou knowest that I would love Thee."[86] There is scarcely a page which lacks its gem of thought or phrase; it is indeed as William Bates declared in his *Funeral Sermon*, "a book for which

80. *Ibid.*, p. 95.
81. *Ibid.*
82. *Ibid.*
83. William Orme, *op. cit.*, Vol. XXII, p. 129.
84. *Ibid.*, Vol. XXIII, p. 209.
85. *Ibid.*, p. 415.
86. *Ibid.*, p. 419.

multitudes will have cause to bless God forever."[87] As an example
of that multiude, we may cite the case of Henry Martyn, who wrote
in his *Journal*: "December 28th 1803; That blessed man, Baxter,
in his Saints' Rest, was enabled to kindle such a degree of
devotion and love as I have long been a stranger to."[88] Thus
his illness gave birth to a classic of true devotional literature, a
book which will endure as long as men require a star of hope in
a world of tears and trouble.

Baxter's work in Kidderminster reached its full height in the
years that followed. "I went to Kidderminster where I was kindly
received," wrote George Whitefield on December 31, 1743; "I was
greatly refreshed to find what a sweet savour of good Mr. Baxter's
doctrine, works, and discipline, remained to this day."[89] The whole
of his crowded sojourn there was less than fifteen years, and his
work was over by the age of forty five. There were fifteen months
from April, 1641, to June, 1642, and then twelve years and nine
months from June, 1647, to April, 1660. He brought to his task
the unqualified consecration of time, toil and talent, and he soon
won a hold over men of shrewd and independent outlook. He
was seldom free from pain and weakness as a result of stones in
the kidney, and he found that he was never "at ease but in a
sweat."[90] Hence each day for health's sake he would walk for
an hour before dinner and for an hour before supper. Then he
would sit by a huge fire in his room to keep him "near to a sweat,
if not in it."[91] His own ailments made him pity the poor, and
for "five or six years," he had to act as their physician as well as
their minister.[92] His wife was to make a remark in a letter to
his cousin William which shows that his services as a physician
were well known and highly thought of: "Mr. Baxter's name and
fame for skill in physic," so she wrote, "will help you."[93] Baxter

87. *Ibid.*, Vol. I, p. 740.
88. Henry Martyn, *Journals & Letters*, Vol. I, p. 75.
89. George Whitefield, Letter 544, Vol. II, p. 47.
90. J. M. Lloyd Thomas, *op. cit.*, p. 12.
90. *Ibid.* 91. *Ibid.*
92. *Ibid.*, p. 78; cf. "about six or seven years," *Poor Husbandman's Advocate*, p. 187.
93. J. T. Wilkinson, *op. cit.*, p. 186.

found that he was besieged with those in need, partly because he would never take a penny from those who came: "I was crowded with patients, so that almost twenty would be at my door at once."[94] But want of time made him discontinue it all when he was able to persuade "a godly diligent physician" to reside among the people.[95] His own time was spent in yet more anxious thought for their spiritual weal or woe, and his patient dealing with their souls in public and in private was not without rich reward. They thronged the Church and sat spellbound as he declared the Word of Truth until the fear of God came down with power. It soon became necessary to erect five capacious galleries to house the large congregation and the time came when he could say that not less than one third of the townsfolk had passed from death to life. "I know not a congregation in England," he wrote in 1658, "that hath in it proportionately so many that fear God."[96] Kidderminster was the only church in which he ever dispensed the Lord's Supper, and that only to those who would consent to discipline:[97] and there were not twelve of his six hundred communicants of whose sincerity he did not have good hope.[98] And his converts grew in grace and godly conduct in a way which would have distinguished them in any company. "Some of them," he said, "were so able in prayer that very few ministers did match them."[99] There was hardly one home in each street where God was worshipped when he first came, but there were some streets where there was scarcely a house where God was not worshipped before he left. It was always to give him great joy to recall the Lord's Days in Kidderminster when one might have heard a hundred families singing psalms or repeating sermons as one passed through the streets.[100] This was success of the kind that would please the heart of the Shepherd on the hills of glory.

He was seldom away from his people during those years except for an occasional day or two which he spent with his brethren

94. J. M. Lloyd Thomas, *op. cit.*, p. 78.
95. *Ibid.*
96. Frederick J. Powicke, *op. cit.*, Vol. I, p. 305.
97. J. M. Lloyd Thomas, *op. cit.*, p. 222.
98. Frederick J. Powicke, *op. cit.*, pp. 98, 303.
99. William Orme, *op. cit.*, Vol. I, p. 119.
100. J. M. Lloyd Thomas, *op. cit.*, p. 79.

in the County. But there was a memorable visit to London in 1654 when he entered quite a new world. He had been to London at least three times before, but that had been in a private capacity; now he went just before Christmas at the invitation of Lord Broghill to join a small group of Divines who had been asked to draw up a list of fundamental doctrines. It was as a guest in the home of Lord Broghill that he met James Ussher, the "learned, humble and pious" Primate of Ireland,[101] and it gave him endless pleasure as he looked back on the friendship which was then brought into being. "Sometimes he came to me," so he naively recalled, "and oft I went to him."[102] He was more than pleased to find that Ussher was so willing to share his own larger knowledge with him, and he always spoke of Ussher's goodness of heart and great learning with a reverence and an affection such as he felt for no other Divine. But this visit also brought him into contact with a greater man still, for Lord Broghill and the Earl of Warwick arranged for him to preach before Cromwell; "which," said he, "was the only time that ever I preached to him save once long before when he was an inferior man among other auditors."[103] Baxter's sermon was preached in the Abbey on Christmas Eve, and his great hearer was not spared. "I knew not which way to provoke him better to his duty than by preaching on I Cor. 1:10 against the divisions and distractions of the Church."[104] It was his aim to show up the mischief that is caused when politicians nurse such factions for their own ends so that they might fish in troubled waters and keep the Church in a state of weakness. "The plainess and nearness, I heard, was displeasing to him and his courtiers: but they put it up."[105] Baxter was twice summoned before Cromwell, who tried in vain to win him round, but he was as forthright with the mighty Cromwell as he had been with the meanest trooper. His old misgivings had been revived by the Regicide, and he thought that the Lord Protector had now "forced his conscience" in order to justify his

101. *Ibid.*, p. 141.
102. *Ibid.*
103. *Ibid.*, p. 139.
104. *Ibid.*, pp. 139, 140.
105. *Ibid.*, p. 140.

cause.[106] There was insight as well as cold severity in his sketch of Cromwell's career, but he was still too close to its events in point of time to write without bias. Yet he was not blind to Cromwell's greatness and he prized the blessings which were due to his rule. "So I perceived that it was his design to do good in the main and to promote the Gospel and the interest of godliness more than any had done before him."[107] He was yet to bless God who had given him a freedom for the preaching of the Gospel under one whom he had opposed such as he could not have under a king to whom he had sworn true obedience.[108] A long life was to teach him in old age that it was not by means of Charles I nor Charles II but by the stern hand and iron rule of Cromwell that England was like to have become "a land of saints and a pattern of holiness to all the world."[109]

In January, 1655, Baxter returned to Kidderminster, and the next five years were the most fruitful of all. He shared his time between the books in his study and the people in his parish, and he allowed nothing else to compete with these priorities. The idea of marriage had no place in his thoughts while at Kidderminster, for he held that it is better for a shepherd of souls not to marry unless by the constraint of some necessity. For, he wrote, "the work of the sacred ministry is enough to take up the whole man, if he had the strength and parts of many men."[110] His views on this subject were so well known that they were remembered to his disadvantage. "Whereas," he wrote in 1681, "one of them reports that I said unto him that I thought the marriage of ministers had so great inconveniences that though necessity made it lawful, yet it was but lawful; that is, to be avoided as far as lawfully we may; I answer that I did say so to him, and I have never changed my judgment."[111] His experience at Kidderminster was well summed up in his own words: "I found that my single life afforded me much advantage, for I could

106. *Ibid.*, p. 88.
107. *Ibid.*, p. 70.
108. *Ibid.*, p. 80.
109. *Ibid.*, p. 84.
110. J. T. Wilkinson, *op. cit.*, p. 155.
111. *Ibid.*

the easilier take my people for my children, and think all that I had too little for them, in that I had no children of my own to tempt me to another way of using it."[112] It was during these five years that he worked out the method which proved to be his most telling approach to men. The whole method hinged on the way in which he mapped out the parish so that he could interview and catechise every member of every household. Two days each week Baxter and his assistant took between them fourteen families, "he going through the parish, and the town coming to me."[113] He would carefully examine them in the catechism which he had prepared for the purpose: then he would take each one apart for a personal interview and would urge them "tenderly and earnestly to immediate decision."[114] There were few who left him before they had been moved to tears, and the untutored reverence of a contrite people grew up round their pastor. But the love of God in the soul of man could not be hid, and the fame of that work soon spread beyond his own parish. There were few who could vie with him in the spiritual authority which he began to wield, for anxious pastors and godly laymen from near and far began to seek his counsel and support. "I thought it best," he wrote, "to draw in all the ministers of the County with me that the benefit might extend the farther."[115] He held a monthly conference to meet the need of preachers and pastors; he urged a solemn discipline to rule the life of parish and people. He engaged his brethren to interview and catechise their flock in the way that he was doing and the results went far beyond the most sanguine dreams of those who followed it out. "Was there such a ministry, or such love and concord, or such godly people in the Prelates' reign?" So he asked in July, 1658, and the answer was plain. "There was not. I lived where I do, and therefore I am able to say, There was not. Through the great mercy of God, where we had ten drunken readers then, we have not one now; and where we had one able godly preacher

112. J. M. Lloyd Thomas, *op. cit.*, p. 80.
113. *Ibid.*, p. 78.
114. James Stalker, *Richard Baxter* in *The Evangelical Succession*, Second Series, p. 237. See *Works*, Vol. XIV, pp. xxi, xxii.
115. J. M. Lloyd Thomas, *op. cit.*, p. 97.

then, we have many now; and in my own charge, where there was one that then made any show of the fear of God, I hope there are twenty now."[116]

Baxter even wrote a book and published it in order to enforce this ideal. He called the book *Gildas Salvianus*, "because," he said, "I imitated Gildas and Salvianus in my liberty of speech to the pastors of the chuches."[117] He chose the names of those two men as a sign of his strong belief that he was now faced with similar conditions and was bound to voice a similar call to repentance. The book is now better known by its sub-title as *The Reformed Pastor* and it remains as one of the finest products of the Puritan period. He sent it forth in the month of April, 1656, with the prayer that God would richly own it, and he lived to see the answer to that prayer in a way which went beyond all dreams. "I have very great cause to be thankful to God," he wrote, "for the success of that book . . . in that it prevailed with many ministers to set upon that work which I there exhort them to . . . If God would but reform the ministry, . . . the people would certainly be reformed. All churches either rise or fall as the ministry doth rise or fall, not in riches and worldly grandeur, but in knowledge, zeal and ability for their work."[118] It is perhaps the most powerful homily which has ever been penned for those who are charged with the care and cure of souls. "We look to it," he said, "that though we can not do the height of what we would, we be not found wanting in what we may."[119] It was written with a verve and warmth of spirit which he never excelled, and the ease of its style marks it out as perhaps the best written of all his books.[120] Baxter surveys the whole field of pastoral duty and personal conduct with rare insight and wisdom. There are digressions from the major theme and allusions to the passing world which are lost on the modern reader; but to abridge it in text or chapter is to disturb it in strength and effect. It is a book in which the sense of awe and the voice of love are found in

116. William Orme, *op. cit.*, Vol. XIV, p. xvi.
117. J. M. Lloyd Thomas, *op. cit.*, p. 97.
118. *Ibid.*, p. 97; see also *Works*, Vol. I, pp. 558-559.
119. William Orme, *op. cit.*, Vol. XIV, p. xliii
120. Frederick J. Powicke, *op. cit.*, Vol. I, p. 131, footnote.

impressive partnership. It rings with the trumpet blast of warning in its address to reason and conscience; it burns with the lam-
bent flame of longing in its appeal for mercy and goodness. There
are aphoristic sayings which make the truth clear and memorable.
"A sin but once committed is morally continued in till it be
repented of!"[121] "Truth loves the light, and is most beautiful
when most naked."[122] "An erring conscience is not conscience,
for conscience is a sort of science, and error is not science."[123] It
is as though Baxter himself were to step out of its pages, take
the reader by hand, and tell him what God would have him become: for the Reformed Pastor was in fact an unconscious photo-
graph of the author as a guide and shepherd of souls. "What have
we time and strength for, but to lay out both for God? What is a
candle made for, but to burn? Burnt and wasted we must be,
and is it not more fit it should be in lighting men to heaven and
in working for God than in living for the flesh?"[124]

Baxter's fame grew with the years as a preacher of great power
and pathos. Continued suffering made him feel a sense of tremendous urgency, and taught him to live with the fact of death
before his mind. He was readily sensitive to the thought of personal
destiny, and this made him "preach as a dying man to dying
men."[125] It was for this very reason that he could preach with
such force and feeling as a living man to living men. He was tall
and spare in figure, with a stoop which became more marked with
the passage of time; and the black gown and white bands which
he wore in the pulpit would set off the pallor of his lean and pain-
worn features. An old portrait which still hangs at Rous Lench
Court shows us a young Divine, not much more than thirty,
whose eyes and looks were calm and grave and of striking sincerity.
We see his broad and ample brow and the high Roman nose, his
hair falling down in love-locks on his shoulders and the hidden
smile which seems just ready to light up his features. When
those piercing eyes swept over the pews packed with earnest

121. William Orme, *op. cit.*, Vol. XIV, p. 114.
122. *Ibid.*, Vol. XIV, p. 123.
123. *Ibid.*, Vol. XIV, p. 373.
124. *Ibid.*
125. J. M. Lloyd Thomas, *op. cit.*, p. 79.

hearers, he must have looked the part of an aristocrat to the tip of his long slender fingers.[126] God had blessed him with "a familiar moving voice which is a great matter with the common hearers."[127] That voice rang out in a style of oratory which touched their hearts with a mysterious power like that of music and which helped to quicken all the latent yearnings of the human spirit. His face kindled with the fire of his own feeling. "His ethical severity was tempered by tender pity as well as by lyrical devotion,"[128] and there were times when it would soar aloft on the wings of poetic eloquence. The sand glass at his side measured the length of the sermon, which was never less than an hour, and his custom was to read it from a closely written manuscript. "I use notes as much as any man when I take pains," he said, "and as little as any man when I am lazy or busy, and have not leisure to prepare."[129] His preaching and preparation were, he said, his recreation and the work of spare hours.[130] And he observed with a guileless candour that should disarm any critic that he often put in something which would pass clean over the heads of his hearers: and he did this that they might be kept humble and willing to learn.[131] But there were no trifles in his preaching, and no languor in his preparation. All his sermons were aimed at heart and conscience and were preached with a fire and passion which could not be ignored. That fire might burn at white heat, but it shone with a clear flame,[132] and it spread from soul to soul in Kidderminster like the Pentecostal flame in Jerusalem.

When in 1683 Baxter found the sermon on John 16:22 which he had meant to preach as his final message in St. Mary's twenty-two years before, he sent it to his old congregation as his special farewell. "With what shame and sorrow," he had thought to say, "do I now look back upon the cold and lifeless sermons

126. Frederick J. Powicke, *op. cit.*, Vol. I, pp. 11, 14.
127. J. M. Lloyd Thomas, *op. cit.*, p. 79.
128. *Ibid.*, p. xvi.
129. Frederick J. Powicke, *op. cit.*, Vol. I, p. 256.
130. J. M. Lloyd Thomas, *op. cit.*, p. 78.
131. *Ibid.*, p. 82.
132. Frederick J. Powicke, *op. cit.*, Vol. I, p. 51.

which I preached?"[133] But in his *Self-Analysis,* written in 1663
or 1664, he said that when he was younger, he had been more
fervent and affectionate in preaching than he could be later:
"but yet what I delivered was much more raw . . . and my dis-
courses had both less substance and less judgment than of late."[134]
It was not at Kidderminster alone that men felt the spell of his
great pulpit oratory: his passion for preaching gave him command of his hearers from his early days at Dudley to his latest
years in London. The poor nailers at Dudley not only filled the
roomy church within, but clung to the window leads without.[135]
The crowds which came to hear him in London were so large
at times that it was impossible for some to get within sound
of his voice at all. Men who did hear him felt that he spoke
as one who had come from the unseen presence of God and
they listened as men would listen for the voice of eternity. Dr.
William Bates spoke of the moving eloquence of his rich and
resonant voice and the "noble negligence" of his plain and powerful style.[136] Samuel Wesley as a young man heard him in
his old age, and he never forgot how his sermons seemed to
glow with what he described as "a strange fire and pathos."[137]
His words were like point-blank gun-shots fired at the breast of
a startled congregation: men had to be forced to listen when the
stake was nothing less than their souls. His great strength lay
in his power to convince of sin: there was an edge to his language
which cut through all pretence. But while he did not spare the
knife, it was held and controlled by the sure hand of love. He
might denounce sin in words of appalling energy, and its sores
were exposed in the light of absolute holiness: but it was all to
urge men to flee from the wrath to come and to lay hold on the
hope of heaven.[138] "If I were in your unconverted carnal state
and knew but what I know, believed but what I now believe,
methinks my life would be a foretaste of hell . . . . I should have

133. *Ibid.,* Vol. I, p. 319.
134. J. M. Lloyd Thomas, *op. cit.,* p. 104.
135. William Orme, *op. cit.,* Vol. I, p. 120.
136. John Howe, *Works,* Vol. VI, p. 303.
137. Luke Tyerman: *The Life and Times of the Rev. Samuel Wesley,* p. 386.
138. William Orme, *op. cit.,* Vol. I, p. 486.

small felicity in anything that I possessed, and little pleasure in any company . . . so long as I knew myself to be under the curse and wrath of God."[139] Thus his warnings were forged with the thunder of wrath and the terror of hell, but they were matched by the persuasive tenderness with which he strove to win men back for God. The flash and gleam of his skilful logic shone side by side with the fire and glow of his wistful appeal. There were both the penetrating vision of a prophet who knew the need of man and the elevating rapture of a mystic who knew the heart of God. Baxter was a man who toiled and preached with heaven and hell before his eyes, and men who heard him in the day of his power were constrained to make their choice in full view of the Great White Throne where all at last must stand.

It was through the friendly encouragement of the learned Ussher that he began to write as well as preach on the theme of personal conversion. "He was oft from first to last importuning me to write a Directory for the several ranks of professed Christians which might distinctly give each one their portion; beginning with the unconverted, and then proceeding to the babes in Christ, and then to the strong."[140] The Primate had perceived wherein his great strength lay, and he brought the question forward when they first met. Baxter was not convinced. "I reverenced the man, but disregarded these persuasions," he wrote, "supposing I could do nothing but what is done as well or better already."[141] He went back to Kidderminster "without the least purpose to answer his desire; but since his death his words often came into my mind."[142] Thus he resolved to act on Ussher's counsel and in 1657 he brought out his *Treatise of Conversion*. He had come to think that "vehement persuasions" were more suitable than mere directions for the unconverted,[143] and we can still hear the echo of his sermons in its pages. It was followed later in the same year by *A Call to the Unconverted*, which he described as "a wakening persuasive" for men who did not so much as purpose to

139. *Ibid.*, Vol. VII, p. cccxxxix.
140. *Ibid.*, Vol. VII, p. cccxxxi.
141. J. M. Lloyd Thomas, *op. cit.*, p. 96.
142. William Orme, *op. cit.*, Vol. VII, p. cccxxxi.
143. J. M. Lloyd Thomas, *op. cit.*, p. 96.

turn.[144] It pleased God to bless this book with success beyond his dreams. "In a little more than a year there were about twenty thousand of them printed by my own consent and about ten thousand since, besides many thousands by stolen impressions."[145] He knew of whole households which were converted through this small book, and he was so encouraged that he began to write a whole series of books of a similar character. The most famous after his *Call to the Unconverted* was a graphic appeal which came out in 1663 with the title *Now or Never*. There were many books on personal conversion before Baxter began to write; some indeed were famous. But no one else had yet produced a whole series of such stirring appeals to the ignorant and the ungodly. Baxter was the first to take up his pen for this purpose, and he brought it to a perfection which has seldom been rivalled. His books were like pioneer manuals in this field of literature; they struck out a new line for the recovery of souls. He wrote with an impassioned earnestness which men could not resist: sometimes grand and impressive in style, sometimes soft and persuasive in tone.[146] Severity in warning was balanced with solemnity in appeal, and the whole was designed to turn the will to God. On his deathbed he made humble reply to a friend who sought to cheer him with a remark on the good he had done by his writings: "I was but a pen in God's hands, and what praise is due to a pen?"[147] But no one on earth can number the souls now in heaven who make up his crown of joy and eternal rejoicing in the presence of God and of the Lamb.

But there was a liberal element in Baxter's theology which caused other repercussions in the pulpit and in his books. He had faced the struggle with doubt in his own mind and had laid its spectre as the result of a severe conflict; but there had been hazards, and he carried the scars of that struggle in more than one respect. Thus he was not in full accord with the Reformed doctrines on Original Sin and Justifying Faith, nor was

144. William Orme, *op. cit.*, Vol. VII, p. cccxxxi.
145. J. M. Lloyd Thomas, *op. cit.*, p. 96.
146. Josiah Pratt, *The Life and Remains of the Rev. Richard Cecil*, p. 151.
147. William Orme, *op. cit.*, Vol. I, p. 400.

he in absolute sympathy with the current teaching on the Reprobation of the Lost and the Perseverance of the Saints. All these aberrations from the orthodox tradition sprang from a mind which was concerned to think out the truth for itself and which clung to the thought that there is a wideness in God's mercy like the wideness of the sea. He could never repress the hope that the God of Love would somehow provide for the ultimate salvation of all. He would have liked to give up the doctrine of hell altogether, and he only preached on this theme with a sense of profound anguish. But since he found its dread reality in the revelation of the Scriptures, preach it he must. Just as the joy of God's presence is the heaven of saints, so the loss of God is the hell of the sinner.[148] "Hell," he said, "is a rational torment by conscience, according to the nature of the rational subject."[149] Men may taste "the pleasures of sin" for a season, but no one could mistake the deep pathos in his question: "Do you think there is one merry heart in hell?"[150] It is perhaps the most splendid witness to his utter sincerity that he defied his own feelings and preached on the terrors of hell with such forceful purpose: but hell was not half so real to him as heaven, nor his fear of hell so deep as his love for God.[151] It has been said that the predominant cast of his faith was so intellectual that it made him hard-grained towards those with whom he did not agree,[152] and it is true that he engaged in the controversies of the time with a zeal which could scarcely wait to discern what was merely verbal mistake from what was a fundamental issue.[153] He took pleasure in such dialectics as an exercise of the intellect and a means of enlightenment: but he would not shut the door of heaven against those who could not tread in his steps. His variations from orthodoxy all take their bent from his sympathetic yearning for our wayward humanity, and the gleam of deep personal reverence shone through all the dangerous arguments which he

---

148. *Ibid.*, Vol. XXII, pp. 415-425.
149. *Ibid.*, p. 339.
150. *Ibid.*, p. 412.
151. Frederick J. Powicke, Vol. I, p. 279; cf. *Works*, Vol. XIV, p. 284.
152. Frederick J. Powicke, Vol. I, p. 242.
153. J. M. Lloyd Thomas, *op. cit.*, p. 105.

sometimes employed. Criticisms of his theology do not weigh more than a feather when thrown into the scale with his transparent devotion, and he preserved a more elevated tone of devotional thought in the clash of his controversies than was often the case with men who walked in more favored retreats.

Baxter's comment on the tepid spirit of Sir Ralph Clare, the knight who owned Caldwell Hall at Kidderminster, led him to a further remark: "Indeed we had two other persons of quality that came from other places to live there . . . who did much good, Colonel John Bridges and at last Mrs. Hanmer."[154] Bridges was a Puritan gentleman who had bought the patronage of Kidderminster and who lived in the town when not away with the army. He was a close friend of Thomas Foley, to whom he sold the patronage of St. Mary's, and their unfailing devotion to the work of Baxter was a source of strength and comfort to him. "You dwell together," he wrote, "in my estimation and affection."[155] Mrs. Hanmer's maiden name was Mary Hill, and she had married Francis Charlton of Apley Castle in 1630. He was the head of an old and honored House in Shropshire, the Sheriff in 1626, "a grave and sober worthy man."[156] We know that the Charltons were a godly couple, for their daughter was to confess it as a great mercy that God had made her the child of godly parents and many prayers.[157] Francis Charlton did not marry until "he was aged and gray and so died while his children were very young."[158] Mary was born in 1631, Margaret in 1636, and Francis in 1639, and their father died in 1642. Apley Castle was stormed by the Roundheads in the year of his death, and this induced his widow to marry Thomas Hanmer for the protection of her family. He was strong for the King and in 1643 Apley Castle was garrisoned by Royalists. But her only living brother-in-law, Robert Charlton, was a Roundhead, and in 1644 the castle was stormed and sacked at his instigation. Mrs. Hanmer and the children were all "threatened and stripped of their clothing" while the dead

154. *Ibid.*, p. 83.
155. Frederick J. Powicke, *op. cit.*, Vol. I, p. 158.
156. J. T. Wilkinson, *op. cit.*, p. 67.
157. *Ibid.*, p. 76.
158. *Ibid.*, p. 67.

lay before their eyes;[159] it left an impression on the child Margaret which was never effaced. Robert Charlton carried off the children, but their mother contrived to rescue and remove them to Essex until the wars came to an end. She then returned to the Castle and managed the estate until her son was old enough to take it into his own hands. She was then once more a widow, and she planned to rent a house and live in Kidderminster. Baxter had not met her before, and he thought that she ought not to leave her son at Apley Castle. But she had set her heart on this idea and in January, 1657 she returned and took a house without his knowledge:[160] and there she lived "as a blessing amongst the honest poor weavers of Kidderminster, strangers to her, whose company for their piety she chose before all the vanities of the world."[161] Meanwhile her son Francis had settled at Apley Castle and her daughter Mary was married at Oxford. Margaret had been living with her married sister but now joined her mother as the one "who deserved her dearest love."[162] But this gifted girl, of gentle birth and fortune, tender and fragile in nature, found the township dull and drab after the gay and careless life of Oxford. She felt estranged from the people, who were as strict as they were poor, and she liked to dress in costly clothing and amuse herself with romantic literature. "She thought that she was not what she should be, but something better (she knew not what) must be attained . . . But in a little time she heard and understood what those better things were which she had thought must be attained."[163]

Thus the need for personal conversion, as she now heard Baxter preach it, was pressed upon her heart as the seal on the wax. All the spiritual anxieties of a virgin conscience were brought to life, and her rebel mood passed away beneath the spell of those unseen realities which now dawned on her soul. This was perhaps a year, perhaps much less, before April, 1660.[164] But the dawn of saving

159. *Ibid.*, pp. 68, 106.
160. Frederick J. Powicke, *op. cit.*, Vol. I, pp. 159; 216.
161. J. T. Wilkinson, *op. cit.*, p. 69.
162. *Ibid.*, p. 68.
163. *Ibid.*, p. 70.
164. *Ibid.*, p. 86.

faith in her heart was soon followed by a grave and sudden illness from which there seemed small hope of her recovery. Godly neighbors, "laymen that were humble praying persons," began to pray for her.[165] Baxter had not joined them on the various occasions when they had met before, but he was "with them at prayer for this woman."[166] Margaret herself afterwards said that December 30, 1659 was her worst day: "I did not then think to be alive this day: I ought not to forget it."[167] Baxter was at her side in the role of pastor and physician and the fourth day was kept as a fast day to pray for her recovery: "And God heard us and speedily delivered her."[168] April 10, 1660 was appointed for thanksgiving, and St. Mary's Church was filled with the song of praise. Baxter had asked what she would have them give thanks for, and she prepared a short paper which was handed to him in the morning as they began. It was in this paper that she declared: "He hath made me desirous this day to give up myself and all that I have to Him, taking Him only for my God and my chief felicity."[169] But she also wrote out that day the words of a personal covenant with God as one who had resolved "to get and keep a fresh sense of His mercy on (her) soul."[107] "Why should my heart be fixed where my home is not?" So it moves to an end; "heaven is my home: God in Christ is all my happiness: and where my treasure is, there my heart should be. . . . Away then O my carnal heart! Retire to God, the only satisfying Object. There mayest thou love without all danger of excess. Let thy love to God be fixed and transcendent. Amen."[171] Baxter was to transpose some of her words into verse and to publish it in his *Poetical Fragments* after her death. This poem on "The Covenant and Confidence of Faith" is so spontaneous in feeling and so tender in expression that it has now become widely known as the hymn whose first lines are: "Lord,

165. *Ibid.*, p. 74.
166. *Ibid.*, p. 74.
167. *Ibid.*, p. 91.
168. *Ibid.*, p. 74.
169. *Ibid.*, pp. 76-77.
170. *Ibid.*, p. 77.
171. *Ibid.*, p. 80.

it belongs not to my care whether I die or live."[172] But there was still another document, "yet more of that day's work," which came to light only after her death,[173] and thought may still gather round that girlish figure writing out her inmost experience in the stillness of night. "And let me strive to keep such a moderate sense of sorrow of my soul as occasion requireth. I have now cause of sorrow for parting with my dear friend, my father, my pastor. He is by Providence called away and going a long journey: what the Lord will do with him I can not foresee; it may be He is preparing some great mercy for us and for His praise."[174] One long passage in this paper is so like a passage in *The Saints' Rest* that it suggests that she must have known it by heart. Baxter transcribes the last sentence in the *Breviate:* "April 10 on Thursday night at twelve of the clock: a day and night never to be forgotten by the least of all God's mercies, yea, less than the least, Thy unworthy, unthankful, hard-hearted creature, M. Charlton." [175]

On April 12, 1660, Baxter left Kidderminster for London, partly for consultation with the Earl of Lauderdale and partly "for other reasons."[176] The Earl knew that his was the most influential voice on behalf of the moderate Puritans and he hoped to win him over to the plan for the King's recall. Baxter was torn between loyalty to the Throne and misgiving for the future; he was in favour of the King's return, but not without anxiety as to the King himself. He was clear-eyed and quite deliberate in his support for the Restoration, though he plainly foresaw what it would mean: "We all look to be silenced, and some or many of us imprisoned or banished; but yet we will do our parts to restore the King, because no foreseen consequence must hinder us from our duty."[177] On April 30, he preached before members of the House of Commons in St. Margaret's Westminster and on May 10, before the Lord Mayor in St. Paul's Cathedral. Those

172. *Ibid.,* pp. 177, 178.
173. *Ibid.,* p. 80.
174. *Ibid.,* p. 84.
175. *Ibid.,* p. 86.
176. J. M. Lloyd Thomas, *op. cit.,* p. 142.
177. *Ibid.,* Note p. 288; see p. 128.

who had hitherto been known as Puritans now began to find themselves described as Presbyterians, unless they had joined the Independents, Anabaptists, or some other sect which was held in greater odium.[178] But Baxter still meant to do all that could be done to save the Church from ruin and his ceaseless meditation was as to how he could secure peace and concord within the fold. On May 29, Charles rode into London, and he told the Puritan ministers who gave him a richly adorned Bible that it would be "the rule of his actions."[179] He did not as yet know how far he could depend on the Commons, and this made it imperative for him to court men like Baxter. The first step was to nominate ten Chaplains-in-Ordinary, among whom were Baxter, Manton, Bates and Reynolds. Baxter was assured by Lord Broghill and the Earl of Manchester that this was the wish of the King, and on June 25, he took the oath as a Chaplain. The next development was a meeting in the rooms of the Lord Chamberlain when the King — with the Lord Chancellor and two or three others — conferred with the ten new Chaplains. Baxter was bold enough to tell the King that he must not undo the good which Cromwell and others had done, but must rather outgo them in doing good.[180] Charles then began to play on the foibles of a tremendous earnestness by asking them to draw up their plans for Church Reform. They met daily for the next two or three weeks at Sion College, and drew up a document with their proposals which they laid before the King in July. They were put off at the time with fair words, but they soon knew that their efforts had received an unqualified repulse from the Bishops. Then on July 22, Baxter preached his only sermon before Charles at Whitehall, and it was printed by the King's command.[181] They were then told that the King would put all that he thought proper to grant them in the form of a Declaration, and a copy of the proposed wording was placed in their hands on September 4. They saw

178. *Ibid.*, p. 154.
179. *Ibid.*, p. 144.
180. *Ibid.*, p. 147.
181. The subject was *The Life of Faith*. See J. M. Lloyd Thomas, *op. cit.*, p. 99.

at once that it would not procure concord unless much that was in it were altered, and a Petition drawn up by Baxter was laid before the King. At length, on October 22, the King's Declaration was read at a meeting of Dukes and Earls, Deans and Bishops, as well as the ten new Chaplains. Then a plea for toleration from Independents and Anabaptists was read, a plea which Charles proposed to meet by a fresh clause which would include Papists as well. They were asked to declare their minds but there was a deadly silence. At last Baxter broke the impasse. "For our parts," he said, "we desired not favour to ourselves alone, and rigorous severity we desired against none. As we humbly thanked His Majesty for his indulgence to ourselves, so we distinguish the tolerable parties from the intolerable. For the former, we humbly crave just lenity and favour; but for the latter . . . we cannot make their toleration our request."[182]

Baxter left the Lord Chancellor's house in a dejected frame of mind, for he was convinced that all hope of concord was at an end: "I was resolved to meddle no more in the business, but patiently suffer with other Dissenters."[183] But a few days later he heard newsboys selling copies of the Declaration in the streets and he found that such alterations had been made in the text that he could now gladly accept: "I wondered at it how it came to pass but was exceeding glad of it, as perceiving that now the terms were . . . such as any sober honest ministers might submit to."[184] The King's Declaration promised that the Prayer Book would be revised and that some new forms would be drawn up to provide a degree of variety: "Till this were done, we were uncertain of the issue of all our treaty: but if that were done, and all settled by law, our divisions were at an end."[185] Baxter pressed the point with the Lord Chancellor whenever he could and the result was that in March, 1661, a Commission was authorised under the Broad Seal to deal with the whole matter. Therefore twelve Bishops and twelve Divines met on April 8, at the Savoy Palace, but the Bishops did not even try to conceal their

182. *Ibid.*, p. 153.
183. *Ibid.*, p. 154.
184. *Ibid.*, pp. 154, 155.
185. *Ibid.*, p. 162.

cold dislike for the Divines with whom they were to treat. Baxter's colleagues were irked by haughty demands and callous tactics, and they would have withdrawn at once had not Baxter implored them to go on. The meeting was adjourned so that they could comply with the Bishops' demand to reduce to writing their "exceptions" and "additions" to the Prayer Book. Baxter left his brethren to draw up the list of "exceptions" while he alone prepared the new "additions." "I departed from them," he wrote, "and came among them no more till I had finished my task, which was a fortnight's time."[186] This meant that he had worked through the Prayer Book and had composed new forms of prayer, as he thought were desirable. He still had to wait a fortnight before the others were ready; then he won their support for his suggested liturgy.

On May 4, the Bishops and Divines held their second meeting and the Puritan Exceptions were laid on the table. Baxter's Reformation of the Liturgy was brought forward at a later meeting, but the Bishops would not allow any kind of discussion. Baxter at length read a Petition for Peace which his colleagues had asked him to prepare and which proves how firmly he had grasped the issues at stake. But the Bishops behaved as if they were impervious to the appeal of strong moral sincerity, and their conduct put an end to all hope of a peaceable conference. The commission was limited by its terms to four months and the time was wasted until only ten days remained. It was arranged that these ten days should be employed in a formal debate by three members of each party, and this in turn reduced itself to an academic clash between Gunning and Baxter in the very spirit of the mediaeval schoolmen. It was at length agreed late on the last evening that the meetings should be discontinued and that they should only furnish the King with a report in terms of vague good-will. Baxter had been foremost in labour and learning, tireless in counsel and debate, and no man could have toiled with more eager desire to reach a firm understanding. "The reason why I spake so much," he wrote, "was because it was the desire of my brethren and I was loth

186. *Ibid.*, p. 163.

to expose them to the hatred of the Bishops . . . . And I thought it a cause that I could comfortably suffer for, and should as willingly be a martyr for charity as for faith."[187] But it was all to no avail. The twelve Divines met once more by themselves and prepared a statement to lay before the King. Baxter was its author and had it in his hand when they approached the Lord Chancellor. But he said that it would be more acceptable if it were left in the hands of Manton, Bates and Reynolds. Baxter would have withdrawn, but he was called back from the stairs and went in with them to the King. He kept in the background and only spoke briefly when called on by the King. These were the last words which he was ever to speak at Court; "and this was the end of these affairs."[188]

Baxter had become a preacher at large during his first year in London, for the Restoration had changed the whole course of his life. He preached up and down the city at the invitation of friends, but his heart was still in Kidderminster. He had never meant to desert his flock at St. Mary's, and he knew that they longed for his return. He would hear how the old Vicar — like so many others — had been restored to his living; he would also hear how Sir Ralph Clare had been at work to restore the old way of worship. But he was still tethered to his post in London and could only hope that nothing would prevent his return. He was sounded out in September with an offer of the See of Hereford, but he refused to think of it because the first draft of the King's Declaration retained "the old Diocesan frame" of Church Government.[889] But when the King's Declaration came out, Baxter was with the Lord Chancellor, who at once made him the direct offer of a Bishopric. The text of the Declaration had removed his scruples, but he wanted time to reply. The Lord Chancellor soon grew impatient and asked for his answer when he met him two days later: "He asked me of my resolution," wrote Baxter, "and put me to it so suddenly that I was forced to delay no longer, but told him that I could not accept it for several reasons."[190]

187. *Ibid.*, p. 170.
188. *Ibid.*, p. 170.
189. *Ibid.*, p. 155.
190. *Ibid.*, p. 157.

He gave his reasons in a fine letter which was written on November 1, 1660. He knew that they would not offend, and this encouraged him to ask a favour which he would have valued far more than a Bishopric. "Instead of it," he wrote, "I presumed to crave his favour to restore me to preach to my people at Kidderminster again."[191] He hoped that the Vicar might be offered some more suitable appointment so that his name might be nominated for the vacant living: but he would be content to preach as his curate if he might not take his place as Vicar. The Lord Chancellor was not unwilling, but he let it drag on for months. The fact was that Sir Ralph Clare knew that he could rule the town as he liked if Baxter were far enough away: and he prevailed on Bishop Morley of Worcester who in turn prevailed on the Lord Chancellor to do nothing. At length in July or August of 1661, Baxter took the road for Kidderminster to see if he could come to terms with the Vicar. He was allowed to preach "twice or thrice" in his old pulpit, but that was all.[192] He then offered to serve as a curate, or to preach for nothing, but the Vicar would not consent, would not even allow him to preach a farewell sermon. Baxter knew that this change of front was due to Sir Ralph Clare and the Bishop, and he resolved to lay his case before them in person. He saw Bishop Morley, who had before promised to grant him a license; but he now refused to grant him permission to preach in his diocese at all.[193] He then saw Sir Ralph Clare, perhaps in the Bishop's chamber, but the conversation came to an end with an ultimatum: "Sir Ralph Clare did freely tell me that if I would conform to the Orders and Ceremonies of the Church and preach Conformity to the people, . . . there was no man in England so fit to be there: for no man could more effectually do it; but if I would not, there was no man so unfit for the place; for no man could more hinder it."[194] There could only be one reply to that ultimatum: it left him no alternative but to withdraw. His last sermon in his old church was on the text: "Father, forgive them, for they know not what they do"

191. *Ibid.*, p. 159.
192. *Ibid.*, p. 171.
193. *Ibid.*, p. 172.
194. Frederick J. Powicke, *op. cit.*, Vol. I, p. 185.

(Luke 23:34). But the farewell sermon which he had hoped to preach in St. Mary's was not allowed, and he gave his final address at a private meeting in the house of a friend. This took place on the eve of his return to London in November, 1661; henceforth they were to hear his voice no more.[195] It cost him far more to leave his flock at Kidderminster than it had done when he refused the Diocese of Hereford; but it was years before he could even write to them lest it should involve them in conflict with the authorities.[196]

Baxter was in London again before mid-November, and he took up his old lodgings to the west of Aldersgate Street. He had obtained a license from the Bishop of London to preach at large in his diocese, and this he had already done for more than a year.[197] It was perhaps in May or June of 1661 that he began to preach twice a week at Milk Street: this meant that he gave a week-day lecture for which he was allowed forty pounds per annum.[198] There was now no reason why he should not also preach at a fixed place on Sundays, and he joined William Bates at St. Dunstan's, Fleet Street, where he preached once a week.[199] But an accident brought his ministry in this church to an end, and he preached out the rest of the quarter in St. Bride's Church at the other end of Fleet Street.[200] In the early months of 1662 he was preaching once each Sunday to a crowded church at Blackfriars and twice during the week to the Milk Street congregation. But the troubles of the Puritan ministers were now on the increase, and none of them could see very far into the future. "We were called all by the name of Presbyterians, the odious name," he wrote, "though we never put up one petition for Presbytery."[201] Baxter was in no sense Presbyterian, still less Congregational, in his views of the Church. And he never withdrew from the Communion or the Liturgy of the Church of England. But he

195. *Ibid.,* Vol. I, pp. 206, 207, 316.
196. *Ibid.,* Vol. I, p. 315.
197. J. M. Lloyd Thomas, *op. cit.,* p. 159.
198. *Ibid.,* p. 160.
199. *Ibid.,* p. 159.
200. *Ibid.,* p. 160.
201. *Ibid.,* p. 171.

believed in a much less complex form of Episcopal Church Government than the ruling diocesan system, and he had hoped against
hope that the King's Declaration would lead to a modified arrangement. Thus he hoped, but he feared as well; and his fears were
better grounded than all his hopes. The King's Declaration brought
forth no fruit: it just withered and died. Instead, on May 19,
1662, the Act of Uniformity was passed and three months were
allowed for men to take the oath by which they would conform.
August 24, St. Bartholomew's Day, was fixed as the zero hour
when all who would not conform would be compelled to leave
the Church. Baxter had no doubt at all as to the course of duty.
On May 25, less than a week after the Act was passed, he preached
what he believed would be his last public sermon unless God were
to cause "an undeserved resurrection."[202] He meant to let authority
know at once that he would obey in all that was lawful; and he
had a greater reason as well. "I would let all ministers in England
understand in time whether I intended to conform or not; for
had I stayed to the last day, some would have conformed the
sooner upon a supposition that I intended it."[203] Baxter was in
fact the first to dissent, and his dissent was a signal for the whole
land. Three months passed by, and then it was August 24. On
"this fatal day" when the Black Act came into operation, near
"two thousand ministers were silenced and cast out."[204] Those who
would not conform lost their livings, and "those that would not
cease preaching were thrust into prisons."[205] The Church had
no men more honourable as scholars or preachers than men such
as Howe and Owen, Bates and Manton, and a host of others who
were expelled; but the pre-eminence in that band of Non-Conformists fell to Richard Baxter. He could never hide the feeling
that he and his brethren had been driven out of the Church by
an Act of terrible perfidy. He could only say of that dark hour
of separation: "I lay in tears, in deepest sorrow."[206]

Meanwhile there were other developments in the life of Baxter

202. *Ibid.*, p. 161.
203. *Ibid.*, p. 175.
204. *Ibid.*
205. *Ibid.*, p. 176.
206. Frederick J. Powicke, *op. cit.*, Vol. II, p. 15.

which could not be concealed. It had been on April 10, 1660, that he had held a day of Thanksgiving for the recovery of Margaret Charlton. It was perhaps the last duty to which he had addressed himself in his Church at Kidderminster, for on April 12 he had left for London. He had ample reason to know that her heart had been touched with the sacred flame of devotion to God; he was not as yet to know that it had also begun to glow with the kindred fire of human affection. But she had to school her feelings and curb her dreams, for how could he requite her love? Her covenant had recognised the truth, although it closed with "a sense of triumph" for God.[207] It was composed in the spirit of one who had fixed her desire on things above, for in heaven there is neither marrying nor giving in marriage. But the very picture of the rose as the flower of love in the garden of the spirit, is the language of a lover's intensity.[208] But that private paper written in the stillness of night was still more frank in its revelation of the secrets of her inmost being. She would "be in earnest" for all her friends; but her thoughts moved on at once to Richard Baxter.[209] She seems to have known that he was about to leave Kidderminster, and the thought of separation was hard to bear. But it was not merely that she was in love with Baxter, and that there seemed no hope of an answering affection: she was also conscious that such "creature love" for Baxter was a challenge to the supremacy of her love and obedience to God.[210] After her death, Baxter found among her papers some "resolutions" which must have been written on or about April 10. The last resolution is frank enough: "I resolve, if Providence concur, to go to London as soon as I can after the Day of Thanksgiving, for the reasons mentioned in another place."[211] Baxter could not find those reasons, but the fragment which he went on to quote hints that it was because of the love which she had for him. "I should . . . expect my greatest comfort from Him, and not from men and means themselves: this is no more than what I thought I had

207. J. T. Wilkinson, *op. cit.*, p. 33.
208. *Ibid.*, p. 33.
209. *Ibid.*, p. 33.
210. *Ibid.*, p. 34.
211. *Ibid.*, p. 93.

known long ago, but I never knew it indeed until now."[212] She could not bear to be severed from him, but the mail-coach kept her in touch with him. His letters were treasured; his counsels were transcribed. Did he detect her love for "the creature" in her "few sad complaints"?[213] It would seem so, and she was to copy his words: "How hard it is to keep our hearts in going too far even in honest affections towards the creature while we are so backward to love God who should have all the heart and soul and might."[214] He told her that "creature love" would only cool love for God; and such words could hardly refer to love for her mother.[215] He longed for her nearness to Christ as the secret of all: "Keep your heart as near as possible to the heart of Christ, and live as in His arms."[216] Perhaps she had told him of her resolution to go up to London, and he wrote a pointed rebuke: "It is not lawful to speak an idle word . . much less to go an idle journey . . . Do your duty with a quiet mind, and follow God in your removes."[217] She ended the counsels which she had thus transcribed with a soliloquy in her own words: "The best creature-affections have a mixture of some creature-imperfections and therefore need some gall to wean us from the faulty part. God must be known to be God . . . and therefore the best creature to be but a creature! O miserable world (how long must I continue in it, and why is this wretched heart so loath to leave it?) where we can have no fire without smoke, and our dearest friends must be our greatest grief, and when we begin in hope and love and joy, before we are aware, we fall into an answerable measure of distress. Learn by experience when any condition is inordinately or excessively sweet to thee, to say, From hence must be my sorrow. (O how true!)"[218]

Baxter had been surprised to find that Margaret Charlton was as much in love with him as she was with the hope of heaven, and he had done all he could to check such earthly desires. He

212. *Ibid.*
213. *Ibid.*, p. 97.
214. *Ibid.*, p. 98.
215. *Ibid.*, p. 99.
216. *Ibid.*
217. *Ibid.*, pp. 104. 105.
218. *Ibid.*, p. 105.

had written with a studied reserve as if his own heart were dead to human passion, yet he had failed to quench the flame of her longing for him. It was not long before he was still more dismayed to find that his own heart was not quite so cold as he had fondly supposed, and he strove the more to quash the warmer feelings which were kindling within. The real origin of his love for Margaret has not been traced, but the course of events is clear. Mrs. Hanmer was an ardent friend of Baxter and she must have known the true state of her daughter's feelings. Perhaps it was in the summer months of 1660 that she escorted Margaret up to London and found lodgings for them both in Sweeting Alley. They would follow Baxter with a loving concern through those days of trial and growing hostility. They were now his only direct link with the old days at Kidderminster, and he was sure to feel the charm of their rich and vivid sympathy. They would be two of his hearers when he preached at Milk Street or St. Dunstan's; he would find a welcome at their home in Sweeting Alley when he called as friend or pastor. Then in January, 1661, Mrs. Hanmer died and Margaret found herself alone: who but Baxter would have sought to comfort her in sorrow? Baxter had thought to live single and die alone, but this must have been one of "the strange occurrences" which was to lead to his marriage.[219] It was noticed that there was more than a pastoral tenderness between the two; but their disparity in age and rank as well as his well-known views in favour of a celibate ministry made it all a "matter of much public talk and wonder."[220] Thus their names were linked in rumour and they were said to be married almost a year before it came to pass: "Insomuch," wrote Baxter, "that the Lord Chancellor told me he heard I was married, and wondered at it when I told him it was not true."[221] But the gossip was not only widespread; it was unkind, and such as he never heard charged against any man but himself: "And it everywhere rung about, partly as a wonder and partly as a crime . . . And I think the King's marriage was scarce more talked of than mine."[222] Bax-

219. *Ibid.*, p. 109.
220. *Ibid.*
221. J. M. Lloyd Thomas, *op. cit.*, p. 174.
222. *Ibid.*

ter's words make it clear that the thought of marriage was in his own mind as well as in the minds of other people during 1661, but there were checks "and long delays" before it came about.[223] But they were drawn to each other in the bonds of a love in which souls are wed for ever, and there was no escape from the final union of two whose hearts were so tenderly intertwined. In August, 1662, the Act of Uniformity was passed and he was cut off from the old tasks which had been enough to take up all his time and labour. "At last, on September 10th 1662," when he was forty-six and she was six and twenty, they were married in the Church of Bennett-Fink near the Royal Exchange.[224] "At last," he wrote, as though it might have been before; and so indeed it might. But he did not marry until he found himself driven out and silenced, with no flock and no cure of souls.[225]

Baxter was the Origen of his century in sheer literary output; it would be hard to find a more voluminous author in the list of English theologians. The flow of books never came to an end because he had reserve stores of thought and knowledge which were as yet untouched. His own remark at the close of his life was made with a naive simplicity: "I have written about one hundred and twenty-eight books, but I would commend to the poor but a few."[226] The list of his printed works is known to number at least one hundred and sixty-eight books, and they could not have been comprised in a uniform edition of less than sixty octavo volumes with a total of some thirty-five thousand closely printed pages. There were "great folios, thick quartos, crammed duodecimos, pamphlets, tractates, sheets, half-sheets and broadsides."[227] Henry Rogers points out that in view of the vast mass of letters among the Baxter Manuscripts, many of them as long as a modern pamphlet, and most of them now bound up in six large folio volumes, one would think that letter writing must have been his major occupation.[228] Not more than a fragment of his correspondence can have survived, but he wrote

223. J. T. Wilkinson, *op. cit.*, p. 109.
224. *Ibid.*
225. *Ibid.*, p. 156.
226. *Poor Husbandman's Advocate*, p. 217.
227. *Dictionary of National Biography*, "Richard Baxter."
228. Henry Rogers, *Life of John Howe*, pp. 57, 58.

each letter with as much care as if it had been a sermon: indeed they were often a long statement on some controverted question, and not seldom a full treatment of some spiritual difficulty.[229] There were as well prefatory commendations which he furnished at the request of friends, and long papers which he prepared to state the case for the moderate Puritans as new crises arose. That he could still manage in the midst of so much toil to produce his own eight score and eight publications was a feat of solid labour which was without equal in that prolific period. His books were a true cross-section of the age to which they belonged, and their pages still have the glint of a world in conflict. He was "all his life long a sort of knight-errant" in the service of Truth,[230] and the coat-of-mail in which he rode to battle made him a most valiant chevalier on the field of controversy. He loved to fling down his challenge to the reckless spokesmen of each new and strident error; then, not without a due sense of the strength at his command, he would calmly wait their attack. But few who took up the gauntlet could boast of much success: they were pigmies, trying to break the lance of a man of giant strength. Yet he was to confess when he looked back on his early disputes: "I knew not how hardly men's minds are changed from their former apprehensions, be the evidence never so plain. And I have perceived that nothing so much hindereth the reception of the truth as urging it on men with too harsh importunity and falling too heavily on their errors."[231] But he seldom fought a battle in which he failed to show "a streak of blood" drawn from the heart,[232] for it was the salvation of men rather than the triumph of the intellect which he desired. He once said that it was illness which moved him to write his first book,[233] but from that time forward he looked upon writing as his special duty. Preaching and its preparation were the work of spare hours: "For my writings were my chiefest daily labour, which yet went the more slowly on that I never one hour had an amanuensis to dictate

229. Frederick J. Powicke, *op. cit.*, Vol. I, p. 140.
230. Henry Rogers, *op. cit.*, pp. 274, 275.
231. J. M. Lloyd Thomas, *op. cit.*, p. 106.
232. James Stalker, *op. cit.*, p. 233.
233. J. M. Lloyd Thomas, *op. cit.*, p. 94.

to."[234] But his wasting infirmities had filled him with such a jealous regard for the value of time that the amount of work which he achieved was like the work of a dozen lesser craftsmen; he was driven out in 1662 to pass the rest of life in trial, in pain, in hiding, in prison, yet in labours which were never to flag while strength endured.

Baxter's great output was due in part to the consuming eagerness with which he wrote; and this in turn meant that he paid little regard to the art of writing. "When I peruse the writings which I wrote in my younger years," he once remarked, "I can find the footsteps of my unfurnished mind."[235] There were others who found in them the signs of a hurried and reckless style, but this gave him little concern. His wife thought that he would have done better to have written fewer books, and to have written those few better: he thought that the literary imperfection of two was a lesser evil than the possible omission of one.[236] Archbishop Tillotson was to allude to the same fact in his letter to Matthew Sylvester in 1692: "I have oft pressed him to let his books lie by him some time, and to review them again and again; but could never prevail with him who said, they must come forth so or not at all."[237] He might regret the lack of an amanuensis, but he used shorthand and wrote with astonishing rapidity.[238] *The Saints' Rest* was written in a few months while he was ill; *The Reformed Pastor* in a few weeks at the height of his work; his *Aphorisms on Justification* apparently in a few days while he was still engaged on *The Saints' Rest*.[239] He did at length admit that in his own judgment, fewer well studied and polished had been better: "but," he went on to add, "the reader who can safely censure the books is not fit to censure the author unless he had been . . . acquainted with all the occasions and circumstances."[240] He could not pause to choose a word or trim

234. *Ibid.*, p. 78.
235. *Ibid.*, p. 104.
236. J. T. Wilkinson, *op. cit.*, p. 131.
237. Frederick J. Powicke, *op. cit.*, Vol. II, p. 293.
238. *Ibid.*, Vol. I, p. 133.
239. J. M. Lloyd Thomas, *op. cit.*, Note p. 290.
240. *Ibid.*, p. 102.

a phrase, and he had no time to write a sheet twice over or to blot a page once written. He was driven by the spur of necessity, and "was fain to let it go as it was first conceived."[241] His mind outpaced his pen, strive as he might to keep them both abreast; and when thought drove him on too fast, it was always his pen that first began to flag. But though at times his style might seem hurried and careless in method, it was always earnest and forceful in spirit; and though he did not mind about literary grace and finish, his works abound in prose that is clear and spontaneous. He could always use homely and lucid language when he wrote to inform; he never failed in solemn and telling diction when he wrote to exhort. He was tender or full of awe at will, always suiting words to his thoughts, always matching thoughts with his heart. When he gave rein to his feelings, there were spells of moving beauty and picturesque utterance; when he found vent for his longings, there were moods of melting pathos and unconscious majesty. He wrote with an unsought charm and distinction which "survives in language that gains in idiomatic freshness by touches of delicious archaism."[242] Many of his themes are now dead, but his work cannot die; the qualities of permanence are as real in Baxter as they are in pure gold.[243] Those large volumes are the work of a man who could never write fast enough for the ideas which were ever welling up in his mind. That man in his finest moments wrote with a verve that ranks with the purest prose in English theology. His works survive because they are rich in thoughts and prose of timeless truth and beauty.[244]

The reign of Charles was one of great storm and stress for Baxter; he was never left long in peace. After his marriage in September, 1662, he lived for some months at Moorfields, but he knew that he was closely watched lest he should preach in private.[245] He went to a parish church on Sundays and heard men like Wilkins and Tillotson: "And as oft else as I had fit opportunity, I privately

241. *Ibid.*
242. *Ibid.*, p. xv.
243. Frederick J. Powicke, *op. cit.*, Vol. II, p. 61.
244. *Ibid.*, Vol. II, p. 254.
245. J. M. Lloyd Thomas, *op. cit.*, p. 187.

preached and prayed myself, either with Independents or Presbyterians that desired me."[246] But he felt that London agreed neither with health nor with study and in July, 1663, he moved to the country air of Acton. The Plague drove him away to Hampden, Bucks, in September, 1665, and he returned in March, 1666, to find the church grounds at Acton "like a ploughed field with graves."[247] His house faced the door of the church and he was there every Sunday for the morning service: the rest of the day he would spend at home with a few poor neighbours who met beneath his roof.[248] While the Conventicle Act of July, 1664, remained in force, he preached only in his household and there were few who came from the town to hear him; but when the Act expired at the end of October, 1668, "there came so many that I wanted room, and when once they had come and heard, they afterward came constantly."[249] He would take his hearers with him to church for the service, and the service ended, they would follow him home to hear him preach again. "It pleased the doctor and parson that I came to church and brought others with me; but he was not able to bear the sight of peoples crowding into my house though they heard him also."[250] But in due course complaints were laid before the King and a warrant was signed for his arrest. He was apprehended in June, 1669, and was asked to swear the Oxford Oath of 1666. This he refused to do, and was sentenced without bail to six months' imprisonment in Clerkenwell. This was no worse than an easy restraint except that he suffered from the extreme heat of summer and that he could not sleep for noise at night. But his wife brought her best bed with her to prison, where they had a large room and were allowed to walk in the garden. "And my wife," he wrote, "was never so cheerful a companion to me as in prison."[251] "I think she scarce ever had a pleasanter time in her life than while she was with me there."[252] They kept house in prison

246. *Ibid.*, p. 190.
247. *Ibid.*, p. 198.
248. *Ibid.*, p. 190.
249. *Ibid.*, p. 204.
250. *Ibid.*, pp. 204, 205.
251. *Ibid.*, p. 207.
252. J. T. Wilkinson, *op. cit.*, p. 113.

with full as much content as if they were at home, and he had
the sight of more friends in a day than he had in six months at
home.[253] He was released in a few weeks because of an error in
the warrant, but the Five Mile Act now drove him away from his
home at Acton. Thus in October, 1669, he withdrew to Totteridge,
where he spent the winter in a farmer's lodgings which were cold
and smoky. At last he and his wife were able to rent a house where
they lodged with more health and ease than he had thought possible.[254] It was here that, in the name of the King, the Earl of Lauderdale offered him the choice of a church or a college or a Bishopric north of the Tweed: but he held on his way, heedless of threats
and bribes alike.[255] Six months after the King's Declaration of Indulgence, in March, 1672, Baxter applied for a preaching license
on condition that he might have it without the title of Presbyterian
or Independent or any other party, but only as a Non-Conformist,
and on November 19 he preached for the first time after ten years'
silence in a lawful public assembly.[256]

In February, 1673, the Baxters left Totteridge for a house in
Southampton Square in London. The King's Declaration was then
declared to have no force in law, but he began to preach in rooms
which were hired by his wife in the market house at St. James. A
large congregation of young men made him feel that all his pains
were easy to bear.[257] Baxter tried to protect the meeting from interference by a notice which was meant to show that it was not a
conventicle: "We meet not under colour or pretence of any religious
exercise in other manner than according to the Liturgy and practice
of the Church of England."[258] The lease was not renewed when it
expired in the latter part of 1674, but he was still preaching at New
Street on Thursdays and sometimes in private houses. But in February, 1675, Non-Conformists lost their license to preach, and he

253. J. M. Lloyd Thomas, *op. cit.*, pp. 207, 208.
254. *Ibid.*, p. 222.
255. *Ibid.*, p. 214.
256. *Ibid.*, p. 221.
257. *Ibid.*, p. 230.
258. Frederick J. Powicke, *op. cit.*, Vol. II, p. 81.

was the first to suffer from the renewed hostility.[259] His wife had
leased a site for the erection of a chapel in Oxenden Street, but he
was now dogged by spies and exposed to "the constant irritation of
hostile surveillance."[260] Twice at least in 1675 he was summoned
before magistrates at the instigation of an informer for his New
Street preaching. The first case was dismissed, but in June he was
fined £60 by Sir Thomas Davis, and the fine was to be levied on his
goods and chattels. It was at this time that his wife hid his books
or gave them away to save them from the hands of the bailiffs.[261]
She still earnestly encouraged him to preach when and where he
could, without regard to the threat of fines or imprisonment. The
new chapel was opened in August, but after one sermon he was
compelled to retire to Charlesworth. He found himself able to
preach for the next ten Sundays, often twice, in local pulpits, and
the people flocked in crowds to hear him: "Those heard that had
not come to church of seven years, and two or three thousand heard
where scarce a hundred were wont to come."[262] It must have been
with some regret that he left such eager hearers to return to London
where he was forced to refrain from preaching for some six months.
Then in April, 1676, he ventured to resume in a chapel in Swallow
Street, and for the next six months he was unmolested. But in
November a warrant was issued for his arrest and a guard was
placed on the door of the chapel for twenty-four Sundays in succession.[263] Mrs. Baxter at length arranged to let the chapels in
Oxenden Street and Swallow Street so that constant preaching
could be maintained in each: "Be it by Conformists or Non-Conformists," he wrote, "I rejoice that Christ is preached."[264] It was his
wife who now arranged for him to preach both at Southwark and
at Covent Garden, although it is not certain how long either arrangement continued. He kept up his Thursday lectures at New
Street and occasional sermons elsewhere, and he never ceased to

259. J. M. Lloyd Thomas, *op. cit.*, p. 230.
260. A. H. Ladell, *Richard Baxter: Puritan and Mystic,* p. 105.
261. J. T. Wilkinson, *op. cit.*, p. 121.
262. J. M. Lloyd Thomas, *op. cit.*, p. 238.
263. *Ibid.*, p. 241.
264. Frederick J. Powicke, *op. cit.*, Vol. II, p. 95.

preach in his own household. But on August 24, 1682, "just that day twenty year" since the Act of Uniformity, he preached for the last time at New Street and took his leave of public preaching "in a thankful congregation."[265] Not long after, his books, his goods, even the bed on which he lay, were seized and sold, and his illness alone saved him from gaol at a time when most of his friends were in prison.[266] He was driven into months of pain and hiding such as he had never known, and compared with which prison itself would have been a palace to him.[267] At length, late in 1684, a fresh warrant was signed for his arrest, and six men stood outside the door of his study all night and kept him from both food and sleep. They brought him "scarce able to stand" before the court,[268] and bound him by a four-hundred pound bond. In December, 1684, and again in January, 1685, he was forced in all his pain and weakness to come before the court again, although he had to be carried because he was too ill to stand. A month later, Charles II died and the reign of the Merry Monarch was at an end.

Romance and marriage, however, were to throw a mantle of consolation over his life which no man ever needed or valued more. Baxter had learned to know and love his wife while she was still greatly given to fear, and he may not have been prepared for the bright change which now transformed her state of mind. But she was no ordinary woman, and she was to become a wife in a thousand. She was timid and reserved by nature, gentle and refined in spirit, yet she was to display a quiet courage in the face of adversity which was without its peer among women of the Restoration. John Howe rightly observed that by her marriage with Baxter she "gave proof of the real greatness of her spirit."[269] Her old melancholy vanished and she found her soul in the loss of self. "Counsel did something to it, and contentment something, and being taken up with our household affairs did somewhat."[270] All her natural

---

265. J. M. Lloyd Thomas, *op. cit.*, p. 250.
266. *Ibid.*, p. 251.
267. *Ibid.*, p. 252.
268. *Ibid.*, p. 253.
269. J. T. Wilkinson, *op. cit.*, p. 190.
270. *Ibid.*, p. 110.

gaiety seemed to escape as if from a prison and poured itself out in pure and selfless service. All the generous affections of which her heart was the centre found an outlet and filled each hour of the day with glad and holy consecration. She stepped out with him to face the dark times at hand, and she never lost heart or hope through all the years of trial which then ensued. Her tastes and habits, her plans and pleasures, were all cast in beautiful harmony with those of her husband, and their wedded life was one long summer day of mutual love and devotion. "These near nineteen years," he wrote, "I know not that we ever had any breach in the point of love . . . save only that she somewhat grudged that I had persuaded her for my quietness to surrender so much of her estate to a disabling her from helping others so much as she earnestly desired."[271] There was not one selfish wish in her love for him, and his daily routine of toil and study was cheered and relieved by true domestic happiness. Powicke observed that there was in her a charm for others which was lacking in him,[272] and he himself frankly declared that her "winning conversation" drew their hearts to goodness in a way that sermons could never do.[273] Baxter indeed went much further in his testimony to her insight: "Except in cases that required learning and skill in theological difficulties, she was better at resolving a case of conscience than most Divines that ever I knew in all my life . . . Insomuch that of late years, I confess that I was used to put all save secret cases to her, . . . and she would give me a more exact resolution than I could do."[274] She was at his side in sickness and fatigue; he was in her heart in sorrow and slander. Her cheerfulness brightened his hours of melancholy, and her gentleness softened his moods of asperity; her fortitude strengthened his hand in resolution, and her sympathy quickened his heart in benevolence. She shared his lot, now in danger, now in hiding, and was never so bright a companion to him as in prison.[275] There was no child to bless their home, and he observed with a note of wistful regret: "And her

271. *Ibid.*
272. Frederick J. Powicke, *op. cit.*, Vol. II, p. 40.
273. J. T. Wilkinson, *op. cit.*, p. 113.
274. *Ibid.*, p. 127.
275. *Ibid.*, p. 113.

sister's children she loved as if they had been her own, especially three daughters."[276] But this only apart, it was as close to the ideal as may be found in the union of a man and woman. Her tender affection was balm to his lonely character, and he repaid his wife with a love and honor which words could ill express.

But the intensity of her spirit was not without its price, for "she . . . proved her sincerity by her costliest obedience."[277] Perhaps the cost was the dearer because it was so quiet and so controlled. Baxter declared that the "knife was too keen and cut the sheath."[278] Hers was a mind keyed up to a higher level than is the case with most people; it was like the treble strings of a lute which have been strained to the utmost: "sweet, but in continual danger."[279] On June 14, 1681, on the twelfth day of a delirious illness, she passed away, leaving a void in his heart which nothing could fill. It was her love alone which had made the dark world bright in his eyes, and the memory of her gentleness was to shine on his path as he followed to "the door of eternity."[280] He found comfort in the recollection of her dearness, and he wrote her Memoir within a month of her passing. It was "in some passion indeed of love and grief, but in sincerity of truth"[281] that he penned this *Breviate of the Life of Margaret Baxter*: it was indeed "under the power of melting grief and therefore perhaps with the less prudent judgment; but not with the less, but the more truth; for passionate weakness poureth out all, which greater prudence may conceal."[282] Nevertheless he had allowed friends to persuade him to discard certain details on the ground that strangers would not concern themselves about such things so much "as love and nearness made me do."[283] It was "this owned passion"[284] which also led him to publish

276. *Ibid.*, p. 124.
277. *Ibid.*, p. 132.
278. *Ibid.*
279. *Ibid.*, p. 146.
280. *Ibid.*, p. 176.
281. *Ibid.*, p. 149.
282. *Ibid.*, p. 61.
283. *Ibid.*, p. 62.
284. *Ibid.*, p. 66.

his *Poetical Fragments* in 1681, "as her sorrows and sufferings long ago gave birth to some of these poems."[285] But the *Breviate* alone affords us the exquisite story of his love and marriage, and it is a gem of purest biography. It helps us to follow her in mental vision from the early picture of her "frail and flower-like figure" in girlhood to the final portrait of her rich and gracious spirit in maturity.[286] It is a most tender record of one who had become ineffably dear to Baxter, "the most dear companion of the last nineteen years of my life,"[287] one whom he called "Dear Heart," in his letters.[288] But it also brings him before us in a fine picture, full of human warmth and insight, for he could not recall her love for him without letting us see his love for her. The stern restraint, the austere severity of his single-minded pursuit of a heavenly character, is offset by this unconscious disclosure of his own most tender feelings as a man like unto ourselves. The lofty grandeur of Puritan abstracttion from the world is seen in a more attractive light when we have felt the throb of love and grief behind his self-complaint: "For though she oft said that before she married me she expected more sourness and unsuitableness than she found, yet I am sure that she found less zeal and holiness and strictness in all words and looks and duties, and less help for her soul than she expected."[289] Baxter's love for her had grown like "a flower in the garden of the spirit,"[290] and his only regret was that he had proved less worthy of her than she deserved. "My dear wife did look for more good in me than she found, especially lately in my weakness and decay. We are all like pictures that must not be looked on too near. They that come near us find more faults and badness in us than others at a distance know."[291] So he fancied; but what would have been her answer if she had lived to draw his portrait as he has drawn hers?[292]

285. *Ibid.*, p. 176.
286. J. M. Lloyd Thomas, *op. cit.*, Appendix ii, p. 268.
287. J. T. Wilkinson, *op. cit.*, p. 61.
288. *Ibid.*, p. 144.
289. *Ibid.*, p. 142.
290. *Ibid.*, p. 41.
291. *Ibid.*, p. 152.
292. Frederick J. Powicke, *op. cit.*, Vol. II, p. 108.

Baxter wrote an account of his own life and times which reached
to the end of the reign of Charles II, and left it in manuscript form
with his friend Matthew Sylvester. Part One seems to have been
written in his early days at Acton,[293] and its "almost classical conclusion" gives it a place in the front rank of such literature.[294] Part
Two ends with a note which shows that he finished it at Hampden
during his absence from Acton because of the Great Plague.[295]
There was a five-year break, and then Part Three began with the
brief subheading: "November 16, 1670. I began to add the memor-
ials following."[296] It may have been Baxter himself who crossed out
parts of the primary manuscript; other parts were changed or left
out at the editor's discretion.[297] It was published by Sylvester in
1696 with the title *Reliquiae Baxterianae,* but this huge and shape-
less folio has never been reprinted. Calamy's Abridgement was
published in 1702 and has become a classic of Non-Conformist
literature; but it was an unfortunate mixture of Calamy's stately
diction and Baxter's lively narrative, and did not do justice to one
or the other. Then, in 1925, J. M. Lloyd Thomas edited an abridgement of Sylvester's Folio which preserves the direct and piquant
style of the original and which provides a mass of basic material
for future historians. Baxter watched the course of affairs with a
flair for acute observation and was "guilty of few errors in his statement of facts."[298] He tried to write with the detached restraint of an
objective spectator, though he did not hide his verdict either on men
or on events.[299] John Wesley's *Journal* bears witness to his success:
"July 30, 1757: I read Mr. Baxter's Account of his own Life and
Times. It seems to be the most impartial account of those times
which has ever yet appeared. And none that I have seen so accu-
rately points out the real springs of those public calamities."[300]

293. J. M. Lloyd Thomas, *op. cit.,* p. 93.
294. *Ibid.,* p. xx.
295. *Ibid.,* p. 192.
296. *Ibid.,* Note p. 291.
297. *Ibid.,* p. x.
298. *Ibid.,* p. xx.
299. *Ibid.,* p. 103.
300. Nehemiah Curnock, *The Journal of The Rev. John Wesley,* Vol. IV,
p. 221.

But the book lives because of its basic human appeal as the self-disclosure of a man of immense moral stature in an age of profound contradiction. It lays bare the complexities of an ascetic and yet attractive figure, at once stern and tender, with the highest virtues of mind and soul. It shows that he was too many-sided for complete understanding in his own age, and too comprehensive for honest recognition even today.[301] He loved England with the love of a man who was keenly alive to all the wrongs in Church and State, ever anxious for the common weal of King and people.[302] He had been a moderate Puritan who loved the Church in which he was ordained, and had become "a mere Non-Conformist" who thought separation a sin second only to the sin of persecution.[303] He stood head and shoulders above most men in the rival parties and he never ceased to strive for peace and concord in the Church as a whole. This is borne out by the Prefatory Letter to his *Apology for the Non-Conformist Ministry,* which was written in 1669 but not published until 1681. It was his most moving appeal to the wiser Bishops, whom he mentioned by name: "I beg of you as on my knees, for your own sakes, for England's, for the Church's, for Christ's, that you will agree with us on these terms. I ask nothing of you for my own self: I need nothing that you can give me. My time of service is near an end: but England will be England, and souls and the Church's peace will be precious, and the cause will be the same when all present Non-Conformists are dead; and Bishops must die as well as we."[304] Baxter was the strenuous opponent of intolerance in the Bishops and intransigence in the Divines; the cordial advocate of genuine unity and Christian charity; both too critical and too catholic to win universal recognition; one who died as he lived in the eager pursuit of healing and comprehension for all the godly within the Church of England.

Sincere and profound in his Puritan convictions, Baxter was never eccentric, but not without prejudice. He could have been content to live like a recluse, feasting his mind on the books which

301. J. M. Lloyd Thomas, *op. cit.,* p. xii.
302. William Orme, *op. cit.,* Vol. XXII, p. 346; Vol. XXIII, p. 108.
303. Frederick J. Powicke, *op. cit.,* Vol. I, p. 23.
304. See J. M. Lloyd Thomas, *op. cit.,* p. xxviii.

he loved. "I must confess," he wrote, "it is much more pleasing to myself to be retired from the world and to have very little to do with men, and to converse with God and conscience and good books."[305] But in 1670 he said that for almost ten years he had been banished from his library, and in more recent months from the few books which he still had by him.[306] Then in 1672, after twelve years during which he had been kept a hundred miles from his books, he "paid dear" to have them brought to Totteridge.[307] But in 1675 he was compelled to hide them, sell them, or give them away to save them from the hands of the bailiffs,[308] and his only comment was that such a loss was "very tolerable."[309] But his life was "always marked by a rare sobriety and ripeness of judgment,"[310] and he loved men even more than his books. He had a wide circle of friends; the names which he recites add up in scores.[311] He had little patience with men who thought that he would debate a point with them "as if an hour's talk would serve instead of . . . seven years' study."[312] But his ample knowledge and his moral insight were put without reserve at the service of the humble-hearted. His breadth of soul is seen in his friendship with men like James Ussher of Armagh and John Eliot of New England; his wealth of mind is seen in his friendship with men like Sir Matthew Hale at Acton and the Hon. Robert Boyle in London. There was nothing drab or joyless in his inner life of faith and worship, though we find him grieving for his sins and deficiencies: "O Lord," we hear him pray, "for the merits and sacrifice and intercession of Christ, be merciful to me a sinner, and forgive my known and unknown sins."[313] He spoke as much to his own heart as to the hearts of his hearers, and they always knew that what he had to say was meant as well for himself: "O that the Lord would lay us at His feet in the tears of

305. *Ibid.*, p. 124.
306. Frederick J. Powicke, *op. cit.*, Vol. II, p. 38.
307. J. M. Lloyd Thomas, *op. cit.*, p. 235.
308. Frederick J. Powicke, *op. cit.*, Vol. II, pp. 88, 89.
309. J. M. Lloyd Thomas, *op. cit.*, p. 236.
310. *Ibid.*, p. xvi.
311. Frederick J. Powicke, *op. cit.*, Vol. I, p. 153.
312. J. M. Lloyd Thomas, *op. cit.*, p. 132.
313. *Ibid.*

unfeigned sorrow for this sin!"[314] He found strength to bear great pain and distress through faith in Him who makes us able: "The Lord teach me more fully to love His will, and rest therein, as much better than my own that oft striveth against it."[315] Devotion was the element in which he loved to move, and praise as well as prayer was his supreme delight: "I feel that Thou hast made my mind to know Thee, and I feel that Thou hast made my heart to love Thee."[316] His whole being was stirred by the sound of sacred music, and he found great delight both in singing and in poetry. "For myself," he wrote in the Prefatory Epistle to his *Poetical Fragments,* "I confess that harmony and melody are the pleasure and elevation of my soul, and have made a Psalm of Praise in the Holy Assembly the chief delightful exercise of my religion and my life."[317] But the concern which he felt was only for church music as an aid in praise and worship: "I scarce cared for it anywhere else; and if it might not be holily used, it should never have been used for me."[318] He knew the Psalms by heart and sang them as long as he lived: one of his latest tasks was to prepare his own metrical paraphrase of the Psalms for use in worship.[319] There is charm as well as pathos in his remark: "It was not the least comfort that I had in the converse of my late dear wife that our first in the morning and our last in bed at night was a Psalm of Praise."[320] Such was the man who bowed in faith before the gale of God's Spirit, and rose up to withstand the storms which beat against him from every human quarter.

On February 6, 1685, the Duke of York came to the Throne as James II. He had vowed long before to smash Non-Conformists with an iron hand, and his reign was marked by intensified persecution in the case of the few prominent Puritans who still survived. Thus, on February 28, Baxter was flung into King's Bench Prison

314. William Orme, *op. cit.,* Vol. XIV, p. 160.
315. J. M. Lloyd Thomas, *op. cit.,* p. 253.
316. William Orme, *op. cit.,* Vol. XXI, p. 391.
317. J. M. Lloyd Thomas, *op. cit.,* p. xxii.
318. *Ibid.*
319. Frederick J. Powicke, *op. cit.,* Vol. II, p. 163.
320. J. T. Wilkinson, *op. cit.,* p. 57.

on the warrant of the Lord Chief Justice. The sole pretext was that *The Paraphrase of the New Testament* which he had just published was said to veil a series of libels on Bishops and statesmen.[321] Baxter had been long and fondly engaged on this volume which had developed from a paraphrase of the Epistle to the Romans: "When I had done that," he wrote, "the usefulness of it to myself drew me farther and farther till I had done all."[322] He knew that he would fall under censure in some quarters for what he had written, or failed to write, on the Revelation of St. John the Divine; but he forgot that he also had to reckon with the malice of a veteran opponent, Roger L'Estrange. It was L'Estrange who laid the charge that the main scope of the book was "to make broad signs to the people that they are under a persecuting and superstitious government, and to propagate the very same doctrine from the Press which the author of it throughout the whole course of his life has hitherto done from the Pulpit."[323] Powicke remarks that we have it on the word of Archbishop Tillotson that the frail old man was summoned before Jeffreys in his own house where his treatment was such as to constrain "his lady to desire him to be more fair."[324] He was discharged from gaol under a writ until the day for his trial was announced, and he retired to the country in a state of extreme weakness: he was feeble with age and much older than his years, worn out with physical suffering and praying daily for early release. On May 6, the charge was filed against him in Westminster Hall, and on May 14, he lodged his plea as not guilty. On May 18, his counsel sought further delay on the ground of extreme ill-health, but this was not approved. It was the day on which Titus Oates stood in the stocks at the New Palace Yard, and Jeffreys burst into a storm of rage. "I will not give him a minute's time more to save his life!" he cried. ". . . I know how to deal with saints as well as sinners. Yonder stands Oates in the pillory and he says he suffers for the truth, and so says Baxter; but if Baxter did but stand on the other side of the pillory with him, I would say two of the greatest rogues

321. See *The Paraphrase* on Matt. 5:19; Mark 3:6; 9:39; 11:31; 12:38, 40; Luke 10:2; John 11:57; Acts 15:2.
322. J. M. Lloyd Thomas, *op. cit.*, p. 253.
323. Frederick J. Powicke, *op. cit.*, Vol. II, pp. 141, 142.
324. *Ibid.*, Vol. II, p. 143.

and rascals in the Kingdom stood there."[325] The trial took place
on May 30 in the Guildhall, and it ranks in interest and importance
with the trial of the seven Bishops four years later. Baxter entered
the court with dignity and composure, now an almost spectral figure, "nothing but skin and bones."[326] Jeffreys followed a few moments later, his "face ablaze with anger and brandy."[327] Baxter's
friend Sir Henry Ashurst had engaged six leading counsel on his
behalf, but the jury was packed with men who throve on bribes
and were the tools of the Tory sheriffs. The trial itself was a bar-
barous travesty in the name of English justice and its course of
events was farcical and disgraceful in the extreme.

It soon became clear that the Lord Chief Justice meant to conduct
the trial in a way which would make both counsel and witness
quite irrelevant. He brushed aside those who tried to speak in Baxter's defence, and he denounced Baxter with vicious invective and
vulgar ridicule in turn. He began by saying that Baxter loathed the
Liturgy and would have nothing but cant and long-winded prayers
without Book. Then he turned up his eyes, clasped his hands, and
began to sing through his nose in imitation of what he took to be
Baxter's style of praying: "Lord, we are Thy people, Thy peculiar
people, Thy dear people."[328] Baxter was "an old rogue"; he had
"poisoned the world with his Kidderminster doctrine"; he was "an
old schismatical knave, a hypocritical villain."[329] "What ailed the
old stock-cole unthankful villain that he could not conform — was
he better or wiser than other men?"[330] And then Jeffreys lost all
semblance of self-control: "This one old fellow hath cast more reproach upon the constitution and excellent discipline of our Church
than will be wiped out this hundred years; but I will handle him
for it, for, by God! he deserves to be whipped through the City!"[331]
When his counsel tried to plead, he was gagged with angry shouts
and scornful jibes. At length Jeffreys called on Baxter to speak:

325. *Ibid.*, Vol. II, pp. 143, 144.
326. J. M. Lloyd Thomas, *op. cit.*, Appendix i, p. 258.
327. *Ibid.*
328. *Ibid.*, Appendix i, p. 259.
329. *Ibid.*
330. *Ibid.*, Appendix i, p. 260.
331. *Ibid.*

"Come, you, what do you say for yourself, you old knave! Come, speak up; what doth he say?"[332] Baxter declared that these things would surely be understood one day, what fools one sort of Protestants are made to persecute and vex the other. Then he looked up and said: "I am not concerned to answer such stuff, but am ready to produce my writings for the confutation of all this."[333] When his counsel said that he had written honorably of the Bishops of the Church of England, Jeffreys could not contain himself. "Baxter for Bishops!" he exclaimed; "a merry conceit indeed!" Baxter's words were then read out from the place where he had said "that great respect is due to those truly called to be bishops among us." But the Lord Chief Justice would not have it: "This is your Presbyterian cant," he said; "truly called to be Bishops! That is himself and such rascals, called to be Bishops of Kidderminster and other such places, Bishops set apart by such factious, snivelling Presbyterians as himself: a Kidderminster Bishop he means."[334] Jeffreys summed up in a statement full of political bias and asked for a verdict on the ground that Baxter had been guilty of a political offence: "He is as modest now as can be, but time was when no man was so ready at 'Bind your king in chains and your nobles in fetters of iron' . . . . Gentlemen, for God's sake, don't let us be gulled twice in an age."[335] Baxter then asked if he thought that any jury would convict the accused on such a trial as this. But the Lord Chief Justice knew his court and replied: "I'll warrant you Mr. Baxter; don't you trouble yourself about that."[336] The jury did not even retire, but brought in the verdict of guilty at once. Sir Henry Ashurst led him through the crowd and drove him away by coach, for the sentence was not pronounced until June 29, a month after the trial. Nothing but the intervention of Jeffrey's colleagues saved Baxter from a savage sentence which would have had him whipped through the streets of London; but he was fined five hundred marks, and was condemned to lie in gaol until it had been paid. And yet the last word may well be that of Archbishop Tillotson in his letter

332. *Ibid.*, Appendix i, p. 261.
333. *Ibid.*
334. *Ibid.*, Appendix i, p. 262.
335. *Ibid.*, Appendix i, p. 263.
336. *Ibid.*

to Matthew Sylvester in 1692: "Nothing more honourable than when the Rev. Baxter stood at bay, berogued, abused, despised: never more great than then . . . . This is the noblest part of his life, and not that he might have been a bishop."[337]

Powicke thinks that it is doubtful whether he was ever confined in the King's Bench Prison, and that he was allowed to endure his imprisonment in a Patent Shop near the gate of the prison itself.[338] Here his superb belief in the Father's House of Many Mansions helped to lift his mind far beyond the reach of human tyranny. His mind was free from dawn till night to roam on the sunlit hills of glory, for did he not believe that a prison was as near a way to heaven as his own home?[339] The good and wise came to see him and took away his tender greetings and noble maxims. He was never at ease for more than a few hours at a time, and that was mostly at night. Yet the strongest man in his prime, working at the full stretch of his mental capacity, could not have done more than he did while he was in prison.[340] Manuscript evidence shows that both in reading and in literary output, he got through more in that time of vindictive confinement than in any other equal segment of his long life.[341] Thus for eighteen months he enjoyed a true solace in his imprisonment for which Bloody Jeffreys in his robes of ermine might sigh in vain. At length, in November, 1686 — as a result of the intervention of Lord Powis — he was released from the fine which had been imposed. This was in some sense by the King's favour, although he still remained under a bond for good conduct. Baxter himself was to observe: "Had not the King taken off my fine, I had continued in prison till death."[342] He was anxious to know whether he was still bound by the Hicks Hall bond of £400 imposed in 1684, and a bond of £300 to the Marshall of the King's Bench: but he was told at length that should he choose to reside in London, he might do so without fear from the Five Mile Act.[343]

---

337. Frederick J. Powicke, *op. cit.*, Vol. II, p. 294.
338. *Ibid.*, p. 151.
339. *Ibid.*, p. 135.
340. *Ibid.*, p. 159.
341. *Ibid.*, p. 160.
342. *Ibid.*, p. 285.
343. *Ibid.*, pp. 158, 159.

He did not leave his rooms outside the King's Bench Gate until February, 1687; then he went to reside with Matthew Sylvester in Charterhouse Square. The King's Declaration of Indulgence in April, 1687, allowed him to begin preaching once more, and he arranged to preach on behalf of Matthew Sylvester on the Lord's Day and on every other Thursday in the mornings. But he refused to join in the Address of Thanks for the Declaration of Indulgence, and he used all his strength to build up good-will between Churchmen and Non-Conformists. Then in December, 1688, the long storm of persecution blew itself out, and William of Orange drove James from his throne and kingdom. Baxter must have rejoiced in the course of events which led to the Revolution, and one of the last books which he lived to write, but not to publish, was a little tractate on the abdication of James II. He was among the few who had been forced out in 1662 and who were yet alive; but he was worn with the rigours of the years in between and he was now not far from the crossing of the river. It was in the mercy of God that there should now be a season of calm, and that he should go down to the banks of that river in peace.

Baxter had always been frugal and was content with a meagre income, while all his life he gave away all that he could for the sake of others. When he settled at Kidderminster in 1641, he was allowed £60 per annum;[344] while he was at Coventry, he had free board in the Governor's residence;[345] during his time in the army, he was paid at the rate of 2/- a day.[346] On his return to Kidderminster after the wars, he was promised £100 a year and a rent-free house; but he never received more than "eighty pounds per annum, or ninety at most, and house-rent for a few rooms in the top of another man's house."[347] He made it his practice to lose his tithes rather than seem zealous to exact them, still less to go to law for them. His father and step-mother came to reside with him about the year 1650 and no doubt shared in the expense of the household during the next ten years.[348] When he removed to London in April,

344. J. M. Lloyd Thomas, *op. cit.*, p. 24.
345. *Ibid.*, p. 43.
346. Frederick J. Powicke, *op. cit.*, Vol. I, p. 73, footnote.
347. *Ibid.*, p. 82.
348. *Ibid.*, p. 92, footnote.

1660, he preached up and down for nothing at the request of his friends for "about a year."[349] Later at St. Dunstan's he was allowed "some maintenance,"[350] and at Milk Street he received £40 per annum.[351] After 1662 he could only preach in private, until he received a license late in 1672 and began his lectures in the New Street Chapel. But in 1673 he had to voice a strong protest against those who spread it about that his object was gain: "I know not to my remembrance," he wrote, "that I have received a groat as for preaching these eleven years but what I have returned."[352] There had been one primary condition for his marriage in September, 1662: "That I would have nothing that before our marriage was hers, that I who wanted no outward supplies might not seem to marry her for covetousness."[353] Baxter's wife honoured his independence and shared all his generous impulses. "It was so far from offending her (as it would be with many ministers' wives that were in want and might have such maintenance as is their due) that I neither conformed nor took any place of gain, that it was as much by her will as my own that for the first nine or ten years of my ejected state, I took not so much as any private gift to supply my wants except ten pounds a year from Serjeant Fountain."[354] It was only her passion for doing good that ever induced her to think otherwise: "She at length refused not to accept with thanks the liberality of others and to live partly on charity that she might exercise charity to them that could not so easily get it from others as we could do."[355] How then did he live when the Black Act of 1662 drove him out of his church and cure? We can only conclude that the income from his books was enough for all his needs, and we know that it did sometimes amount to £60 or 80 a year.[356] Fines and confiscations which he sustained in the latter part of his life did not prevent him from being able to say after his wife's death: "Through God's mercy and her prudent care, I lived in plenty and

349. J. M. Lloyd Thomas, *op. cit.*, p. 159.
350. *Ibid.*
351. *Ibid.*, p. 160.
352. Frederick J. Powicke, *op. cit.*, Vol. II, p. 73.
353. J. T. Wilkinson, *op. cit.*, p. 109.
354. *Ibid.*, pp. 120, 121.
355. *Ibid.*, p. 121.
356. Frederick J. Powicke, *op. cit.*, Vol. I, p. 104.

do so still, though not without being greatly beholden to divers friends; and I am not poorer than when I married; but it is not by marriage nor by anything that was hers before."[357] It was after her death that he suffered his worst calamities; his goods, his books, his bed, his all, were seized by the law of distraint, and he was forced to take secret lodgings at a distance with a stranger. "But," he wrote, "I never wanted less what man can give than when men had taken all. My old friends (and strangers to me) were so liberal that I was fain to restrain their bounty. Their kindness was a surer and larger revenue to me than my own."[358]

Baxter's last years found him able to do little more than revise or complete old manuscripts as occasion arose: but there was one notable exception. On October 18, 1691, less than two months before his death, he finished a tractate called *The Poor Husbandman's Advocate* and signed it as "Moriturus G. Salvianus." He had employed the joint-name of Gildas Salvianus as the first and leading title of *The Reformed Pastor in* 1655. It was next used when he published the *Sermon on Repentance* which he preached before the House of Commons on the eve of the King's recall. Dr. F. J. Powicke found the third part among the manuscripts in Dr. Williams' Library with the inscription, "Repent, O England: the third part of Gildas Salvianus." He was to have preached it as a sermon at the Merchant's Lecture in 1679.[359] The fourth and last part was this plea for poor tenants addressed to "Rich Racking Landlords"; but it remained with his other unpublished manuscripts until it was found and printed by Dr. Powicke in the *John Rylands Library Bulletin* in January, 1926. Towards the end of this little tractate, Baxter mentioned in an incidental manner that he was the author of about one hundred and twenty-eight books; and this was his farewell. Powicke observed that he wrote as was his habit, straight on without stopping to revise or correct, careless of style and spelling, eager only to get it done before the flame of life went out.[360]

357. J. T. Wilkinson, *op. cit.*, p. 155.
358. J. M. Lloyd Thomas, *op. cit.*, p. 252.
359. *Poor Husbandman's Advocate*, p. 176.
360. *Ibid.*, p. 171.

There are signs that he wrote with a trembling hand, nor can the pages hide a waning vigour of mind. But he wrote from the heart and there was no failure of true spiritual vision or strong moral indignation. Baxter was himself a landlord, though of minor degree, and he took pains to clear his own name and motive in so writing. His last visit to his father had been while he was at Kidderminster in the latter half of 1661 when his father lay in great pain some twenty miles away.[361] On his death, in February, 1663, Baxter had inherited the patrimony in some houses and lands at Eaton Constantine, and in 1667 these were let on lease with provision for his step-mother to continue in residence.[362] There she died at a great age in 1680, and the income from the rents was then set apart for his poorer kinsmen. The rents themselves were fixed at the lowest figure and the tenants were exceedingly well treated: "I let all to tenants that never offer to remove. The small tenements I give them leases freely and take little rent, and none of one. The bigger tenement I let at £30 per annum . . . and the tenants are well contented."[363] Thus he could speak with all boldness to Rich Racking Landlords: "I do not partially persuade others to what I would not do myself."[364] This small tractate allows us to place his transparent devotion to God side by side with his warm humanity and love for his neighbour. The great thing which at once arrests thought is its character and intention. Baxter declared that his object was "that the poor Husbandmen may not be so toyled like beasts, endangered for want of necessary warmth and distracted with cares to pay their rents, as to disable them to mind their soul concerns and to read God's Word and worship Him in their families, and to educate their children in civility and piety, and that thereby the land degenerate not into Atheism, Infidelity and Barbarism."[365] He was deeply concerned for their spiritual necessities as well as their social welfare, and we hear the authentic cry of a true pastor in his appeal: "O pity

361. J. M. Lloyd Thomas, *op. cit.*, p. 172.
362. Frederick J. Powicke, *op. cit.*, Vol. I. p. 205, footnote.
363. *Poor Husbandman's Advocate*, p. 213.
364. *Ibid.*
365. *Ibid.*, p. 178.

them that through poverty and necessity can neither read nor educate their children to read! Pity them that know not what a Bible is, to whom it is of no more significance than a chip!"[366]

Baxter was cared for in his last years by the good Mrs. Bushell who had kept house for him since the death of his wife, but he never ceased to miss the fragrance of her company or the sweetness of her ministry. "I had never much known worldly cares," he wrote in 1681; "before I was married I had no need; afterwards she took the care on her and disuse had made it intolerant to me. I feel now more of it than ever I did when yet I have so little a way to go."[367] He did not know that he had yet ten years to go, years of trial and calamity in which he missed the touch of her hand more than words could tell. But he would not complain and he filled his days with noble employ. Sylvester indicates that he preached as often as his strength would allow until late in 1691. Then he kept up daily worship in his own house where he opened his doors each morning and evening to all who would join him. At length he was confined, first to his room, then to his bed; for old age and disease, with poverty and privation, had done their work. He had been a life-long victim of illness and ailments of every kind, and the solemn catalogue of his chronic afflictions is an astounding document. It fills us with respect for the mental vigour and the moral courage which had borne him through a long life of untiring exertion. But it was the wearing distress of pain and need which had lifted his eyes beyond this world and had fixed them upon the world to come. His life had hung by a thread so slender that he had lived each day as though it were his last.[368] He had gone on his way like the gentle Herbert, with the bells of that Church which is beyond the stars ringing their glad chimes in his ears, and he preached to the end with great freedom about that Realm above: "like one," wrote his friend Calamy, "that had been there and was come as a sort of an express from thence to make a report concerning it."[369] And his passing at the end was in deep harmony with it all. His

366. *Ibid.*, pp. 189, 190.
367. J. T. Wilkinson, *op. cit.*, p. 126.
368. J. M. Lloyd Thomas, *op. cit.*, p. 124; see Powicke, Vol. I, p. 87.
369. William Orme, *op. cit.*, Vol. I, p. 399.

concern for London was voiced in an exclamation on the Sunday before he died: "Lord, pity, pity, pity the ignorance of this poor city!"[370] On the Monday, Dr. Bates and Mr. Mather found him wasted with pain as the result of a large stone in the kidney, but they heard him tell them: "I have pain; there is no arguing against sense; but I have peace, I have peace."[371] At five o'clock in the evening, he was seized with cold and trembling which wrung from him "cries for pity and redress from heaven."[372] This was the sharp advent of the last long night of pain and weakness, and the hours moved slowly towards the dawn of a winter morning. At last at four o'clock in the morning, Mrs. Bushell heard him murmur "Death, death," and Matthew Sylvester caught his last whisper: "O I thank Him, I thank Him; the Lord teach you to die."[373] There was no rapture of speech or feeling, but his heart was at peace. Thus at the age of seventy-six, in the cold dark dawn of December 8, 1691, his life moved to a close. He was buried beside his wife, in the ruined Chancel of Christ Church Newgate Street: but his spirit passed away; away from a life of pain and trouble to the everlasting rest of the saints in light.

370. J. M. Lloyd Thomas, *op. cit.*, Appendix i, p. 266.
371. *Ibid.*
372. Frederick J. Powicke, *op. cit.*, Vol. II, p. 165.
373. *Ibid.*

Now it belongs not to my care
 Whether I die or live:
To love and serve Thee is my share:
 And this Thy grace must give.

If life be long, I will be glad,
 That I may long obey:
If short: yet why should I be sad,
 That shall have the same pay?

Christ leads me through no darker rooms
Than He went through before:
He that into God's Kingdom comes
 Must enter by this door.

Come, Lord, when Grace hath made me meet
 Thy blessed Face to see:
For if Thy work on earth be sweet,
 What will Thy glory be?

My knowledge of that Life is small;
 The Eye of Faith is dim:
But it's enough that Christ knows all;
 And I shall be with Him.

   — Richard Baxter in *Poetical Fragments*

BIBLIOGRAPHY

Frederick J. Powicke, *A Life of the Reverend Richard Baxter,* 1615-1691, 1924.

Frederick J. Powicke, *The Reverend Richard Baxter Under the Cross,* 1662-1691, 1925.

William Orme, ed., *The Practical Works of the Reverend Richard Baxter, with a Life of the Author and a Critical Examination of His Writings* (23 Vols.), 1830.

RICHARD BAXTER, *A Paraphrase on the New Testament, with Notes, Doctrinal and Practical,* 1701.

Richard Baxter, *The Poor Husbandman's Advocate* (published in John Rylands Library Bulletin, January, 1926).

J. M. Lloyd Thomas, *The Autobiography of Richard Baxter, Being the Reliquiae Baxterianae, with Introduction, Appendices and Notes,* 1925.

J. T. Wilkinson, *Richard Baxter and Margaret Charlton. A Puritan Love Story. Being the Breviate of the Life of Margaret Baxter by Richard Baxter, 1681, with Introductory Essay, Notes and Appendices,* 1928.

A. R. Ladell, *Richard Baxter: Puritan and Mystic,* 1924.

James Stephen, *Richard Baxter* (see *Essays in Ecclesiastical Biography,* New Edition), 1875.

James Stalker, *Richard Baxter* (in *The Evangelical Succession,* Second Series), 1883.

Dictionary of National Biography, "Richard Baxter" (Vol. I), 1950.

Thomas Babington Macaulay, *The History of England from the Accession of James II* (Everyman's Library edition), 1927.

INDEX

Index